The Cellphone

The Cellphone

*The History and Technology
of the Gadget That
Changed the World*

GUY KLEMENS

McFarland & Company, Inc., Publishers

Jefferson, North Carolina, and London

LIBRARY OF CONGRESS CATALOGUING-IN-PUBLICATION DATA

Klemens, Guy, 1973 –
   The cellphone : the history and technology of the gadget that
changed the world / by Guy Klemens.
          p.   cm.
   Includes bibliographical references and index.

   ISBN: 978-0-7864-5867-7
   softcover : 50# alkaline paper ∞

   1. Cell phone systems.   I. Title.
TK5103.485.K58   2010
621.3845'6 — dc22   2010029782

British Library cataloguing data are available

Cover images ©2010 Shutterstock

Manufactured in the United States of America

*McFarland & Company, Inc., Publishers
   Box 611, Jefferson, North Carolina 28640
   www.mcfarlandpub.com*

Table of Contents

Introduction

Many areas along the Congo River probably meet the definition of an undeveloped region. There is little electricity or plumbing, and certainly few telephone lines. In 2005 an American reporter found a woman selling fish who kept them in the river since there was no refrigeration, taking them to customers when requested.[1] She cannot read or write, so sending a note will not help. Someone who wants to buy fish will just have to call her cellphone.

The cellphone, or cellular phone in its full appellation, a device that as recently as 1990 was an oddity, has long since reached ubiquity. Market saturation in the usual developed countries of North America and Europe approached or surpassed 100 percent at the turn of the century, meaning that some countries have more cellphones than people. But this new medium is more than the latest plaything of the prosperous.

Unlike many technological advances, the cellphone has not bypassed the developing world. By 2004 the number of subscribers in Africa had surpassed 75 million and continues to grow. The cellphone is too vital for developing countries not to adopt. For many in the world, the cellphone brings a flowering of opportunity, with the century of technology finally making drastic improvements to their daily lives. For others, the cellphone is not always so welcome.

Far from the hardships of the Congo River, and well into the most affluent of societies, a cellphone rang in a Niagara Falls courtroom on March 11, 2005.[2] When no one would admit to owning the offending device, the presiding judge ordered 46 people in the courtroom be taken into custody and transported to jail. Two years later a state commission ruled to remove the judge from office for this action, but the message is clear. These devices can be an annoyance. The cellphone has a significant role in society, although no one is quite sure what that role is or what it should be. Almost everyone uses a cellphone, but it is still an object of mystery.

What is inside these devices, how do they work and how did they originate? On a related thread, why did cellphones come into being? The story consumes a large part of the technological developments of the past several decades. A comprehensive history must therefore tread beyond names, dates and events, and explore numerous technical concepts.

An examination could begin with the many components that make up the device. First, of course, a cellphone is a telephone, but it is also a radio receiver and transmitter, calling for an understanding of radio waves, antennas, and the history of radio. Microscopic circuits perform the various functions, a liquid-crystal display provides an interface for the user, and none of it would work without a battery. All of these parts need explanation in order to understand the cellphone, and their sum presents more facets to examine.

The handset is only a small part of a larger cellular system, created to meet the demands of mobility under the constraints of limited bandwidth. All of the history of cellphones from the beginning and into the foreseeable future springs from the limitations of bandwidth. And the bandwidth under discussion here is not the vague entity of common usage. The bandwidth of a message is an exact number, as is the available bandwidth of a communication channel such as a radio link. A careful understanding of this fundamental topic is therefore essential to a history of the cellphone. The technological aspects are many, but the phenomenon of the cellphone certainly extends beyond the inanimate.

Engineers create cellphones and then release them into the world for people to use, so the technology and the design process is only part of the story. The industry itself is a large business, using enormous amounts of resources and personnel. And cellphones add efficiency that help other businesses, and the economy in general, prosper and expand.

On an individual level, the cellphone has reached universal acceptance. People throughout the world carry them, use them, and sometimes wonder if they are harmful. As it has for technology such as the automobile and the television, society has reshaped around the cellphone. The history of the cellphone is therefore also about people and their use of this device.

This book uses the terms *cellular phone* and *cellphone* rather than *mobile phone* because it focuses on a specific type of wireless connection. Cordless phones, for which the handset is in radio contact with a wired unit in the same room, are not under discussion here. Also outside the topics covered are wireless local-loop systems, in which fixed radio connections replace some of the street-level telephone wires. Instead, this history deals with wireless systems built around the cellular concept, in which wireless users operate in small local areas (the cells). This is the principle that allows personal communication systems to overcome the limitations of bandwidth and to give the users the mobility needed for continuous contact.

The term cellular phone also has the ability to describe several families of devices. For its first decade the cellular phone existed only as a car phone. It then became a bulky portable unit, and then shrank into the modern handset. In this recent phase of the cellular phone's existence it is the familiar *cell-phone*. In the following story, there is a gradual transition in terminology, using "cellular phone" to refer to the general device and system-level and technology-level concepts, and then using "cellphone" to indicate the device that the current consumer experiences as a cellular phone.

This book makes no attempt to shield the reader from technical concepts, not only because to abridge the scientific explanations would be to remove much of the story, but also because such protection is unnecessary. The philosophy followed here is that an adequately careful explanation can clarify any topic. And so this book offers more than narrative history, it is also a lesson in the concepts and subjects important to understanding the cellphone as a device and as a phenomenon.

The fundamental theme in the history of the cellphone is how many trends had to reach an apex and converge at the right time. If someone were to take the complete plan for a cellphone back in time to only 1970, there is little that anyone could have done with it. Circuit miniaturization, batteries, displays and other essential components were still following their own independent development paths. Besides technology, society had to change in order to demand the cellular phone. Then there are the legal and business aspects. There were no frequencies available, and the telephone monopoly of the time had little motivation to build an expensive system to compete with itself.

This convergence would repeat often in the history, and is still taking place in many ways. The digital cellphone, for example, would have been impossible in 1980. As described in later chapters, the necessary techniques of digital audio compression were just developing, and integrated circuits did not have the necessary computational power. By 1990, not only was the technology in place, but the market demanded the digital cellphone. Large, experienced companies were ready to make the switch, and government agencies recognized the demand and knew how to modify regulations and allocate new frequencies. The history of the cellular phone therefore brings together a wide variety of historical threads.

The organization of this book mixes chapters that have more technical explanations than history with chapters having the reverse ratio. The first two chapters deal with bandwidth and radio, the foundational concepts that motivated and created the cellular phone. The chapter that follows is the pre-history of the cellular phone, with the creation and surprising popularity of the car phone. The demand for a better system takes the story to the 1970's and the development of the first cellular systems. A chapter explaining the analog systems that emerged is followed by a chapter detailing the story of their introduction and growth. But that is only the first phase of the history.

What follows is the switch to digital technology, with a description of digital communications concepts in general and then specifically as they apply to cellphones. Having built the foundation of understanding, the history can proceed with the entry of digital cellphones into the marketplace. By that point, in the mid– to late 1990's, the cellphone had reached universal success, prompting a chapter examining that growth and the effects on the business world. Another set of topics that forms a crucial part of the history, and the subsequent chapter, is the implications that the cellphone has had on health, on the individual and on society. And while this history is backward-looking, the final chapter approaches some recent developments with a look at the multi-featured personal electronic device that the cellphone is becoming.

The overall goal of this book is to impart an understanding of the development of the cellphone and the technologies it encompasses. This book does not take the place of the wireless gurus, who survey the current soup of developing ideas and make predictions about what the cellphone will become. But knowledge of what brought the cellphone to its current state is the best preparation for entering that milieu. Before going to the advanced topics, one must understand the fundamentals. And the most basic topic for cellular phones is the subject of bandwidth.

1

Bandwidth

The term bandwidth has passed from the mathematically trained to the technically inclined, to those that use technology, and finally into the common lexicon. Everyone wants more bandwidth, even if they are not sure what it is. The limitation of bandwidth in the realm of mobile communications drove the creation of cellular phones, and is still motivating their advancement. Without the limitations of bandwidth, the wireless phone could have remained as it was when introduced in 1946. A careful understanding of the concept of bandwidth is therefore useful, or more precisely, essential to a history of cellular phones.

The aim of this chapter is to explain the concepts important to bandwidth with a focus on wireless communications. While the topics are mathematical, equation-based explanations are not necessary for conceptual understanding. To demonstrate some of the concepts, the flow switches from the analog world to the digital world, where the manipulations are easier, and then back. A later chapter will deal with digital signals in more depth, with the topic here remaining the foundations needed to introduce the analog cellular phone.

Decomposing Signals

The story begins with trigonometry, which is usually defined as the study of triangles, but for the purposes of this history trigonometry deals with angles. An angle describes how two lines separate after a meeting point. To put numbers to it, consider the meeting point to be the center of a circle with a radius of one unit. The distance along the circumference between where the lines cross the circle is the angle. Around 2,200 years ago the Greeks started dividing the unit circle into 360 parts, perhaps due to influence from their astronomy, creating the system of angular degrees still in use.[1] They based their system of trigonometry on the chord, which is the straight line distance between the intersection points. After Greek civilization lost its luster, the study of angles went east.

The relevant contribution of Indian civilization, among many, was to start using the half-chord to make calculations. This first appeared around the year 400 in the *Siddhantas*, a series of texts dealing with various topics such as religion and astronomy. The Sanskrit word for half-chord, *jya-ardha* became shortened to simply *jya*, which Arabic scholars wrote as *jiba*. When Robert of Chester was translating Arabic texts in or about the year 1150, he read this word as *jaib*, the Arabic word for bay,[2] and wrote the Latin equivalent *sinus*, from which the term sine originates. In his defense, Arabic is often written without vowels, which may have contributed to the confusion. Despite its simplicity, the sine of an angle has many uses, with one use of particular importance here.

Plotting the sine of the angles produces the sine wave, the fundamental shape that underpins much of modern technology. In a strict mathematical sense, the sine wave cannot exist in nature, since it extends into infinity in both directions. Even if the requirement of infinite extent is taken away, few waves in nature look like sine waves. Among them are waves on the surface of water, or waves created by plotting measurements of air displacement for sound or from plotting the voltage across antenna ports for radio waves. These are *signals*, which may not have any periodicity and might not even look like waves. Leaving the connection between signals and sine waves for later, the sine wave itself is worthy of examination.

Two numbers describe a sine wave, the less important of which is the *amplitude*, giving the height of the peaks. Human hearing, for example, responds to sound amplitudes over such a wide scale that measurements are nearly always reported on a logarithmic scale.* Similarly, radio receivers

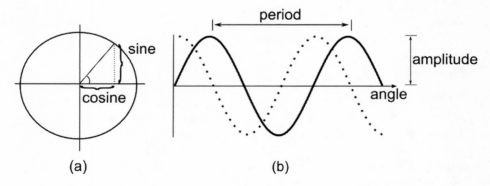

(a)   (b)

Figure 1. The sine and cosine of an angle are distances in the unit circle (a); plotting the sine (solid line) and the cosine (dotted line) for all angles produces sinusoidal waves (b).

*Each unit representing a factor of ten is a Bel, which is commonly multiplied by ten to produce the decibel scale (dB). A ten-fold increase is therefore 10dB, one hundred is 20 dB, one thousand is 30 dB, etc. For sound measurements, near silence is the baseline of 0 dB, while a typical conversational voice may be at 60dB, one million times louder.

encounter incoming waves with amplitudes that can vary by factors of millions. In both cases, the wave amplitude does not need to be an exact quantity.

The second descriptor of a wave is the *frequency*, and this quantity strongly determines the wave's character. Whether dealing with hearing or radio waves, two waves of different frequency produce qualitatively different responses. As for an exact definition, the frequency is the number of times the wave repeats in a second, expressed with the unit label hertz (Hz), but also sometimes with cycles-per-second.

The time between repetitions is the *period*, which is the reciprocal of frequency. For example, a wave with a frequency of one kilohertz, one thousand cycles-per-second, has a period of one millisecond, or each cycle consumes one thousandth of a second. Measuring a wave at one point in space, such as in a microphone, produces waves that vary in time but do not go anywhere. Waves can also, however, move through space.

A moving wave has another descriptive quantity, the *wavelength*, which is related to the frequency. If a radio wave could be frozen in time while in mid-air, then measuring the voltage at each point along it would produce a sine wave in space. The distance, in meters, from one peak to the next is the wavelength. Unfreezing time, the entire wave would continue traveling at the speed of light. It may be apparent that since radio waves all travel at the same constant speed, the wavelength and the period are related. The frequency, period and wavelength of such waves are locked together.* For example, a frequency of 100 MHz corresponds to a period of $1/100,000,000$ Hz $= 10^{-8}$ seconds. The speed of light is 3×10^8 m/sec, so the wavelength is 10^{-8} seconds $\times 3 \times 10^{-8}$ m/sec $= 3$m. Raising the frequency to 200 MHz halves the wavelength to 1.5 m, or halving the frequency to 50 MHz would double the wavelength to 6 m. These characteristics of radio waves are interdependent, but they are also only for describing one solitary wave. Multiple waves oscillating or traveling together introduce another aspect that determines their effects.

Signals generally consist of multiple sine waves, making the relative positioning of the waves important. If two waves of equal amplitude and frequency exactly overlap, then a measurement would show one wave with twice the amplitude of the two waves. If one wave is shifted by half of a period relative to the other, then the measurement will yield nothing since the two always have equal and opposite values, leading to cancellation. Any other positioning would produce something in between those cases. The *phase difference* is a measure of how closely waves align. A phase difference of zero degrees is perfect alignment, and the waves are in-phase. A phase difference of 180 degrees is perfect misalignment, or put another way, the waves are 180 degrees out of phase. The phase dif-

---

*In this case a few equations may clarify the interrelations. Let the period be represented by T, the wavelength by L, the frequency by f, and the speed by c. Then $T=1/f$, $L=c/f$ and $L=cT$.

ference between waves that share the same frequency and start together, although with some offset, will remain constant for all positions and times, since their peaks and valleys always have that same offset.

A special case is when the phase shift is ninety degrees, called a cosine wave. The sine and the cosine wave are only distinguishable in comparison with each other. When measuring one wave alone, there is no reason to call it a sine wave or a cosine wave. The shape is a *sinusoid*, without categorization as a sine or a cosine. But when two waves exist together, they have a measurable phase difference. If that phase difference is 90 degrees, then the leading wave can be called the cosine wave and the lagging wave can be assigned to be the sine wave. A ninety-degree phase difference is special and has its own name, the waves are in *quadrature*. Such waves have an important role in wireless communications, both analog and digital, as will be seen later.

The connection between signals and sine waves, and their relevance to bandwidth is crucial to communications. To gain a basic understanding, however, it helps to leave these analog waves behind and examine their equivalents in the digital domain.

Operations with Walsh Codes

The Walsh codes are digital numbers that perform similar functions to the sinusoids. Their use extends into the nineteenth century, but they are mostly known from a study published in 1923 by mathematician J. L. Walsh,[3] several decades before digital electronics became prominent. Interest in Walsh codes at that early date arose because they are a *complete* and *orthogonal* set of numbers. The Walsh codes are introduced here for two reasons. First, they demonstrate these important properties which also apply to sine waves. And Walsh codes themselves play a prominent role in modern digital cellular communications, which will be discussed in later chapters.

A simple procedure gives the Walsh codes of any length. Binary numbers are usually represented with the values "0" and "1," but "-1" and "+1" are used here to simplify some operations. The Walsh code of length one is simply +1. To create Walsh codes of greater length, copy the previous Walsh codes to the right, below, and diagonally, and reverse the signs for the diagonal copy.

The following examples use the Walsh codes of length four:

$$w_0 = +1 +1 +1 +1,$$
$$w_1 = +1 -1 +1 -1,$$
$$w_2 = +1 +1 -1 -1,$$
$$w_3 = +1 -1 -1 +1.$$

Making use of the Walsh codes requires another element, an operation denoted here by $\otimes$. For a number with a length of one, the operator performs multiplication:

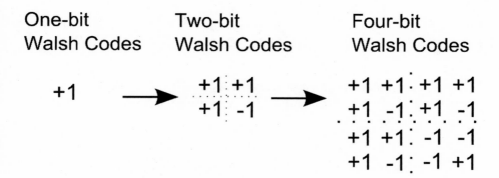

Figure 2. To produce longer Walsh codes, copy the previous set into four quadrants and reverse the bits in the lower right quadrant.

$$+1 \otimes +1 = +1,$$
$$-1 \otimes -1 = +1,$$
$$+1 \otimes -1 = -1,$$
$$-1 \otimes +1 = -1.$$

For numbers longer than one digit, carry out the multiplication digit-by-digit and add the result. As a final step, divide the sum by the length of the numbers. For example

$$+1\ -1\ +1\ -1$$
$$\otimes\ +1\ +1\ -1\ +1$$
$$+1\ -1\ -1\ -1 \xrightarrow{\text{sum}} -2 \xrightarrow{\div 4} -\tfrac{1}{2}$$

The last step is an example of normalization, and will make the results independent of the Walsh code length. With this operator it is now possible to demonstrate the special properties of these codes.

The first property to understand is that the Walsh codes are orthogonal with respect to the operator $\otimes$, meaning that applying the operator to different Walsh codes always produces zero. Therefore, $w_0 \otimes w_1 = 0$, $w_1 \otimes w_3 = 0$ and similarly for other combinations of Walsh codes. The orthogonality applies even if the signs are reversed for one or both of the Walsh codes, such as $w_1 \otimes -w_2 = 0$.

The exception to orthogonality is when $\otimes$ operates on two copies of the same Walsh code. Due to the normalization step, the result is always one or negative one. For example, $w_0 \otimes w_0 = 1$ and $w_2 \otimes -w_2 = -1$. This property of orthogonality is what renders the Walsh codes useful for analyzing binary numbers, since it creates a special power for the operator.

The operator $\otimes$ acts as a Walsh code filter, finding the Walsh codes within other numbers. As an example, consider the number $a = +1\ +1\ -1\ +1$. Then

$$w_0 \otimes a = {}^1\!/_2,$$
$$w_1 \otimes a = -{}^1\!/_2,$$
$$w_2 \otimes a = {}^1\!/_2,$$
$$w_3 \otimes a = {}^1\!/_2.$$

The number a is composed of the Walsh codes with these weightings. This means that summing the Walsh codes using these results as multipliers produces the original number:

$$ {}^1\!/_2 w_0 - {}^1\!/_2 w_1 + {}^1\!/_2 w_2 + {}^1\!/_2 w_3 = a $$

Another approach is to consider the number to be made up of Walsh codes from the beginning, and then apply each Walsh code in turn. For the first Walsh code,

$$ w_0 \otimes a = w_0 \otimes ({}^1\!/_2 w_0 - {}^1\!/_2 w_1 + {}^1\!/_2 w_2 + {}^1\!/_2 w_3) $$

$$ = {}^1\!/_2 w_0 \otimes w_0 - {}^1\!/_2 w_0 \otimes w_1 + {}^1\!/_2 w_0 \otimes w_2 + {}^1\!/_2 w_0 \otimes w_3 $$

$$ = {}^1\!/_2 \times 1 - {}^1\!/_2 \times 0 + {}^1\!/_2 \times 0 + {}^1\!/_2 \times 0 = {}^1\!/_2. $$

The orthogonality filters out all of the parts of the number a made up of other Walsh codes, and the normalization lets the part of a that is made up of w_0 to emerge undistorted. Repeating these steps with the other Walsh codes finds their contributions to a. The procedure is *decomposition*, in which operations reduce a signal to its constitutive elements.

An important property implied by the ability to perform decomposition is that the Walsh codes are complete, meaning that all digital numbers have a representation as a sum of Walsh codes. Put another way, summing the Walsh codes with the weighting found by decomposition always reproduces the original number. There is no left-over part of the number that the Walsh codes do not represent. As a note, the lengths of the Walsh codes are always powers of two, such as 2, 4, 8, 16, 32 and so on. No Walsh codes exist, for example, of length 50. Placing 14 +1's at the end of a 50-digit number, however, produces a 64-digit number, which does have a representation with 64-digit Walsh codes.

While the Walsh codes are complete, orthogonal sets in the digital domain, the sinusoidal waves perform these functions for analog signals. The equivalent of the $\otimes$ operator is to multiply two analog signals and then add the point-by-point results over one period. Multiplying a sine wave by itself and adding the results over one period is the equivalent of using the $\otimes$ operator on two of the same Walsh code, since it always produces the same number. Adding a final normalization step insures that the final number will always be one.

Using two sine waves with different frequencies is the equivalent of applying the $\otimes$ operator with two different Walsh codes. The result is always zero, meaning that sine waves of different frequencies are orthogonal. Waves that are in quadrature, with a phase difference of 90 degrees, are also orthogonal. So performing multiplication and summation on a sine wave and a cosine wave will produce zero even if they have the same frequency.

These properties lead to the ability to decompose a signal into sinusoidal waves. Or, from another perspective, all analog signals are weighted summations of pure sine and cosine waves. To determine how much of a certain frequency is in a particular signal, multiply the signal by the single-frequency sine wave and sum the results. Repeat this with a cosine wave and then move to the next frequency to continue the decomposition. This procedure can extend to infinite frequency, but in practice the frequency components decrease after some point and approach zero magnitude. The frequency components in human speech, for example, are strong up to a few kilohertz and then decrease sharply in amplitude, so that there is almost nothing above ten kilohertz. Other signals, such as broadcast radio waves, contain waves with frequencies only within a regulated span, with no components at higher or lower frequencies.

The Frequency Domain

The crucial property that the sinusoids are a complete set for the representation of signals came to prominence in the early nineteenth century. French academic Jean Baptiste John Fourier first published the idea in an 1822 study of heat. Today the set of sinusoids and their amplitudes making up a signal is called a Fourier series. At the time, Fourier's treatise came under criticism for lacking mathematical rigor.[4] Does every wave have an equivalent Fourier series? Mathematician Peter Gustav Dirichlet soon provided the equivocal answer: Yes and no.

Not every signal can be decomposed into constituent sine and cosine waves, but the ones that matter physically can. Three major classes of signals exist for which there is no equivalent Fourier series. Signals that reach infinity at one or multiple points are out. So are signals that have an infinite number of peaks and valleys in a finite length. The last category contains signals that have an infinite number of discontinuities in a finite length. The discontinuities are points where the value of the signal moves instantly between values, without an intermediary slope. A series with a finite number of discontinuous points can have a Fourier series, although that series can be long.

The notable aspect of signals without Fourier series representation is that they are based around the concept of infinity. While a valid mathematical concept, infinity has little bearing on what happens at the human scale. A measured voltage, for example, may go to a high value, but it will not reach infinity. And a radio wave may contain billions of peaks and valleys within one second, but that, too, has not reached infinity. So any measured signal can be represented by a Fourier series, even if this does not apply to every mathematical signal. And this representation of a signal as a set of single-frequency sine waves creates the notion of bandwidth.

The first definition of bandwidth is the space of frequencies needed to describe the time-domain signal. Representing sound with a Fourier series requires frequencies up to 15 kHz, so that is the bandwidth. In actuality, the terms with the most amplitude in human speech are in the lower range of these frequencies, so telephones only transmit up to approximately 4 kHz. There is some ambiguity in the usage of the term bandwidth, which could mean the frequency-domain extent of a signal, or it could mean the range of frequencies that a communication channel can transmit. So an audio signal's bandwidth can be 15 kHz, while the telephone's bandwidth is 4 kHz. In all cases, the aspects of the signal important for communications are in its frequencies.

The Fourier series of a signal is its frequency domain representation. This is different from actual measurements, during which signals act in the time domain. A measurement of an audio signal, for example, gives the air displacement at each time, or more specifically, the amplitude of the electrical current in the sensor. After making the measurement for some length of time, the time-domain results can be operated upon to decompose it into sinusoidal waves of different frequencies. The switch has been made from the time-domain to the frequency-domain, and a switch can be made to go back again. In both cases, information from an entire section of one domain, not just one point, figures into the calculations. A Fourier series consisting of only one frequency, for example, would be just a single-frequency sine wave. The full spectrum of frequencies must be included to find the time-domain signal. Similarly, the measurement needs to be made over some length of time to be able to find a frequency-domain equivalent. And the measurement interval is not without repercussions in the frequency domain.

The length of the signal in the time domain determines the resolution needed in the frequency domain, and therefore the size of the Fourier series. As a first consideration, the sine wave is periodic, so the time-domain signal must be made periodic. This is done by considering only one section of the measured time-domain signal, and assuming that segment repeats infinitely. This imposed periodicity is what places limitations on the frequency-domain representation.

The longer the time-domain signal is, the more frequency-domain resolution needed for an adequate representation. Consider, for example, an audio signal of some long duration, out of which one-second is chosen for decomposition. The signal that is actually decomposed is this one second segment repeated infinitely, so the sinusoids that make up this signal must also repeat every one second. The slowest wave that fits has a period of one second, or one hertz in frequency. The next fastest wave that fits has a period of half a second, or a frequency of two hertz. This reasoning continues for higher frequencies, so that the Fourier series contains only the waves with whole-number frequencies. The resolution, which is the difference between the frequencies, is one hertz. To take a different example, use a measurement interval that is one millisecond, or one thousandths of a second. The slowest wave that fits the time interval has a period of one millisecond, meaning one kilohertz. The next slowest wave that fits has a period of half of a millisecond, or two kilohertz. The resolution is therefore one kilohertz, demonstrating that decreasing the time length of the signal decreases its frequency resolution.

While the length of the time-domain signal determines the frequency resolution, the bandwidth remains unchanged. A series extending from one hertz to 4 kHz with a one hertz resolution, for example, would have four thousand terms. A series covering the same frequency span, but with one kilohertz resolution would contain only four terms. While the sizes of the two series are much different, they both cover the same frequency span and therefore represent the same bandwidth. The second series, however, contains much less information than the first, which is fine since that series' corresponding one millisecond-long signal has less information than the first series' one second long signal. To summarize, a longer time-domain signal needs more resolution in the frequency domain for an adequate representation. The converse is also true.

The frequency-domain bandwidth determines the resolution in the time-domain. This makes sense since a high-frequency component represents a fast time-domain wave. For example, a bandwidth of one megahertz implies that the highest possible frequency component is a one megahertz sinusoidal wave, with a period of one microsecond. One microsecond is the fastest change possible within the signal, and is therefore the time-domain resolution.

A duality emerges from the relation between the two domains. The longer a signal consumes, when measured in either domain, the more information it has and the more resolution its representation needs in the other domain. These considerations only affect the method of communication, not the signal itself. Returning to the previous examples, the one millisecond segments give four terms, and the one second segments give four thousand terms. To translate a continuous audio signal into the frequency domain, however, requires one

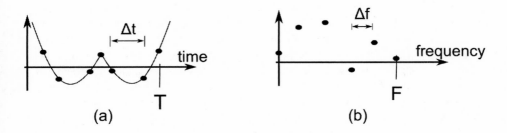

Figure 3. Time-domain representation of a signal over time T with resolution Δt (a); corresponding frequency-domain representation up to frequency F with resolution Δf (b).

thousand one-millisecond segments in a second. The one thousand four-term series brings the total number of terms to represent one second back to four thousand. Whether to use one thousand time segments of one millisecond, one time segment of one second, or something in between depends on the specifics of the equipment and the communication channel.

The duality between the time and the frequency domain affects wireless communications in several ways. The obvious connection is that signals with high information content, meaning many fast variations, require large bandwidth. But there are also physical ramifications. One is that short impulses, such as sparks from motors or lightning, have large bandwidths, putting noise into much of the radio spectrum. The energy of a one microsecond pulse, for example, is mostly in the spectrum up to one megahertz. Unlike a theoretical pulse, which maintains a constant value over a short time, physical pulses such as lightning usually contain shorter pulses. The energy therefore can extend deep into the radio frequency bands.

Another example is in location finding, which often uses the time of an incoming signal for position information. The analog phones of the 1980's and early-to-mid 1990's (the first generation of cellphones) used bandwidths of approximately 30 kHz, which translates to a time-domain resolution of 16 microseconds. This is long enough for a radio wave to travel almost five kilometers, so exact positioning is difficult. One type of the second generation of cellphones from the 1990's, however, uses a bandwidth of 1.25 MHz, corresponding to a time-domain resolution of less than one microsecond, or a travel time of less than 300 meters. Combined with other information, the location of the phone can then be determined to within a few meters. Bandwidth therefore has real physical consequences.

Linearity and Preservation of Bandwidth in a System

Of particular importance in discussing bandwidth is the topic of how a signal's frequency-domain representation changes as it passes through a system. In the case of a telephone, a microphone converts the audio signal into an electrical signal, which then goes through amplifiers and enters into the wire network. Besides miles of wire, the electric signal encounters switching equipment and more amplifiers before reaching the receiver and being converted back into an audio signal by the speaker. The bandwidth may begin at 4 kHz, but what is it at the end of the journey? The answer is that the bandwidth of the signal will not change if the network elements meet one special criterion.

A *linear* device does not change the bandwidth of a signal that it operates upon. The term *device* is general, meaning anything that has an input and an output. Electronic components such as amplifiers are included, as are transmission wires and even distances of empty space that radio waves travel through. The term linear derives from the graphical representation of a device's operation.

A linear device has an input-output plot consisting of a straight line. The line can be steep or shallow, but as long as it is straight, sine waves do not distort as they pass through. An input signal consisting of a single sine wave, for example, would produce an output signal that is also a sine wave and may have a different amplitude, but is otherwise unchanged in shape. This applies just as well if the input signal contains many sine waves.

A common analysis method is to first find the Fourier series representation of the input signal, apply the linear device's input-output relation to each frequency component, and then to sum the Fourier series at the output to find the resulting signal. The device changes the amplitude of each term in the Fourier series, but does not add any new terms. Analyzing the effects of a linear device on each frequency component of a signal is possible since the device acts on each frequency independently of waves at other frequencies. The bandwidth therefore remains the same at the output as it was at the input. As expected, linearity is an important goal in much of wireless design, although it is difficult to achieve in some cases.

Much of the interference in wireless systems originates in the nonlinearity of *power amplifiers*. As the name implies, these amplifiers take the small-scale signals from the electronics and move them to the large-scale for transmission. Ideally the amplifier's input-output plot would be perfectly linear, and it is, but only to a point. Any amplifier has a maximum power level it can deliver, depending on the specifics of the circuit and its components. As the power approaches that maximum, the input-output plot deviates from a straight line, introducing non-linearity. The linear analysis method that treats each frequency component independently no longer applies. A sine wave input would produce a distorted wave at the output, and calculating the Fourier series of the output would show that the device has added new frequency components. Those new waves could interfere with communication taking place in other frequency bands, and are therefore undesirable. Always operating the amplifier well below the nonlinear region may seem to be a way to avoid this problem, but the other important power amplifier parameter has to be considered.

As with much of engineering, a tradeoff exists between two competing and conflicting goals, which for power amplifiers are linearity and efficiency. For an amplifier, the efficiency is the percentage of supplied power that appears in the output signal. The rest of the energy dissipates as heat and is therefore wasted. For a high-power radio station transmitting with thousands of watts, the lost power can be significant. For cellular phone handsets, the lost power may not be as large, but still drains the battery. So the efficiency of a power amplifier must be as high as possible, which introduces the conflict with linearity since the efficiency of a power amplifier circuit rises with the power level.

The push to operate the power amplifier at the highest power level with-

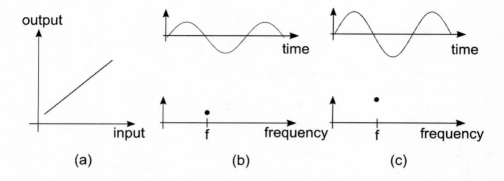

Figure 4: The input/output plot of a linear device is a straight line (a); the device changes the amplitude of the input signal (b) to produce the output signal (c) without altering the frequency.

out entering the nonlinear region drives much of not only power amplifier design, but also the transmitted signal shape. For efficient operation the average signal power should be as high as possible. Peaks in the signal that are too high, however, will stray into the nonlinear range of operation. A signal with a low peak-to-average ratio is therefore ideal.

The peak-to-average ratio starts at two and only rises from there. Consider a signal consisting of a pure sine wave. Power in electricity is proportional to the square of voltage, so the output power is in the shape of a sine wave squared. If the peak of this wave is one, then the average is one-half, giving a peak-to-average ratio of two. Any deviation from a perfect sine wave increases this number. But the deviations carry the information, which introduces the next fundamental communications topic.

Analog Modulation

Audio signals, with frequencies of several hundred to several thousand hertz, may be fast on the human scale, but to a radio system they are far too slow for efficient operation. As discussed later, an antenna's size should be the same order of magnitude as the wavelength of the waves it transmits or receives. A one kilohertz radio wave has a wavelength of 300 kilometers, which is too large for a practical antenna. But a wave with a frequency of 500 MHz has a more practical wavelength of 0.6 meters. Another motivation for changing a signal's frequencies is *multiplexing*, also called *multiple access*, meaning to send multiple signals at the same time. This is familiar through the operation of radio and television, with each station assigned a different band of frequencies. These factors point to the need for placing audio information onto higher frequency waves.

Modulation is the variation of a sinusoidal wave in order to send infor-

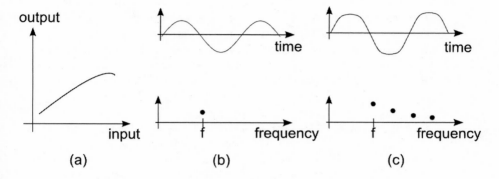

Figure 5: An amplifier deviates from linear operation as it approaches saturation (a); the device not only amplifies the input signal (b), it also adds distortion that creates new frequency components in the output signal (c).

mation. Since a wave has three defining characteristics, any of these three, or some combination, can be varied for modulation. Two variation schemes, amplitude modulation and frequency modulation, are familiar through radio as AM and FM. The phase of a wave is a third property to vary, yielding the less commonly known phase modulation. Each of these methods has different qualities and applications. The first two, Amplitude Modulation and Frequency Modulation, are discussed here while reserving Phase Modulation for a later chapter dealing with digital modulation.

The multiplication of two signals creates amplitude modulation. A device multiplies a high frequency wave, the carrier, with a low frequency wave, the signal, causing the amplitude of the high frequency wave to vary. The trend of the peaks in the modulated wave is in the shape of the low frequency signal. The multiplication process, also called *mixing*, is achieved in several ways. One simple method is to use an amplifier acting on the carrier wave, with the signal wave controlling the amount of amplification. Another method is to pass the two waves through a nonlinear device. The nonlinearity creates many new frequencies, some of which are the product of the inputs. Whatever the mixing process used, the resulting wave is different from its original form, creating new frequency components.

An amplitude modulated wave does not contain either of the frequencies used in its creation. To clarify, let the signal wave have a frequency denoted by f_L (for low frequency), and call the frequency of the carrier f_H (for high frequency). Finding the Fourier series of the modulated wave, made by multiplying the signal and the carrier, reveals it contains two equal-amplitude waves with frequencies $f_H + f_L$ and $f_H - f_L$. Summing these two waves produces an overall wave of frequency f_H with an envelope frequency of f_L. An example of two sinusoids adding to create amplitude modulation is the operation of a tuning fork. The fork produces a tone when struck, as does the instrument being tuned. When the two tones are close, the amplitude varies periodically, sounding like a low hum. Tuning the instrument so that the tones match more closely, the amplitude variation becomes slower and disappears if the frequencies match exactly.* In practical radio systems there is some leakage of f_L and f_H through the mixer, although the elements such as amplifiers and the antenna do not operate at f_L, so that leaked wave is not transmitted. Some of f_H may get through, which is not necessarily undesirable.

To demodulate the AM wave and extract the signal wave, repeat the mixing. In the example, waves with frequency components $f_H + f_L$ and $f_H - f_L$ arrive at the radio. The receiver multiplies that wave by a wave of frequency f_H, producing waves with frequencies at the sums and differences of the inputs. These four waves are $f_H + f_L + f_H$, $f_H + f_L - f_H$, $f_H - f_L + f_H$, and $f_H - f_L - f_H$. The second and fourth waves are back at the signal wave frequency of f_L, while the first and third waves are around the distant frequency of $2f_H$. To demodulate an AM wave, therefore, mix it with the carrier frequency and then pass the results through a filter that only allows waves at audio frequencies to emerge at the output. All the receiver needs, besides the mixer and filter, is its own copy of the carrier wave.

AM radio transmissions include a copy of the carrier wave along with the modulated signal so that the receivers can be simple and inexpensive. A nonlinear device, such as a diode in simple receivers, can accept the three waves at frequencies $f_H + f_L$, $f_H - f_L$ and f_H, perform the multiplication between them, and produce the signal wave at f_L. Whenever two dissimilar metals make contact, there is some diode effect in the junction, so even household objects can emit demodulated AM signals. When the received power is high enough, the audio can be heard without amplification. The heyday of AM transmission has passed, so few stations broadcast with enough power, but there was a time when radio could be heard coming from household objects. Amplitude modulation is simple in principle and in practice, but the story is not all good.

The explanation of amplitude modulation shows that it doubles the bandwidth of the signal. The previous example started with one signal tone at f_L and created, after mixing, two tones with frequencies on either side of the carrier wave's frequency, $f_H \pm f_L$. An audio signal consists of many tones, all of which exist on either side of the carrier frequency in an AM wave. The two sets of tones on either side of the carrier wave's frequency are called side bands, and they are identical to each other.

Some systems, called *single side-band amplitude modulation*, make use of this redundancy by filtering out one of the side bands and only transmitting the other. This saves bandwidth, allowing more stations to broadcast in a given

---

The trigonometric identity cos A × cos B = ½ (cos(A+B) + cos(A-B)) is the mathematical basis for mixing.

frequency band, but introduces complexity within the receiver, since the simple multiplication process described earlier will not work. Of course, modern receivers have become so complicated that this added complexity is nearly trivial. And there is another significant benefit. Lowering the bandwidth also lowers the amount of noise that enters the receiver, which is an important goal in amplitude modulation.

Amplitude modulation is strongly susceptible to *noise*. This noise is any radio signal other than the desired one, including environmental factors such as solar radiation, lightning and nearby electrical equipment. Interference from other transmitters, such as another station operating at the same frequency, is often separated from noise in system design and specifications, but the effect is the same. These waves arriving from other sources distort the carrier wave's amplitude, so that the envelope is no longer an exact copy of the signal.

The way to minimize noise entering into amplitude modulation is to decrease the bandwidth. The radio receiver's filter acts like a window, letting in the small band of frequencies that make up the desired broadcast. But noise also comes in through the open window. Even without incoming waves, engineers designing radio systems assume that the electronic devices in the receiver themselves have an evenly spread minimum noise floor caused by random fluctuations of electrons. That noise floor rises with temperature, reaching a value of 4×10^{-21} watt/Hz* at 25 C. A one megahertz channel therefore begins with 4×10^{-21} watt/Hz $\times 10^6$ Hz $= 4 \times 10^{-15}$ watt of noise before accounting for any received waves. This may not seem like a high noise power, but it is comparable to the power level of some received broadcast waves. By using a smaller window, less noise enters the radio.

Lowering the bandwidth therefore seems to be an all-around win for radio design. With stations using less bandwidth there would be more room in the spectrum. And with less noise getting into the receiver, the transmissions would be of higher quality. Small bandwidth appears to be always good, yet the opposite became true when a new form of modulation emerged.

Another wave parameter that can carry a signal is the frequency, leading to *frequency modulation* (FM). As the name implies, the amplitude of the signal wave becomes a frequency variation in the carrier wave. A large signal amplitude, signifying a loud sound, therefore corresponds to a large deviation in frequency from that of the carrier. In the early FM radio of the 1940's, each channel had an allocation of 200 kHz, of which 25 kHz on each side was left blank for channel spacing, leaving 150 kHz available. This allowed a maximum frequency deviation of 75 kHz.[5] This was later reduced so that each FM channel could broadcast the two signals needed for stereophonic programs. Analog cellular phone systems gave each user about 25 kHz, so the frequency

---

More commonly expressed as -174 dBm/Hz in logarithmic scale. The dBm unit denotes decibels relative to one milliwatt, so that 30 dBm = 1000 milliwatts = 1 watt.

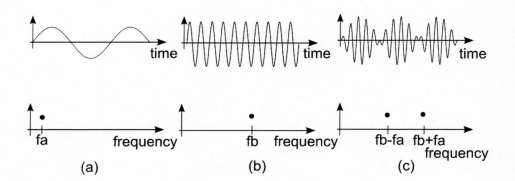

Figure 6: A low-frequency wave (a) multiplied with a high-frequency wave (b) creates an amplitude modulated (AM) wave (c).

deviation was a more modest 12.5 kHz. In all systems, frequency modulation takes up more bandwidth to send a signal than amplitude modulation would.

A frequency modulated wave requires, at least in the mathematics, infinite bandwidth. This may appear contradictory with the definition of frequency modulation. If the frequency varies by at most f_M around the carrier frequency f_H, then the frequencies of the modulated wave would all seem to be contained within $f_H - f_M$ and $f_H + f_M$. This is, however, the instantaneous frequency, or the frequency for an infinitesimally small period of time.

Measuring a frequency modulated wave over any significant length of time reveals a complicated shape. The Fourier series that corresponds to such a shape contains many waves stretching well past the frequency limits of $f_H \pm f_M$. For example, varying the frequency of the carrier with a single signal tone of frequency f_L, produces a wave with Fourier series components $f_H \pm f_L$, like amplitude modulation. But there are also components at $f_H \pm 2f_L$, $f_H \pm 3f_L$, and continuing to infinity. But the relative amplitude of the waves decrease with distance from the carrier wave, so truncating the series after the first few components does not usually significantly distort the signal.

The perceived lack of benefits of FM over AM hampered the early development of FM radio. An influential paper published in 1922 did the mathematical analysis and found that FM offered no bandwidth savings over AM, and would probably require more bandwidth to avoid distortion. The conclusion seemed definitive: "It is proved that the frequency modulation system using a spacing or compensating wave is inferior to the amplitude variation systems both as to the width of the frequency band occupied and as to distortion of signal wave form."[6] This paper was particularly influential since it was written by John Carson, who had achieved prominence in the field by developing single-sideband radio. Yet from a modern perspective, this reasoning cannot be complete, since FM is widely used instead of AM. The flaw was in trying to use FM like AM, rather than creating a completely new type of broadcast system.

Frequency modulation offers many benefits to radio along with the increased bandwidth that it uses, beginning with better reception. While an AM system seeks to reduce noise by using the smallest possible bandwidth, FM lowers the effect of noise by increasing the bandwidth. FM is inherently immune to amplitude variation because the information is contained in the frequency. To increase noise immunity, an FM system designer can increase the maximum frequency deviation (f_M in the previous examples), thereby also increasing the bandwidth. The signal-to-noise ratio after FM demodulation increases by a factor of four each time the bandwidth doubles.[7]

Spreading the transmitted signal over more frequencies helps noise immunity by adding redundancy. When the frequency band is wide then any one frequency component experiencing high noise at some time is less important to the overall received signal. This principle, of spreading the spectrum to reduce the effect of noise, will be one of the fundamental concepts of digital cellular communication. In analog radio, FM not only allows better reception, but the quality stays high over a greater area.[8] For AM, the signal is strongest near the antenna and weakens with distance but the noise level can remain nearly constant. The signal-to-noise ratio therefore declines and the quality drops with distance. In the case of FM, by contrast, the signal-to-noise ratio at the antenna does not directly correspond to the signal-to-noise ratio after demodulation. The quality of the audio remains mostly constant with distance until the signal-to-noise ratio becomes so small that the FM wave completely submerges into the noise.

Another positive attribute of FM is that the receiver can differentiate between competing stations better than AM. When two competing waves at the same frequencies arrive at the receiver, it demodulates the one with the higher power. An AM receiver, however, demodulates the sum of the two waves, producing audible distortion. Experience shows that AM requires a signal-to-interferer power ratio of 100 to 1 for clear audio output, while FM can produce good quality sound with a 2 to 1 power ratio. Experiments of the 1930's showed that an FM station could cover the same broadcast area as an AM station with better signal quality and at one tenth the power.[9]

In addition to the benefits of FM signals themselves over AM, the transmitters are more economical to build. This is because the transmitted wave has a constant amplitude envelope, producing a relatively low peak-to-average ratio. For AM, the peak-to-average ratio can be large, reducing the efficiency of the transmitter's power amplifiers.

The simple receivers of AM do not, however, work for FM. The wave from the receiver's oscillator, which is set to operate at the frequency of the carrier wave, and the received wave go to a circuit called a discriminator. The output is a voltage which corresponds to the difference in phase between the two inputs.

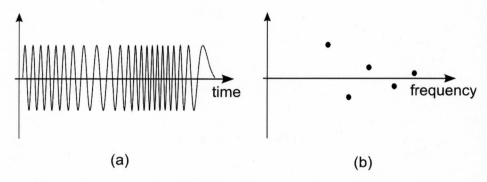

(a)   (b)

Figure 7. A frequency modulated (FM) wave (a) contains many frequency-domain components (b).

The changing phase difference corresponds to the frequency difference between the two waves, so the amplitude of the output voltage from the discriminator carries the demodulated signal. These newer parts, such as local oscillators and the discriminator, are from the developments in radio technology that took place through the 1920's and 1930's, after AM radio became an established technology. Such advancements also solved the problem of the large bandwidth required.

FM radio can use more bandwidth by operating at higher frequencies than AM radio. When commercial radio began broadcasting in the 1920's, frequencies in the hundreds of kilohertz were considered high. The first government spectrum assignments in the USA, made in the late 1920's, only covered up to 1000 kHz (or one megahertz).[10] The AM radio band settled in this range with each station having an allocation of 10 kHz. With the advancement of radio technology, by the 1930's inexpensive, mass-produced oscillators could reach over 100 MHz, opening one hundred times more spectrum for radio. Upon creation in the late 1930's, the FM radio band stretched from 42 to 50 MHz,[11] and the Federal Communications Commission later moved it to the current frequencies of 88 to 108 MHz. With the ample bandwidth, FM stations offered higher audio quality than their AM competition, and could send the multiple transmissions needed for stereo. Yet despite the advantages of FM over AM for radio, the growth of FM was a long and slow process.

Much of the development of FM radio, both technically and commercially, was due to the work of early radio pioneer Edward Howard Armstrong. A lifelong innovator in the field of radio, he was already well known by the 1930's for several significant contributions to the radio field. While facing an uphill battle for the acceptance of FM radio, he was a respected figure in the industry, and was well-rewarded. At the time of his death, Armstrong's net worth was over fifteen million dollars, an enormous sum for 1954. The story of FM radio begins with his involvement in the early 1930's.

Armstrong conducted the trials in 1934 and 1935 that showed the benefits of FM radio. He had taken his proposal to RCA and they allowed him to use their transmitters at the top of the Empire State Building. The receiver was eighty miles away in Haddonfield, New Jersey, which is significant because the antenna on the Empire State Building was approximately 1,250 feet above the ground, giving a distance to the horizon of forty-five miles, showing that over-the-horizon broadcasting is possible. These were the tests that showed FM as giving better reception quality and more broadcast range with less transmitted power than AM.[12] The two kilowatt test station easily outperformed a 25 kilowatt AM broadcast from the same location.[13]

Despite the positive results, RCA decided not pursue FM radio, leaving Armstrong to continue its development on his own. Television was RCA's futuristic research topic at the time, with AM radio doing fine as is. Actually, RCA also owned much of AM radio, which may have added to its reticence to switch to a new technology. Armstrong instead sold some of his shares of RCA to raise $300,000 and founded an FM radio station in 1939. Covering New York City with a transmitter across the Hudson River in Alpine, New Jersey, it was soon joined by other FM stations around the country, and the FCC approved FM for commercial broadcasting in 1945.[14] Despite the benefits of FM, most of the radio industry continued with AM.

The adoption of FM into radio as a replacement for AM was slowed by commercial and regulatory forces. Some of the literature written by FM supporters can be quite bitter (e.g., D. V. Erickson's *Armstrong's Fight for FM Broadcasting: One Man vs Big Business and Bureaucracy*[15]). These accounts typically portray FM as a better system, which is true, held back by the Federal Communications Commission and corporate forces, which may be true.

Others promote the FCC and chairman James Fly as champions of FM radio who held the nascent television industry at bay until the FM systems were in place.[16] The FCC even took back television's channel one, which belonged to RCA's station in New York City, for FM radio. Whatever the intention, the introduction of FM radio was almost guaranteed to be slow.

The problems began with the FCC's restrictions placed on FM broadcasts. While AM stations could broadcast at high powers, all FM stations in a market had to use the same power, which was usually relatively low. The restriction in coverage area resulted in lower revenue, and also led to a popular misconception that FM is a short-range technology in comparison to AM.[17] The FCC's contention was that it was trying to avoid the chaotic situation at the start of AM radio in the 1920's.

Adding to the obstacles, in 1948 the FCC moved the FM band of 42–50 MHz to 88–108 MHz, rendering all FM receivers from before 1948 obsolete. The stated reason was that expected sunspot activity would cause interference, yet the FCC then allocated the old FM radio band to television, which is more sensitive to noise than radio and was by then based on FM as well. The feared solar interference did not occur.[18] By the 1950's, FM radio had a reputation as being a specialty technology suitable for small markets such as enthusiasts and in-store music for businesses.[19] The sales of FM receivers gradually increased, boosted by the introduction of stereo broadcasts, reaching parity with AM in the mid 1970's and then moving ahead to dominate radio.[20]

The struggle between FM and AM radio has parallels in the battles over a digital cellular standard in the 1990's. In both situations, the proposal of a more complicated technique was met with justifiable skepticism, although the new method was demonstrated to be better. The resistance from companies and regulatory agencies continued, however, perhaps due to the large investments that were already in place. Eventually, as the new method entered successful use, its benefits became apparent and the method gained acceptance. The difference is the time involved. The ascendancy of FM happened from 1935 to approximately 1980. As discussed in later chapters, the competition between the digital cellular techniques of TDMA and CDMA lasted approximately one decade, from 1989 to 1998.

Limited Bandwidth

When advancing technology extended the usable commercial spectrum from one megahertz to over one hundred megahertz, the bandwidth may have seemed almost limitless. Even FM stations, with their relatively wide 200 kHz channel allotments could be accommodated along with military, shipping, emergency services and other uses. Since the 1930's though, the applications have increased dramatically, while the spectrum has not.

Modern technology and manufacturing methods allows for receivers that could operate up to one hundred thousand megahertz, so there would appear to be plenty of available spectrum. But not all of those frequencies are useful for wireless communications. The problem is in the frequency-dependence of the loss for a radio link.

Radio waves lose power in two ways, one of which does not vary with frequency and one that does. The first source of loss arises from the way that waves expand as they propagate away from the source. The source spreads its power, P, onto the surface of a sphere around it. Since the area of a sphere is $4\pi r^2$, with r being the radius, the energy density in units of watts-per-square-meter is $P/4\pi r^2$. As the wave propagates outward, the area increases at a rate of r^2, so the energy density of the wave decreases by the same amount, and receiving antennas collect less power. The wave does not lose energy from the spreading, but the energy travels in directions other than toward the receiving antenna. This type of loss varies only with distance, but there is another loss mechanism that does increase with frequency.

Radio waves propagating over terrain experience loss from absorption. Soil, water, vegetation, houses and other features all remove some energy from the radio waves that travel along the ground. The electromagnetic waves excite small electrical currents in the terrain, which dissipate the energy as heat. A few watts spread over many square kilometers of land creates an imperceptible amount of heating, but from the perspective of the wave the energy loss is significant. And unlike the loss to the communication link through wave spreading, this loss usually rises with frequency.

The frequency-dependence of radio wave propagation loss is difficult to characterize generally, since it varies with the specifics of the terrain. For example, one published propagation model states that radio waves traveling over leaf-bearing trees experience a loss in decibels proportional to approximately $\sqrt[4]{f}$, with f being the frequency.[21] Similar studies in many other environments, including urban settings, have found a significant frequency-dependent component to propagation loss. As a general guideline, cellular systems operating at 1900 MHz need approximately 1.5 times more base stations than systems using 800 MHz due to the lower effective broadcasting range.

Another source of radio wave loss that rises with frequency is the effect of objects and their shadowing. The ability of an object to stop a wave is dependent on its size relative to a wavelength. This is demonstrated by the ability to hear around large objects, but not see around them. Light waves have wavelengths of approximately half of a micrometer, so common objects are millions of wavelengths in size. Almost any object can stop light and can cast a sharp, dark shadow. The wavelengths of sound waves, however, are in the range of several centimeters to three meters, which is approximately the same as terrain obstacles. The objects that are a few wavelengths across will stop some of the waves, but others will be able to go around, so the shadow is not as complete as in the optical case.

Radio waves are in the same size category as sound waves, so human-scale objects will attenuate but not block the waves. A radio wave with a frequency of one gigahertz has a wavelength of thirty centimeters. At two gigahertz the wavelength is fifteen centimeters. The wavelength continues shrinking as the frequency rises, and the relative size of objects in the propagation path grows. An object five meters across, for example, is 16.6 wavelengths across for waves of one gigahertz but 33.3 wavelengths across for waves of two gigahertz. As the relative size of the object grows, its shadow becomes more complete. So, once again, low frequency waves experience less loss than their higher-frequency counterparts.

Most broadcast applications are therefore in competition for the first one or two gigahertz of spectrum, with some exceptions. Short range communication, such as a few meters, is possible at high frequencies. Also, communication with satellites can be at a high frequency such as 10 GHz, since the waves travel upward rather than along the ground. Fixed microwave links, with high-gain antennas pointed directly at each other are also examples of high-frequency radio communication. But Earth-bound broadcasting communications links over more than a kilometer benefit from using frequencies toward the low end of the scale.

Most of the history of cellular phones was driven by scarcity of spectrum. There are other important factors, such as portability and battery life, but bandwidth was the original motivation. In a given area, thousands of users might like to make a wireless call, but how can the system accommodate all of them with the allotted spectrum? And just as the technology seemed to meet the needs for voice calls, the demand for pictures, sound, video, and internet access raised the bandwidth requirements further, so the progress continues.

2

Radio

The previous chapter focused on communications concepts such as signals, modulation, transmission and reception. A communication network could use electrical or fiber-optic links for their implementation, but the story of the cellphone lies elsewhere. The communication medium is radio, which emerged in the late nineteenth and early twentieth century as an alternative to wired communications. This chapter is the pre-history of the cellphone, describing how scientific and technological developments built up through the nineteenth century reached a crescendo with wireless communications.

Electric Fields

For most of history, electric effects seemed small and inconsequential. The ancient Greeks knew that rubbing a piece of amber (hardened tree sap) with fur would allow it to pick up some light items such as feathers. From a modern perspective, this is static electricity, but for centuries this was assumed to be a unique property of amber.[1] The Greek word for amber is *elektron*, from which the vocabulary of electricity derives.

While interesting and amusing, this effect did not seem particularly important at the time and remained largely unexplored until the seventeenth century. By then the technology had developed to create powerful static charges for study and demonstration. This was the same process of rubbing fur against amber, but mechanized to create large charges. A typical setup would have a strip of material such as fur or silk looped belt-like around a set of wheels. A crank would get the belt moving, rubbing the belt first against one material to pick up a charge and then against an object, such as a metal globe, to deposit the charge. Observation of electric phenomena could proceed in earnest and theories began to emerge. Practitioners saw that electrically charged objects could either attract or repel each other, leading to debates over how many types of charges there are and how they interact.

The theory that eventually reached acceptance presumed two types of charge, positive and negative, that exist in matter in equal quantities. The equality of the two charges balances to produce no overall charge in most objects. Removing some of one type of charge from an object leaves an overall charge surplus of the other type. The main proponent of this theory was American inventor and statesman Benjamin Franklin, who wrote persuasively on the subject. While he could describe the effects of electrical charges, Franklin could make no hypothesis as to what they are physically, leading to one unfortunate choice that has led to confusion ever since. He guessed that the positive charges are the main mobile charge carriers, so that in an electrical circuit current flows from the positive terminal to the negative terminal. Over a century later it was known that electrons, with a negative charge, are the usual mobile charge carriers. Electrical current is still formally defined as flowing from positive to negative, even though the physical flow is from negative to positive. Franklin's contributions were many, though, and his exploration of lightning in particular was important from a historical perspective.

Benjamin Franklin's proof that lightning, a mysterious phenomenon of great power, is electric in nature brought electricity to the public's notice. Franklin reached his conclusions through a series of careful observations and deductions, publishing his results in 1750. His work also described a possible experiment to prove the electrical origin of lightning, which interested researchers soon carried out in France. Whether the famous kite experiment of June 1752 actually occurred, and what scientific conclusions could have been drawn are subjects of historical controversy. According to the story, Franklin built a kite of silk and wood connected to a metallic wire and flew it in the rain. At the end of the wire he placed a metal key to accumulate charge. After that was a length of silk strand that he could hold while flying the kite. If the silk length became wet, it would conduct and the charge on the key would be lost through his body into the ground, so Franklin held the end of the kite string while standing inside a shed and his son got the kite flying. After some time, Franklin raised a knuckle to the key and received an electric spark, showing that the metallic wire was gaining charge. But by the time this supposedly occurred the French experiments had already been conducted and established the fact that lightning is an electrical discharge.[2]

The effect on public awareness on the subject was profound. Electricity was no longer confined to a small set of inconsequential experiments. It was a large part of nature, and further propelling electricity into the public consciousness were discoveries into its role in biology. Experiments revealed that electricity is closely connected to the workings of living organisms.

Sometime near the end of the eighteenth century, Italian physician Luigi Galvani, or someone in his lab (the exact origin and date are unknown), found that applying electricity to a dissected frog's leg would cause it to twitch.[3] Galvani and others soon brought this effect out of the laboratory and presented it to the public in demonstrations throughout Europe. Some were conducted after executions, where applied electric currents would bring movement back to the limbs and faces of the deceased, as if the body were close to being brought back to life. This view of electricity as some sort of key to life may have partly inspired Mary Shelley to write *Frankenstein*.[4] Electricity never reached its expectations of the nineteenth century, the dead were not reanimated, but its importance was clear and researchers created the basis of understanding that would usher in the electronic age of the twentieth century. Out of the many advancements made, of concern here in the development of radio waves is the electric field.

The electric field is a way of describing the effects that take place between two charged objects. Oppositely charged objects experience a force drawing them together, while objects with the same charge repel each other. Experiments found characteristics of these forces, such as that they decrease as the square of the distance between the charges. With enough observations, by the early nineteenth century scientists could describe much about the electric force. While they may not have understood its origin, researchers could predict the amplitude and direction of electric forces.

The distribution of electric force around a set of charged objects could be mapped with a small charge. In this experiment the small object, or test charge,

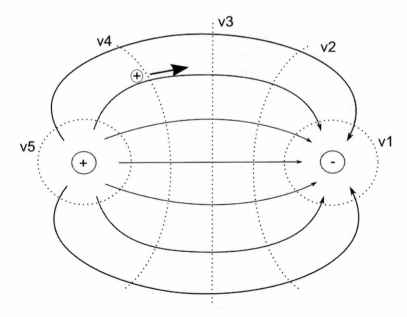

Figure 8: The electric field lines (solid lines) show the path a small charge would follow; dotted lines show constant voltage contours in ascending order from v1 to v5.

is moved in the space around the other charges, and the force experienced by the test charge, both magnitude and direction, is noted at each location. Assuming the test charge to be small enough not to significantly disturb the other charges, the map shows the distribution of the forces. That map of forces, normalized by dividing by the magnitude of the test charge, is the electric field. The sole function of an electric field is therefore to move electric charges.

Moving charged objects against an electric force requires energy, and releasing the objects and allowing the electric force to move them produces energy. The unit of energy per unit of charge is the familiar Volt, named after Alessandro Volta, who assembled the first battery in 1799.[5] Voltage is the potential energy that exists around charged objects, and is related to the electric field. Any two points in an electric field have a voltage associated with them, corresponding to the energy required to move an object between the two locations, or this is the energy released when the object is let go at one point and moved by the electric force back to the first point. A common analogy is to compare the voltage with height and the electric field with the slope of a terrain. The charged object could then be a ball that is either pushed up a slope, or allowed to roll downhill.

A fundamental limitation of the electric field in communications is that it is firmly tied to the charged object that produces it. The high rate of decrease in its strength with distance limits the use of an electric field to short ranges. Adding to the hardship is the difficulty in producing large charge imbalances. What radio needs is a way to create an electric field without the bulky and wasteful static electricity apparatus, and then a way to get that electric field over a large distance. Accomplishing this requires another element, which was also coming into fruition in the nineteenth century.

Magnetic Fields

The history of magnetism followed an independent development to that of electricity, since the effects of the two seem entirely different. The ability of some metals to move other metals had been noticed since ancient times, as had the workings of the compass. The connection between the two was made in 1600 by William Gilbert, court physician to Elizabeth II. He reasoned that the Earth is itself a magnet, causing the magnetic needle of the compass to move into position. The next discovery important to the story of radio came in 1820, when Hans Christian Ørsted, a professor in Copenhagen, observed that current flowing through a wire caused a nearby compass needle to move,[6] establishing a link between magnetism and electricity.

Like the electric field, a measurable force describes the magnetic field. French scientist André-Marie Ampere characterized this force soon after learning of Ørsted's discovery. The magnetic field causes two currents that are running parallel to each other and in the same direction to experience a force drawing them together. Conversely, if the currents are running in opposite directions, they experience a force moving them apart. As with the electric field, the thought experiment of moving an infinitesimally small segment of current around a set of currents and noting the magnitude and direction of the force at each point can chart the magnetic field. Despite the similarities in the definition, however, the magnetic field has fundamental differences with the electric field.

Magnetic fields are always associated with electrical currents, with the magnetic field in loops that curl around the current. In the case of permanent magnets, that current is the movement of electrons at the atomic scale. Unlike the electric field, which begins at a positive charge and ends at a negative charge, magnetic fields only exist in closed loops. If there were magnetic charges, matter would probably have an equal quantity of both, leading to cancellation in the overall material. Instead, each atom has its own magnetic field loop. With the random orientation of atoms in most materials, the individual atomic fields are as likely to be directed against each other as to be co-directional, leading to no overall magnetic field at the large scale. But the atoms of some materials, particularly metals, can arrange in a regular order, allowing the magnetic fields to reinforce each other into a large overall magnetic field. So while the odds of finding a naturally occurring rock or metal with a large external electric field are vanishingly small, discovering a magnetic material is not uncommon.

Since an electric current creates a magnetic field, some may wonder if a magnetic field can create a current, but it cannot. If a magnetic field could be made to loop around wire, that could initiate a current in that wire. But mag-

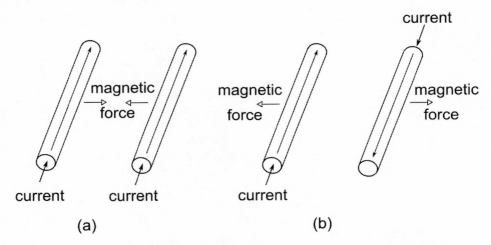

Figure 9: The magnetic field is the force drawing together two co-directional electrical currents (a) and pushing apart contra-directional currents (b).

netic fields only loop around their source currents. There is no way to arrange current sources to create a magnetic field that curls around another object such as a wire. Yet magnetic fields are at the core of electric power generation. The distinction is that the fields discussed above are steady in time, while the fields to be discussed below are varying in time.

A changing magnetic field does create an electric field, and therefore it can create a current. This is the process of *induction*, as found by English scientist Michael Faraday in 1821, and at nearly the same time by American Joseph Henry. Moving a magnet around a loop of wire, or moving the loop of wire around a stationary magnet, creates a current in the wire. In both cases the magnetic field in the wire loop changes with time, which moves the charges, the electrons, within the wire. If the magnetic field is introduced and then becomes constant, the charges would simply realign once and then remain static. To keep the charges circulating, the magnetic field must be perpetually changing. This is the basis of electrical generation, in which various methods such as steam or wind spin loops of wire within a band of magnets, or else spin the magnets within the wire loops, so that the magnetic field within the wire loops are always changing. This periodic motion produces sinusoidal waves of voltage and current at the loop terminals.

By the mid–nineteenth century, scientists had established the link between the electric and magnetic fields, almost reaching the radio wave. There were some concepts that needed embellishment, and one more element to discover. Fortunately a single scientist emerged who could assemble the pieces.

Electromagnetic Waves

The modern understanding of the interplay between electric and magnetic fields, including electromagnetic waves, came from the work of Scottish scientist James Clerk Maxwell. Michael Faraday had been a proponent of explaining experimental results with the concept of fields, and Maxwell continued developing this idea. While Faraday was a brilliant experimentalist, Maxwell was also a gifted mathematician, and was able to place electric and magnetic field theory on a mathematical basis.

Maxwell spent the middle decades of the nineteenth century working on this topic, leading to the publication in 1873 of a two volume compendium of electrical knowledge that explained all of the observations made up to that time of electric and magnetic phenomena. Maxwell's style was to introduce the fields as mathematical objects defined by equations. Using mathematics, he would show the properties that those objects must have. Then he would compare the derived properties with experimental results and, finding a match, declare the mathematical objects to be the electric and magnetic fields. While outlined here in three sentences, the actual explication consumed several hundred pages of scientific and mathematical reasoning. And his contributions went well beyond compiling and explaining previous knowledge.

Maxwell used his mathematical field theory to add a new element that no one had observed. Faraday's law of induction, stating that a changing magnetic field produces an electric field, was well known at the time. Maxwell's physical reasoning told him that the converse must also be true, that a changing electric field can produce a magnetic field. His mathematical theory reinforced this notion, since this mechanism was needed to make the equations consistent. In one of the great achievements in the history of physics, Maxwell condensed the entire theory into twelve equations. All twelve are still considered true, although some have been combined and others have been redefined as supporting equations, leaving four equations that are known today as Maxwell's equations. Toward the end of the two volumes, Maxwell had one more major addition to the theory.

Maxwell's equations lead him to the supposition that waves of electric and magnetic fields could travel through space. As Maxwell described, a changing magnetic field generates an electric field, and a changing electric field generates a magnetic field. Under the right conditions, therefore, an electric and magnetic field could support each other and exist independently. Maxwell, working with his equations, found that these waves travel at the speed of light as it was known at the time. While acknowledging that this does not prove that light is made up of electromagnetic waves, the theory is not contradicted.[7] Later advancements would demonstrate conclusively that light and radio waves are, in fact, these waves that Maxwell described.

This is an *electromagnetic wave*, containing both electric and magnetic field components that reinforce each other. The changing electric field creates a magnetic field which is itself changing, thereby creating an electric field and continuing the process. Its method of travel is propagation, indicating that it moves by recreating itself in a new position. While an electric or magnetic field is tied to its source, an electromagnetic wave leaves its source completely behind, propagating outward as an independent entity. And like a pebble dropped into still water or an insect's wings beating against air, an electromagnetic wave can start with a modest source and travel great distances.

Yet the assertion of electromagnetic waves, while momentous from today's perspective, was not immediately seen as a high priority by contemporaries. Maxwell founded Cavendish Laboratory at King's College in London, where many of the experiments leading to the creation of quantum theory took place, but pursuing Maxwell's electromagnetic waves was not on the agenda. Instead, the first measurements were made in Germany by Heinrich Hertz in 1887, almost ten years after Maxwell's death.

Hertz used metal rods as the transmitting and receiving antennas, with a spark to generate the waves. He would then look for a spark to appear at the receiver. With this primitive equipment Hertz measured several wave properties such as their speed and how the waves reflected from metal surfaces, and found that they were consistent with Maxwell's calculated predictions. While

Maxwell's work had not spurred much interest in electromagnetic waves, Hertz's results did. The use of hertzian waves, as they came to be called, became an active endeavor.

The Introduction of Radio

After Hertz, a period followed in which several experimentalists were trying out their own systems and advancing the state of the art. Pointing to one figure as the inventor of radio is therefore probably inaccurate. The first wireless patent was actually issued long before Hertz's experiments, when people noticed that a strong spark could cause another spark to appear elsewhere. District of Columbia dentist Mahlon Loomis conducted a demonstration in 1866, sending a signal 20 miles from one mountaintop to another in Virginia, using kites with metal wires to act as what later became known as antennas. He received a patent in 1872, but never set up a commercial system, as the Chicago fire of 1871 had financially weakened some of his backers and the funding disappeared.[8]

At the time, spark transmission was mysterious. People did not know how it worked but could put together simple equipment to use it. The developments of Maxwell and Hertz put electromagnetic wave transmission and reception on a solid theoretical and technological basis. Researchers could begin to systematically improve the equipment and techniques for radio.

Various experimentalists contributed to the early development of radio. English physicist Oliver Lodge introduced using an oscillator as the source, thereby transmitting a wave of one frequency, rather than a spark. Recall that a spark contains a broad spectrum of frequencies, so an oscillator-based transmitter could produce a stronger and clearer signal by putting all of the energy into one wave. The receiver further improved efficiency by containing a circuit that responds to only one frequency of the incoming waves. Alexander Popoff of the University of Kronstadt, a Russian town near Saint Petersburg, made several improvements to radio equipment around 1895, and is therefore often acknowledged in Russia as the inventor of radio.[9] But in much of the world the label of radio's inventor comes down to two engineers, with one especially well known.

Guglielmo Marconi is the radio pioneer most closely associated with its early development. While not a formally trained scientist or engineer, in 1894, at the age of twenty, he read about Hertz's results and proceeded to create his own experiments. By 1896 he could transmit over two miles on the family estate. He tried to sell the idea of radio to the Italian government, but they were not interested, so he instead moved to Britain, where he had government connections though his Irish mother. His most notable experiment was sending a radio wave across the Atlantic in 1901. The original plan was to transmit from Cornwall and receive in Cape Cod, but a storm heavily damaged the receiving station, so a new receiver was built in Newfoundland. At the appointed time, the Cornwall station transmitted a Morse code "S" (three dots) repeatedly for ten minutes, followed by five minutes of silence, then repeating the transmission. Marconi made adjustments to the equipment and was eventually able to receive the letter.[10] Like Charles Lindbergh's flight across the Atlantic twenty-six years later, Marconi's achievement entered the popular imagination as a way that technology was changing the conception of the world.

Besides his contributions to the technical aspects of radio, the business Marconi founded would act as the genesis for much of the radio industry. The Marconi Company was one of the main participants in the founding of the British Broadcasting Company in 1922, which became the British Broadcasting Corporation in 1927. And Marconi-built radio stations would form the basis for the Canadian Broadcasting Corporation in 1932. The subsidiary company Marconiphone was also the primary supplier of radio equipment for Britain for a time. In 1919 General Electric (GE) bought American Marconi for approximately $3 million to create the Radio Corporation of America (RCA). American Telephone and Telegraph (AT&T) and Westinghouse soon bought into or signed agreements with RCA, although AT&T sold its share and left radio broadcasting in 1926, and anti-trust actions compelled GE and Westinghouse to divest from RCA in the 1930's. Still, by the 1930's RCA, the successor to American Marconi, was the dominant force in American radio. Through deals with GE, AT&T and Westinghouse, RCA owned most of the patents, it was the largest manufacturer of radio receivers, and RCA started the first and largest American radio network, NBC, in 1926.[11]

Recent events in Britain have conspired, however, to remove some of the prestige from the Marconi name. The Marconi Company was bought by the General Electric Corporation (GEC, a British company not affiliated with the American GE), and the name disappeared for decades. It reappeared in 1999 when GEC changed its name to Marconi PLC, and shifted its focus from defense contracts to telecom and internet. Given the date and the business, what follows is unsurprising. Marconi PLC went on a spending and acquisition binge, the internet boom ended, and the company was left with $8 billion dollars in debt it could not service. The company's market capitalization began to fall from its height of $50 billion, reaching $2 billion in 2001.[12] Still, Guglielmo Marconi's contributions to the early radio industry are undeniable.

The other contributor to the technology who could claim the title of radio's inventor is the Serbian-born American engineer Nikola Tesla. Tesla made advancements in fields such as electrical motors and power generation, and today has a following among some who see him as the great unsung hero of the early age of electricity. Part of his interest was in wireless transmission, and if his notes are correctly interpreted, he demonstrated the transmission of 20 kHz waves in the 1890's at public lectures. By 1897 he had achieved transmissions over 25 miles, and submitted a patent that year. The two important patents, both granted in 1900, were #645,576, "System of Transmission of Electrical Energy," and #649,621, "Apparatus for Transmission of Electrical Energy." These patents form the basis of Tesla's claims to radio.

Tesla's radio patents deal with electrical power distribution, rather than communications, since Tesla's interests tended toward the industrial. Experiments a few years earlier had shown that air ceases to be an insulator at low pressure, an observation that led to the invention of the vacuum tube. Tesla's patents proposed using balloons to elevate antennas to thirty thousand feet above sea level, where the air pressure, and therefore the electrical resistance, is low. A generator applies millions of volts to one antenna to send power hundreds or thousands of miles across the rarified air to receiving antennas. Tesla was careful to describe how his invention would be used: "It is to be noted that the phenomenon here involved in the transmission of electrical energy is one of true conduction and is not to be confounded with the phenomenon of electrical radiation...."[13] The patents make no specific mention of modulation or communication, although there is a note that the power could be sent in pulses.

Despite Tesla's intended application, his patents provided the most complete description of a radio system up to that time. There were four circuits, all tuned to the same frequency. On the transmitter side is an oscillating circuit, acting as the source, and an amplifier circuit. At the receiving side is a tuned receiving circuit, picking up just the right frequency waves from the antenna, and another amplifier circuit. That he was trying to patent a power transfer system, rather than a communication system, does not diminish the applicability of the patent, which applies to a machine and not an application. On the matter, Thomas Jefferson wrote: "A machine for threshing wheat has been invented in Scotland; a second person cannot get a patent right for the same machine to thresh oats, a third rye, a fourth peas, a fifth clover, &c."[14] As with most legal matters, however, this conclusion is open to debate and some court rulings have been in favor of patents for new applications of existing devices.[15]

The patent disputes and the question of primacy between Marconi and Tesla continued for decades. Marconi's patent, #763,772, "Apparatus for Wireless Telegraphy," filed November 10, 1900, included the basic system elements present in Tesla's patents, but went into greater detail in describing the circuits and components and was specifically about radio-based communication. Nonetheless, the patent office denied the patent in 1903, citing Tesla's two patents. But then, without explanation, the patent office reversed its decision and granted the patent in 1904.

Tesla's supporters maintain that Marconi's successes over Tesla stemmed from his powerful connections. In particular, Thomas Edison and Andrew Carnegie had picked Marconi to back commercially.[16] Without that level of support, Tesla was unable to compete. When Marconi won the Nobel Prize for developing radio in 1911, Tesla tried to sue the Marconi Company for patent infringement, but did not have the resources to continue the case. Another wrinkle in the story came decades later when the Marconi Company brought a patent infringement suit against the United States government for radio usage during World War One. The patents had long since expired, but money was still at stake. On June 21, 1943, five months after Tesla's death, the Supreme Court ruled that Marconi's patent had been invalid, citing Tesla's patents. Whoever the progenitor may be, radio at the turn of the twentieth century was an established means of communication.

The first two decades of the twentieth century saw several necessary pieces added to the technology of radio. These are the elements that would allow radio to be a feasible and reliable communication medium and to become a consumer product.

One large obstacle radio faced was the lack of a compact, efficient electrical amplifier. The ability to grow a signal's power, without changing the signal, is obviously essential to transmission. A signal at the telegraph key, or later the microphone, may have less than one watt of power, while the waves leaving the transmitting antenna must be tens or hundreds of times more powerful in order to enable adequate reception at distant antennas. On the receiving side, an amplifier further increases the possible distance and the reception quality. Despite the crucial importance of the amplifier, a good candidate did not emerge until nearly 1920.

Early radio transmitters relied on switch-based circuits to generate the necessary high-power currents. This type of circuit is based on an element known as an *inductor*, which looks like a coil of many loops of wire, usually wrapped around a metal rod. As the name implies, the inductor uses the phenomenon of inductance, in which a changing magnetic field creates a current. The inductor supplies both the magnetic field and the wire loops.

When the inductor is attached to an electrical source such as a battery, current flows through the wire, creating magnetic fields. Since the wire loops are adjacent and all wound in the same direction, the individual magnetic fields add constructively to form a strong overall magnetic field. Opening a switch in the current path breaks the circuit and stops the current, causing the magnetic field around the inductor to collapse. This quickly changing magnetic field in the loops creates a surge of current emerging from the coils. What is happening is that the inductor is releasing the energy that it stored in its magnetic field.

The switch-based amplifiers created a surge of power that was sufficient for Morse code transmission. The telegraph key could be directly connected to the switch, thereby amplifying the key's movements. An important note is that this is not the spark-gap transmission method used by Hertz, in which the source was a spark between two conductors. The output of radio transmitters by the turn of the twentieth century were continuous sinusoidal waves, not impulses. While the surges from the switch-based amplifiers were quick on a human time scale, they were sufficient to power the circuitry for hundreds, or thousands, of wave periods at the radio frequency.

As the only method available, the switch-based amplifier improved significantly over its approximately twenty-year life span. Companies created amplifiers that could switch hundreds, and then thousands, of times per second. They improved the quality of the power impulses to smooth them in time and create a roughly constant power level. Using this method, the early radio experimentalists achieved many milestones.

The first voice and music show was arranged by another radio pioneer, Reginald A. Fessenden, who broadcast music on Christmas Eve and New Year's Eve of 1906. He did this by introducing the modulation into the strength of the surges created by the switch-based amplifier. At the time, the radio audience would have consisted of a few ships along the Eastern shore, academic receivers, and hobbyists.[17] Those groups would form the whole of the non-military radio community for the following decade. One of the deciding factors in the subsequent spread of radio was the introduction of a new electrical amplifier.

The vacuum tube finally enabled the creation of circuits that could amplify signals steadily and without distortion. There are many types of vacuum tubes, but the exemplary amplifier configuration is the triode. As the name implies, the triode consists of three conductors, separated by a small distance and placed in an evacuated glass tube.

As previously mentioned, the resistance of air drops at low pressure, so conduction is possible across the gaps between conductors in a vacuum tube. The amplifier circuit connects two of the conductors to a strong power source. The third conductor is between the other two and controls the current between them. When there is no voltage on the third conductor, current can pass, traveling between the first two conductors. As the voltage on the third conductor rises, it starts to block the current between the other conductors. A low-power signal on the third conductor can control the high-power current flow between the other two conductors, creating amplification. With the introduction of the vacuum tube amplifier, the quality of radio transmitters and receivers crossed a threshold of usability by the public.

As the technology matured, radio passed from experimentalists to hobbyists. Transmitters and receivers were on the market, and the field of amateur radio was born. Enthusiasts would tune their receivers up and down the frequency spectrum trying to make contact with the most distant, or DX, stations. Depending on atmospheric conditions, contact between continents was possible. Parts of the upper atmosphere are thick with ions and therefore lightly conductive. The effect of conductivity rises with frequency, so radio waves with low frequencies, below approximately 1.6 MHz, pass through the ionized layer into space. Waves with frequencies between 1.6 MHz and 30 MHz experience enough conductivity to be reflected back to the ground, making global contact possible. This is the shortwave frequency range and is of particular interest to the DX'er. The upper atmosphere also reflects waves with frequencies above 30 MHz, but those waves usually experience too much loss for long-distance communication.[18]

The sea was a natural place for radio, and soon found application there. Wires will not reach ships at sea, and the wireless companies, such as Marconi, also were not eager to battle the telephone companies on land. The sinking of the *Titanic* on April 15, 1912 had a powerful hold on the public, and published accounts carefully relayed the role of wireless. As the *Titanic* slowly took on water, the wireless operator made numerous calls for help. Three ships were in the vicinity. The first, the *Lena*, had no wireless system at all. The second, the *California*, did have a radio system, but did not operate it at night. The third, the *Carpathia*, also had a wireless system and had also shut it down for the night. But by chance, the operator had returned in the night and started the system to run some checks, received the distress signal, and the *Carpathia* went to rescue survivors. The tale fascinated the public, and motivated Congress to pass the Radio Act of 1912, which set guidelines for maritime wireless.[19] By 1920 radio was established as a usable, and in some cases mandatory, technology, although it remained the domain of specialists and the technically-minded few. The 1920's were the turning point when radio transformed into a commercial enterprise.

Broadcasting is a term originating in farming in which a container spins and throws seeds in all directions. Similarly, radio broadcasting is one-way communication to a mass audience, unlike the person-to-person communication of amateur radio. This shift from the active to the passive was a fundamental turning point, and would remain the guiding principle of radio, and then television, until the rise of the cellphone and personal wireless communication in the 1990's. For most of the twentieth century, and for most of the population, radio was something that one accepts, not something that one creates. That conception of radio originated with the start of commercial radio broadcasting in the 1920's.

The most likely candidate for the first modern broadcast radio station is KDKA in Pittsburgh. KDKA began as an amateur radio station set up by Westinghouse engineer Frank Conrad in 1916, and operated unexceptionally until October 17, 1919. On that day Conrad placed the microphone next to a phonograph and broadcast music for a few local listeners. Soon he was taking requests, and the audience grew. Conrad, helped by his family, started broadcasting two hour blocks of music Wednesday and Sunday evenings, with readings from the day's news included. The interest generated led the Joseph Horne Company, a Pittsburgh department store, to use the station in its advertisements in mid–1920 to sell amateur radio sets. This, in turn, caught the attention of Westinghouse, the maker of those radios.

Westinghouse added funding and equipment, turning Conrad's amateur operation into a professional radio station. That station, KDKA, began broadcasting on November 2, 1920.[20] The purpose of the station was not to turn a profit by itself, but to sell more radio receivers. Adding to the motivation was the fact that Westinghouse had been left out of the RCA/General Electric/AT&T alliance, and was trying to find a place in the radio industry. The plan worked, and in 1921 Westinghouse was invited to purchase a 20 percent stake in RCA. The idea of broadcast radio was immediately popular and quickly spread.

The emergence of broadcast radio in the early 1920's was exuberant but also chaotic. Hundreds of stations appeared between 1920 and 1922, some lasting only a few days. There was no money in broadcasting and motivations varied. Companies opened stations for advertising, church groups took to the air for proselytizing, and many hobbyists tried broadcast radio. Without regulation, or with unenforced regulation, stations would broadcast at frequencies on top of each other, or too close together. The equipment was still in its early stages, so the transmitters would drift in frequency over time, and receivers could not differentiate between signals that were not far apart. Each city had dozens of stations, although taking the state of the technology into account, there was really only room for seven at a time. Some cities, such as Los Angeles and Chicago, tried relieving congestion by giving stations time slots, rendering profitability almost impossible. Some cities held nights when all broadcast radio stations must shut down to allow for amateur radio enthusiasts to continue their hobby.[21] But the hobbyists were clearly being left behind as significant revenue was at stake.

Regulation from the government over the new and growing medium was also uncertain. The Wireless Ship Act and its extensions through the years restricted radio to between 500 Hz and 1351 Hz, with the Secretary of Commerce apparently in charge. In a 1923 decision, the United States Court of Appeals found that while the Secretary of Commerce could give radio licenses, the office could not deny applications. Government powers in the area were further weakened by a 1926 ruling from the District Court of Northern Illinois, which found that any station following the rules of the 1912 law could broadcast at any frequency without government interference. In response, Congress passed the more detailed Radio Act of 1927, which established the Federal Radio Commission to regulate assigned frequencies. Electrical communication advanced, leading to the more comprehensive Communications Act of 1934, and the creation of the Federal Communications Commission (FCC) to oversee the electromagnetic spectrum.[22]

In only a few years the radio changed from a scientific and technical oddity to a common household appliance. Like the internet decades later, once the commercial potential of radio was acknowledged, and the technology had matured to reliability, the hobbyist and academic users diminished in importance to the industry. In 1922 there was one radio receiver per 500 households, while in 1926 the ratio was one receiver per six households. And the growth was not confined to the United States. By 1926, stations were transmitting on all continents. Outside of North America, Europe was the most active with 170 stations, Latin America had 40, and there were also a handful of stations in Asia and Africa. Worldwide, there were approximately 12.5 million receivers, with half outside the United States.[23]

The Telephone

A previous technological innovation had introduced the telephone, although like radio, the exact origin is a matter of debate. Alexander Graham Bell filed a patent for the telephone on February 14, 1876, and demonstrated it at the Philadelphia Centennial Exhibit of 1876. Elisha Gray, a physicist, filed a patent caveat, not an application, the same day as Bell, but a few hours later, so the office awarded the patent to Bell. There is also a third choice for the inventor of the telephone, since Antonio Meucci demonstrated a working telephone in 1849. He could not raise the $200 needed for a patent application, so he instead filed a patent caveat in 1871, which the Patent Office lost. In 2002 the U.S. House of Representatives passed a resolution recognizing Meucci's achievements in the field. In response, the Canadian Parliament resolved that Bell had been the inventor.[24] Wherever its origins may lie, Bell took control of the new medium and his company brought the telephone to the public.

The first telephone system began operation in New Haven, Connecticut in 1878 with 21 subscribers. Bell had offered the telephone to Western Union, the telegraph company, in 1877 for $100,000 but was turned down. Western Union soon realized the mistake and planned to start its own phone service, to which Bell replied with a patent infringement lawsuit. Western Union backed down and Bell's company, which became American Telephone and Telegraph (AT&T) in 1885, owned the early telephone industry. The company prospered to such an extent that AT&T bought Western Union in 1909, and then sold it in 1914, prompted by an anti-trust settlement with the government. AT&T had become a giant, but was also fixed on future growth.

The strategies that AT&T followed from the late nineteenth century were similar to those of technology companies a century later. The company put significant resources into technological advancements, always looking for more breakthroughs.[25] It established Bell Laboratories in New Jersey which would be a center of technological development throughout the twentieth century. The early development of the cellular phone came almost entirely from Bell Labs. What was not invented at Bell Labs, AT&T bought from inventors, and the company built up a large collection of patents. In business, the focus was on long-range communications, for which AT&T's large size was a benefit. Only AT&T could route thousands of miles of cable around the country. While competition existed at the local level, AT&T's ownership of the long-distance market continued into the 1970's, when challengers such as MCI and Sprint began to develop their own systems.

While profits in the telephone business were ample, the telephone's rise was not meteoric when compared with the spread of later technologies. Using 1890 as a starting point, 67 years passed until 75 percent of the population of the USA had a household telephone.[26] Subsequent innovations, such as radio, television, the internet, and the cellphone would reach the public faster, driven by increased communications and prosperity.

Mobile Communications on Land Begins

As soon as radio technology reached the consumer, the attempts began to use it for mobile communications on land rather than just on ships. First was the Detroit police department, which placed radio receivers into patrol cars in 1921.[27] The 500 watt transmitter installed at police headquarters broadcast at around 2 MHz. The units in the patrol cars were only receivers, so the officer would have to pull over and find a phone to communicate back. The system was unwieldy and difficult to use and maintain, so the challenges were strong, but the need was stronger.

The early adoption of a new communication technology by the police was not an exception. In 1877, only one year after Alexander Graham Bell's demonstration of the telephone, the Albany police department installed five telephones in their precinct offices. By 1880 there were only seven telephones in the city of Detroit, and the police department installed the eighth phone. As another example, in 1916 when radio transmitters still depended on switch-based amplification, the New York Harbor Police was using radios to communicate between boats.[28]

Due to the newness of radio, including the state of the equipment and the concept of broadcast radio itself, the Detroit police system was not an immediate success. The system was licensed as a radio station, but had to change frequency and call letters eight times in six years. For a while in 1922, the police were required to transmit entertainment programs during the day with occasional police dispatches scattered throughout. Even more frustrating, the receivers in the patrol cars were unreliable. The Commissioner of Police closed the radio station in 1927, but reopened it in 1928 with more advanced equipment. The system then began to work, and received attention worldwide as visitors came to inspect the system. The Cleveland and Indianapolis police departments added radio dispatch systems in 1929, soon followed by many other cities.[29]

Two-way radio communication with patrol cars began in 1940 at the Connecticut State Police. The system used FM to take advantage of the capture effect, in which receivers could lock onto a transmission with minimal interference from transmissions at close frequencies. The system designers also realized that received radio amplitudes change rapidly in a moving receiver, an effect that degrades AM reception but has little effect on an FM signal. Another innovation was to separate the direction of transmission by frequency. The station used frequencies around 39.4 MHz to send messages to the patrol cars, while the patrol cars would use 39.18 MHz to transmit back to the station.[30] These improvements became standard in mobile radio systems, and apply to modern cellphones as equally as they did to the relatively primitive equipment of 1940. As often happens, the new technology of radio dispatch went from a novelty, to gaining acceptance, to being perceived as required. An industry was born and new companies emerged to meet those needs.

One such enterprise was the Galvin Manufacturing Company, founded in 1928 to make radio equipment. Started in Chicago by Paul V. Galvin, the company began by making accessories for household radios. When the Depression hit in the early 1930's, the company moved into the still prosperous automotive industry with mobile radios.[31] The product line, called Motorola, proved reliable and less expensive than those of competitors GE and RCA. The Motorola was so successful that it became the company name in 1947. Having found a lucrative niche, the company fully committed to portable radio development.

Motorola brought out radio communicators that an individual could carry coincident with World War II. First was the AM-based Handy-Talkie in 1940, followed three years later by the more advanced Walkie-Talkie. The Walkie-Talkie used FM, so the communication was clearer and the range was several miles. The unit weighed 16 kgs, so much of it was in a backpack that the user had to carry. Motorola would remain at the forefront of mobile radio until the cellular phone era, which it also dominated for several years until competition could catch up.

Assembling the Parts of a Mobile Phone Industry

The elements that would make up the cellular phone, and the wireless industry in general, had emerged by the post-war period, but remained separate. The telephone and the radio were both in common, although not universal, usage. And there was no overlap between the two. This was partly due to the state of the equipment, but also emerged from business, legal and social considerations.

Radio companies did not want to compete with the phone companies, and the phone companies did not see the need for expensive new systems. The radio industry was firmly enmeshed in the broadcasting model, and saw its growth in selling radio receivers and finding listeners. On the telephone side, AT&T had briefly entered the radio broadcast business with the purchase of a few stations, but sold them in 1926 under anti-trust pressure from the government.

More two-way radio communication would use more of the radio spectrum, which the government regulators would have to find and allocate. The introduction of AM radio in the 1920's had been haphazard, with the available spectrum quickly filled by small stations. The government's role clarified after the FCC's founding in the 1930's, but assignment of spectrum also solidified. With broadcast radio, military, police, shortwave, research and other applications assigned frequencies, there was little left over. The promise of television placed further demands on spectrum.

And the overall question of whether a market would emerge was unanswered. Dispatch systems existed, but those were for commercial users, emergency services, and others who needed to communicate in the field. Consumers had phones at home, at the workplace, and payphones elsewhere for special circumstances. There was little indication that any more telephone capabilities were needed.

3

Mobile Phones

Post-war prosperity, and the technological progress achieved by then, allowed the creation of a new frivolity, the car phone. This was the mobile phone in its earliest stage and was the first combination of a radio and a telephone to reach the market. These were not cellular phones, however, since each mobile unit was a city-wide transmitter. But the system connected the user to the telephone network, so it was not a radio dispatch system. Too large to be carried in anything less than an automobile and too expensive for any but the elite, the car phone nonetheless was popular. The systems were actually too popular, prompting improvements both in service quality and in capacity which eventually lead the cellphone.

The Start of the Car Phone Era

Mobile phone service began in 1946 when AT&T started the first system in St. Louis. The equipment was expensive at $2,000, which at that time was more than the price of a typical new car. And despite the expense, the system was not particularly convenient.

In those pre-cellular days, everything, meaning especially the equipment and the usage of available spectrum, was primitive. The FCC allocated six channels of 60 kHz each in the VHF band around 155 MHz. But the early equipment suffered from interference between adjacent channels, limiting the system to only use three of the channels at the same time.[1] The car phone was also not direct dial, so to make a call the user would have to give a phone number to the operator, who would then place the call. For all the trouble, the sound quality was poor and dropped calls were common.[2] If the few available channels were occupied, the user would have to wait for one to become free. As a final inconvenience, the mobile unit was push-to-talk, converting the telephone call into a walkie-talkie experience. The need for improvements was obvious, even without a modern perspective.

Despite the expense and inconvenience, a sizable customer base emerged for the mobile phone. Some relief for the low capacity of the systems came in 1955, when improved technology allowed a channel width reduction from 60 kHz to 30 kHz, thereby increasing the number of channels per city from six to eleven.[3] In 1956 the FCC also added a second band around 450 MHz in the UHF band. By 1964, the United States had 1.5 million mobile phone users,[4] and the mobile phone was established as a viable technology and as a marketable product.

The 1960's brought progress in the form of the Improved Mobile Telephone Service, which would carry through until the cellular era. Besides the previous frequency bands, the FCC added another 10 MHz to the 450 MHz band. The system then had 18 VHF channels and 26 UHF channels of 30 kHz, yielding 44 total channels available per city. Along with more capacity, the new service gave a more phone-like experience. The push-to-talk requirement was gone, and users made calls by direct dial, rather than going through an operator. This was still not a cellular system, since it was built around the idea of each mobile unit being a city-wide radio station. A network resembling a primitive cellular system was introduced on the highway between New York and Boston in 1947, which could pass calls from one transmitter to the next.[5] But this was a rare exception, as other systems maintained city-wide coverage through one central transmitter.

The mobile units weighed about 10 kilograms and put out a steady 20 watts for UHF and 25 watts for VHF.[6] The central transmitters that communicate with the mobile units broadcast 200 to 250 watts.[7] While these power levels are not high for light bulbs, in the context of radio they are considerable. Those high and powerful central transmitters were the main sticking point holding back system expansion.

The central station could reliably communicate with the mobile units up to a radius of approximately 25 miles. Beyond that, up to a radius of 60 to 100 miles, the signal was too weak for consistent service, but strong enough to interfere with any other mobile radio system. As a result, the central transmitters had to be at least 100 miles apart, leaving a 50 mile blank space between them. So a customer could use the sporadic and unreliable service only within the confines of one area.

Service was 10 to 20 times more expensive than regular fixed telephone service, but demand still exceeded supply and there were long waiting lists.[8] And this was not only an American phenomenon. Car phone service had spread not only through the USA, but was available in other countries as well.

The Nordic countries of northeastern Europe would foster much of the European development of mobile and cellular systems. The Nordic countries are Sweden, Denmark, Norway, Finland, and a few related islands and territories such as Greenland. All are Scandinavian and share closely related languages and cultures. The Swedish national phone company, Televerket, established Europe's first mobile phone company in 1955. The system would only have 20,000 customers by 1980, but is nonetheless an example of the Nordic interest and leadership in the field.[9]

Due to the close relationship of these countries there was demand from the start for mobile systems that would work across borders. This premium on standard systems that could be adopted internationally would eventually produce the globally successful GSM cellular standard. Yet Finland, the odd country out with a unique language and history, would have considerable success in the field through Nokia. So the reasons for Nordic success in the field go beyond common cross-border languages and cultures. Examining two of the prime movers in the area's cellular phone industry shows a particular emphasis on international markets.

Ericsson is a Swedish company that would rise to the top of the international cellular infrastructure market. The company of LM Ericsson was founded by Lars Magnus Ericsson as a Stockholm telegraph repair shop in 1876.[10] Twenty years later it was manufacturing telephones and system equipment, particularly for international sales. Given Sweden's large size and sparse population this strategy was a necessity for growth. The domestic market was small, but the long distances called for the latest technology and sizable investments. By the first decade of the 20th century, Ericsson had factories in Great Britain, France and Russia. In research, Ericsson was supported by Televerket, which helped especially in the area of switching equipment. In the 1970's Ericsson developed digital telephone switching equipment that became widely used around the world, and Ericsson maintained that lead in telephone infrastructure. While the public face of the cellular phone industry that the consumer sees are handset makers such as Motorola, the workings of the system are often from Ericsson. When looking at the cellular industry from the perspective of the consumer, another Nordic company is one of the most prominent.

Nokia, which would become one of the largest cellphone manufacturers, began as a paper mill in rural Finland. Why a Finnish company has been so successful has been the subject of much study, with no one clear factor emerging.[11] As mentioned, Finland is culturally set apart from its neighbors, and has a largely rural history that does not point to a technology based economy in the future. In the 1920's forestry products made up one third of the gross national product and 90 percent of exports. Then came the wars of the early 1940's, the interpretation of which is a matter of perspective. From one view, the conflict was an invasion by the Soviet Union that the Finns repelled with German help. To the countries involved in World War II, however, this was another front in the larger war, with Finland on the German side. The Soviet Union demanded large reparations payments after the war, and Finnish politics was dominated by acquiescence until the Soviet Union's break-up in the late 1980's. Yet Finland was able to remain the only border country not saddled with a stifling Soviet system.

Industry and enterprise could flourish, and what there was of the sparsely-populated country's phone industry has always been competitive. Unlike countries with monopolistic phone companies, the phone business in Finland was made up of dozens of local companies, and the government provided no protection from foreign competition.[12] Cellphone giant Nokia is the preeminent result of this environment.

The future electronics giant and largest corporation in Finland began in industrial manufacturing. It started as a pulp mill near the town of Nokia in 1865, adding hydro-electric power generation in the 1890's.[13] Nokia joined in a business coalition with a rubber company and an electrical cable company in the 1920's, and the three companies together produced a wide variety of Finland's products. The group found a particularly lucrative trade in shipping industrial and electrical equipment to the Soviet Union. They used the Nokia brand for international sales, and in 1967 the three corporations merged under that name. The full name is Oy Nokia Ab, where "Oy" is the Finnish designation for a corporation, and "Ab" is the same in Swedish.

After the 1973 oil shortage, the company executives decided to bring the electronics component of the company to the fore.[14] This led to heavy investment in their electronics division. In 1980, 12 percent of all research and development spending in the country of Finland was by Nokia on its electronics division.[15] Nokia also went on an acquisition spree, buying various European companies manufacturing televisions, computers and other consumer electronics. Mobira, a Finnish mobile phone company was one of the acquisitions. Nokia would enter the cellphone market through Mobira when the first Nordic system opened in 1981.

Unlike the quick adoption of the mobile telephone in Northeastern Europe, development in the UK was hampered by the organizations controlling radio bandwidth. Until deregulation in the 1980's, control of British telephones fell to the General Post Office. Phones were General Post Office, and therefore government, property that the customer leased, but did not own. Getting a phone was a matter of joining a long waiting list. The payoff would be a squat, black Type 300 phone. Introduced in 1938, this utilitarian model would serve its basic purpose for decades.[16]

In the time when mobile phone systems were beginning in other countries, the General Post Office cited lack of available spectrum for holding back their introduction in the UK. A mobile dispatch system for commercial vehicles did appear in the early 1950's, but the General Post Office took back the spectrum in 1954 to create ITV as competition to the BBC. Finally, in 1965, a mobile phone service called System I reached the market. Direct dial was unavailable, so the user would ask an operator to make a call in the phone system. And like other non-cellular systems, capacity was limited. The price was also high, and the service was marketed to the wealthy and business executives. While profitable, System I was not a popular success, so by 1980 there were only 14,000 users.[17]

Japan was also an eventual cellular hot-spot that had trouble establishing a popular mobile service. Nippon Telegraph and Telephone (NTT), founded in 1952 by the government, was the monopoly that held control of the phone industry until its partial breakup in the 1990's. Installing a phone line involved a hefty fee of 70,000 yen.[18] Paging was introduced in 1968, and there was recognition of the demand for more mobile telephone access. NTT created a cellular test system for Tokyo in 1975, with the result coming to market in 1979. Japan therefore had the world's first commercially available cellular phone system.

The Drive to an American Cellular Phone

AT&T spent decades requesting spectrum from the FCC for cellular phone systems. Their first trip to the well was in 1947, when AT&T proposed a 40 MHz band somewhere between 100 MHz and 450 MHz for a cellular-based system. The FCC denied the request since there was no spare bandwidth.[19] The matter came under consideration again in 1949, raising the possibility of granting frequencies in the UHF band, but in the end the spectrum went to television. AT&T tried again in 1958, asking for 75 MHz of bandwidth around 800 MHz.[20] Once again, the FCC could not spare the frequencies.

The FCC finally agreed to set aside frequencies for a new type of mobile phone system in 1968. Based largely on the AT&T request from 1958, the plan was for 75 MHz from 764 to 840 MHz.[21] The FCC changed this in 1970 to 806 to 947 MHz, which was found by eliminating television UHF channels 70 to 83. The final allocation came in 1974, with 70 MHz made available and 115 MHz reserved for future use.[22] By then AT&T had already begun to move forward with research into the technology that these systems would need.

Testing and development of cellular phone systems progressed through the 1970's. First came an 18 month feasibility study in 1971 and 1972.[23] As would be repeated later when developing new cellular phone systems, the first tests used vans packed with shelves of electronics to do the job of the phones. Once the system is working, developers can work on a mobile unit for the consumer. Meanwhile, NTT was also conducting trials in Tokyo in 1971, and would start the previously mentioned test system in 1975.[24]

The first trial in America of a complete, working cellular system was held in Chicago in the late 1970's. The department of Justice had banned AT&T from manufacturing cellular phones in 1974, so the Japanese company Oki made the first 200 phones, and was soon joined by Motorola and E. F. Johnson.[25]

The test began with a six-month trial from July 1978 to December 1978 involving 90 Illinois Bell employees as users, and expanded to include customers on December 20, 1978.[26] The system used 10 cell sites, each with an 8 to 10 mile radius, to cover most of the Chicago metropolitan area. With a steady and powerful ten watts of output power, the mobile units could smooth over most reception difficulties. The system met performance expectations, but based on the data acquired, engineers revised the operations, rendering all the equipment obsolete.[27]

Roughly simultaneously with the Chicago trial, Bell Labs set up a test in Newark to measure signal propagation and cell size in an urban area.[28] Three main sites of 1.4 mile radius broadcast and received messages, and six towers around the test area simulated interference by broadcasting noise. The mobile unit was a van that drove throughout the area to take measurements and to send and receive messages.[29] This was a lengthy and expensive way to develop a cellular system but it resulted in the creation of a standard, AMPS, that worked well. AMPS may even have worked too well. Its satisfactory performance lowered the demand for a better system, allowing Europe to take the lead by creating a digital cellular system first.

While AT&T had done most of the cellular phone development until the 1970's, government restrictions would keep it out of the emerging industry. AT&T operated as a monopoly through much of its history, like a power or water company. But its control of the industry was not monolithic, and there were competitors. One was GTE, which started in the 1920's as a local phone service provider in Wisconsin. Decades of expansion, and a merger with Sylvania Electric Products in 1959, turned GTE into a large corporation in the communications field.

Another competitor started in 1968 as Microwave Communications, Inc., with a plan to create a telephone service between Chicago and St. Louis using fixed radio links rather than long-distance telephone wires. Eventually becoming the redundantly named MCI Communications Inc., expansion would also transform this company into a nation-wide provider of telephone service. But the highest pressure that AT&T felt was from the government.

The Justice Department and AT&T engaged in a back-and-forth struggle since the importance of the telephone first became obvious. The government position was to allow AT&T to largely control its field, but to stop its spread into other business areas. So AT&T gave up ownership of Western Union in 1914, and sold its network of radio stations to RCA in 1926. But the company was still a behemoth with control over a large part of American communications, prompting more government involvement.

The anti-trust suit against AT&T was lengthy and the results are still not clear. The process began when the Justice Department filed the suit on January 14, 1947.[30] As the suit progressed, negotiations compelled AT&T to gradually give up markets. With a consent agreement in 1956, AT&T agreed to exit the manufacturing and maintenance of mobile phone equipment.[31] Judgment against AT&T came January 24, 1965,[32] yet the final agreement and results did not arrive until the early 1980's.

The agreement that the Justice Department reached with AT&T had two goals. The first was to provide equal access to the markets for other companies, which led to the break-up of the company. On January 1, 1984, AT&T's 26 local phone businesses were grouped into seven geographical pieces and spun off as separate companies: Pacific Telesis, Nynex, Bell Atlantic, Ameritech, U.S. West, Bell South, and South Western Bell. AT&T would keep the national long-distance service and the research facility of Bell Labs. The second goal was vertical divestiture, meaning that rules barred the new companies from manufacturing equipment or telling other companies how to manufacture products. They could, however, make or influence products sold outside of North America.[33]

Thirty years later, the phone industry is again made up of a small group of large corporations. None of the seven companies from the AT&T breakup still exist, since they have all been swallowed by mergers and acquisitions. By the year 2000, service in the USA was mostly provided by giants such as Verizon (which includes Bell Atlantic and Nynex) and Cingular (including Ameritech, Bell South, Pacific Telesys and Southwestern Bell). When Cingular changed its name to AT&T Mobility, the loop was completed. The same is true internationally as companies like Deutsche Telecom, Orange, and a few others serve most of the world.

From a results-based perspective, it would appear that AT&T was at least partially right. Large corporations with extensive resources can efficiently provide phone service. Equipment manufacturing has also come to be dominated by large corporations such as Nokia, LG, Motorola and a few others, for the same reasons. A small company could custom-build a few high-priced units, but to mass-produce phones at low prices requires economies of scale.

The break-up did, however, yield some positive results. While service may be provided by a small number of corporations, that is still more than one. The competition between the few players is intense and probably translates into savings for consumers. For example, long distance calls that may have cost several dollars per minute in the 1970's could be made for a few cents in the 2000's. The companies also had to become more efficient, which helps the corporations compete in foreign markets.

Ready for the Cellular Phone

The problem with mobile phone service, limited bandwidth, and its solution, a cellular system, were both well understood from the beginning. With only six available channels per city, anything other than the lightest usage would be overwhelming. Over the decades the number of channels increased to 44, but that was also far from sufficient. Instead, the industry looked to another method for meeting demand.

The elements were finally assembling that would enable the cellular phone to emerge. The technology was small and reliable. Businesses could see the success of mobile phones and recognize the revenue potential of expanding the service. Government regulators understood the importance enough to find spectrum. And the public had also become accustomed to the idea of mobile telephone communications, even if few had or could afford the system.

By the late 1970's, the outlook became clear that there would be a large market for the cellular phone. Many in the electronics field and in the general public eagerly anticipated its introduction. But no one could know at the time how large the new industry would become.

4

Analog Technology

The cellular phone entered the world in the 1980's as a short-range FM transmitter and receiver, with the technology taking many forms called *standards*. Physically, a standard is a large set of pages, usually kept in a shelf-full of binders, detailing what a manufacturer or service provider needs to know in order to produce compatible equipment and operate a system. Industry committees, made up of corporations and trade groups, write the standards and approve revisions. Their legal status varies among countries. In the USA, for example, the FCC places restrictions on the usage of assigned frequency bands based on limiting interference with other users, but does not dictate the standard used. In Europe, by contrast, certain bands of frequencies are reserved for specific standards, such as GSM and UMTS.

There is a proliferation of standards, with intense competition between their proponents. Discussion of that rivalry will come in later chapters. While there were many standards in the analog era of cellular phones, each country generally only used one. The fundamental differences that appeared between digital standards were in the cellular phone's future, since the analog standards were largely the same. This chapter examines the AMPS standard in some detail below, since it typifies most of the features of an analog cellular phone system.

Frequency Reuse and Mobility

A cellular phone system is based on the idea of lowering transmit power to allow frequency reuse within an area. This is in contrast with broadcast radio, which transmits with high power in order to be received over as large an area as possible. Pre-cellular mobile phones used this type of system, so only about 44 users could simultaneously communicate in any city.[1] When a central transmitter uses a frequency, it therefore exclusively owns it for a radius of about one hundred miles. After that range of one hundred miles, such as in the next city, the frequency is available for the next transmitter to use. By lowering the power from hundreds of watts to a few watts, or even less than one watt per channel, the minimum distance between stations using the same frequency is smaller, making frequency reuse possible within a city. This is the key characteristic of a cellular phone system, but since the area covered by a transmitter's broadcast is small, it introduces a new challenge of mobility.

The other defining element of the cellular concept is that the system can switch moving users between towers to find the strongest signal. This feature is what separates a cellular phone from a cordless phone or the mobile phones of the pre-cellular era. These defining concepts and the cellular name trace back to the unpublished work in 1947 of a Bell Labs researcher, the fortuitously named Douglas H. Ring.[2] And for the subsequent three decades, Bell Labs performed much of the research that would lead to the cellular phone's eventual emergence.

Even as the mobile phone entered the market, the successor system was already in planning. As described in the last chapter, the lack of FCC–approved spectrum held up development. Although without elements such as the Integrated Circuit and liquid-crystal display, the cellphone as it is currently conceived could not have reached deployment. The cellular phone is an example of an invention that represents the convergence of many strands, including the technical, legal, economic and cultural, in time to be useful. Following success, the order of these developments could reverse, with the cellular phone dictating changes and advancements in these other fields. This was clearly the case by the year 2000, but before that the cellphone was riding along the paths created by other inventions. Yet the cellular phone had good ideas behind it, starting with the notion of the cell itself.

A cell is the area over which clear and reliable radio communication can occur between a central tower and mobile units. Due to terrain such as hills and buildings, cells are irregular in shape, although diagrams usually show cells as hexagons. When the central tower's antennas are omnidirectional, meaning that they broadcast in every direction equally, the towers are in the center of each cell. For the case of directional antennas, which broadcast in one direction, the towers are in the corners between cells. A single tower would then serve three cells with three different directional antennas.

The key words in the definition of a cell are "clear and reliable," and they dictate cell parameters such as size. Subjective tests found that people regard an FM signal using a 30 kHz channel bandwidth to be clear if the signal power is at least sixty times higher than the noise power.* The Newark measurements showed that a cell radius of eight miles would meet the signal-to-noise requirement for an urban environment at the transmit power levels they were using. Further than eight miles from the base station, the power would not reliably

---

*A signal-to-noise ratio of 18 dB in logarithmic scale.

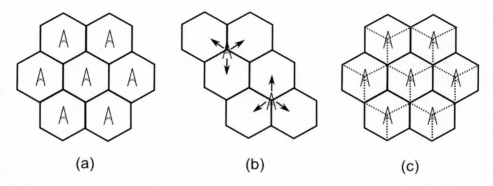

Figure 10: Cells using omnidirectional antennas have a tower in the center of each cell (a); when using directional antennas, each with 120 degrees of coverage, one tower contains three antennas and covers three cells (b), or alternatively, the directional antennas divide each cell into three sub-cells (c).

be strong enough for clear reception but would still show up as interference to other users.

There is always interference between neighboring cells, leading to frequency reuse restrictions. The Newark measurements found that a frequency could be reused after six cell radii of separation. This leads to clusters of 12 cells, with each cell in a cluster using a different set of frequencies. AMPS, for example, used 833 channels, which divided into 12 cells yields 69 channels available for each cell.

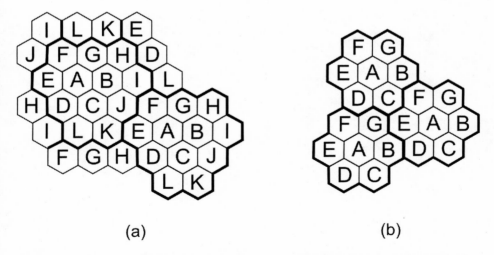

Figure 11: Cells with omnidirectional base stations divide the frequencies among twelve cells (a); using directional base station antennas allows for clusters of seven cells (b).

Measurements also showed that a system using directional antennas allow for frequency reuse after 4.6 cell radii, giving clusters of 7 cells. The 832 AMPS channels then divide into 118 channels in a cell. The directional antennas take all the power that an omnidirectional antenna would spread over 360 degrees and sends it into only 120 degrees, yielding three times the power in that direction. A mobile unit outside the 120 degree beam would receive much less power, and therefore experience less interference. Even with these restrictions, frequency reuse increases capacity significantly within a given area over that of a fixed radio system. The cellular concept transforms a single radio system into numerous semi-independent radio systems.

Each cell acts as an autonomous piece of the overall system. The unit of the central tower and its controlling electrical equipment has many names, but here it will be called the *base station*. The function of the base station is to perform the wireless communication with the mobile units within its cell. The base station also has some control over the mobile units as is needed to communicate. In many standards, for example, the base station periodically measures the received power from the mobile units and sends commands to raise or lower their transmit power. Most of the system commands do not, however, originate at the base station.

Above the base station in the system hierarchy is the *system controller*, which oversees the operation of the entire network. The system controller also acts as the gateway between the cellular phone network and the wired telephone lines. The mobile units use the radio link with the base stations to communi-

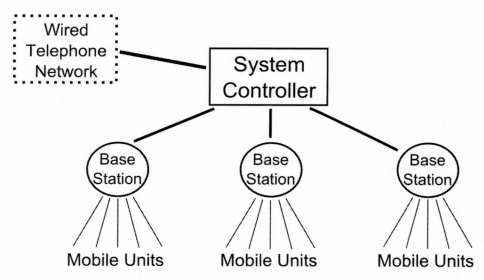

Figure 12: A cellular phone network is hierarchical, with each base station acting as a small radio system.

cate with the system controller. The link between the base stations and the system controller is either with wires or through a fixed wireless link. From its high vantage point, the system controller is also in a position to guide the overall operation of the system. When a mobile unit leaves one cell and enters another, it is the system controller that assigns a frequency to the mobile unit in the new cell.

While the advantages of the cellular concept are numerous, there are also new difficulties. Many of the problems originate in the low transmit power that a cellular system uses. The first cellular test systems used powerful transmitters that could overcome occasional weakness in the radio link. But commercial systems would have to operate with a smaller transmit power in order to reduce interference between cells. Some subsequent digital cellular systems had less stringent interference requirements, but also, as will be discussed, other reasons for reducing the transmission power.

Fades in Signal Strength

Fading is a challenge that affects all mobile radio systems. As the name implies, a fade is a drop in the received power, either at the base station antenna or at the mobile unit. If the power dips low enough, communication may be interrupted. All radios experience fading, but the problem is not difficult to overcome with stationary antennas, since they can be put in a position to receive high power and left there. With the mobility of cellular phones, the receiver may not stay in a good position for long. Users move the phones around the cell and through urban terrain, causing wide variations in received power. While each situation is unique, fades generally fall into one of two categories differentiated by their time-scale.

Slow fades are caused by large motions, such as moving away from the base station or going behind a large building that blocks the radio waves. These are gradual fluctuations in received power that occur on the scale of minutes or, if driving, seconds. Car radios, for example, experience slow fades when driving outside a station's coverage area or under an obstruction such as a bridge. Since commercial radio stations broadcast with relatively high power this is rarely a problem for most listeners. Furthermore, within the listening area, blocking and shadowing by most objects such as buildings and groups of trees are not enough to stop the waves. Considering the low power used by cellphones, all of these effects can be problems. One method of amelioration is to place the base stations high off the ground and above the clutter. Another is to place more base stations in areas with weak coverage. The slow fades may be problematic, and their solution may be expensive, but they are at least straightforward to predict, measure and correct. More difficult to deal with is the other class of fading.

Fast fades come about from multipath interference, in which incoming waves reach the receiver from different paths. Some waves propagate directly from the base station to the mobile unit in a straight line, while others reflect from the ground or other objects. The result is waves reaching the mobile unit's antenna that have traveled different lengths, and therefore have different relative phases. There could be constructive addition of waves that are in-phase, or destructive interference of waves that are out of phase. The interactions are so complicated and so specific to the exact reception spot that the degree of fading is impossible to predict in a practical sense. Moreover, the interference effects can change completely in the space of a few centimeters. The effect is particularly pronounced indoors, where almost all of the incoming waves are reflections of some sort. Those with experience using indoor television or radio antennas will be familiar with this effect. Moving the antenna only slightly can be the difference between strong reception and almost no reception. In an urban environment, remaining motionless is no protection against fast fades, since changes in the surroundings, such as passing traffic, change the patterns of incoming waves. Upcoming chapters discuss what cellular phone systems can do about fast fades.

So far this chapter has explained cellular phone systems from a high-level perspective, with non-specific concepts and the general ideas behind cellular

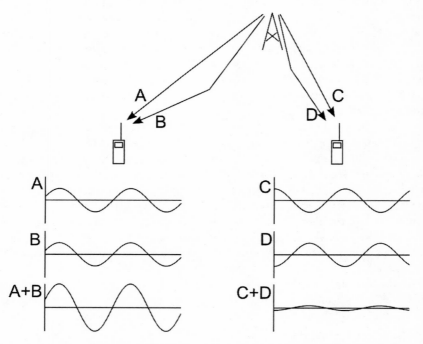

Figure 13: Phase differences between incoming waves following different paths can cause cancellation, leading to fades in power.

phone systems. A more in-depth understanding calls for a closer examination of specific analog cellular phone standards. The one that will be used as the main example is the AMPS standard, which served as a model for most other analog standards.

Advanced Mobile Phone Service (AMPS)

The AMPS standard emerged from the tests in the late 1970's as a workable cellular phone system using the 50 MHz of spectrum that the FCC made available. That spectrum came in two parts. The first 25 MHz, 824 to 849 MHz, were for the reverse link (mobile-to-base), which alleviates some difficulty for the mobile units, since lower frequency waves experience less loss through terrain and shadowing than their higher frequency counterparts. This leaves the higher 25 MHz, 869 to 894 MHz, for the forward link (base-to-mobile). The waves arriving at the base station may be lower power and have more fades, but the base station has the bulky and expensive equipment to better process them. The standard pairs channels from each band, so when the user makes or receives a call, the system controller assigns the mobile unit one reverse channel and the corresponding forward channel. Since the channel size is 30 kHz, the 25 MHz bands yield 832 channels. The form that the broadcasts would take within those channels was a given due to the weak and varying power levels.

Amplitude modulation is susceptible to interference and fades, leaving frequency modulation to carry the audio signal. AMPS uses frequency modulation with a maximum frequency deviation of ±12 kHz, thereby filling 24 kHz of each channel. This leaves 3 kHz of empty spectrum on each side of the signal to act as a spacer and decrease interference between channels. Besides dictating the width and lane markings on the metaphorical roadway of the spectrum, AMPS also carefully describes the vehicles, which are the transmissions that communicate the information.

Along with the conversation, the base station sends a steady signal in each voice channel called the *supervisory audio tone*, which the system uses to maintain the connection. When a call is in progress, the base station sends this constant tone along with the audio signal, and the mobile unit receives and then retransmits it back. While the conversation may lag, the supervisory audio tone is always on, so the system can tell if the connection is still valid. The user does not hear the tone since it is above the 4 kHz cut-off for signals sent to the speaker, but it is always present.

Besides indicating a working connection between the base station and a mobile unit, the system can also use the supervisory audio tone to detect inter-cluster signal leakage. Recall that a cluster is a grouping of cells in which each cell uses different frequencies. A cell's frequencies may be reused by other cells in the system, but those cells will be in other clusters and therefore sufficiently far away not to cause interference. But exceptions always exist.

Under some conditions waves may reach a cell in another cluster using the same frequencies. The base station has no way to differentiate between the two sets of waves, leading to interference. To find such cases, AMPS uses three supervisory audio tones, 5970, 6000, or 6030 Hz, with all of the cells within a cluster assigned to one frequency. If a base station receives the wrong tone, then the system knows that waves are arriving from another cluster. In that case, the system may switch calls away from that channel until the foreign tone diminishes.

Separate from the voice channels, each cell also has a forward setup channel which the base station uses for its own communication with the mobile units. The base station continuously sends strings of 463 bits over the setup channel that include the cell ID number and other system information. There is also space in the message to address specific mobile units. To mitigate the effects of fast fades, the base station splits these messages into 40-bit binary groups and sends each bit group five times. The base station spreads the groups in time by alternating between those meant for mobile units with an even ID number and those meant for mobile units with an odd ID number. The mobile unit receives and demodulates the bit groups as best it can, using a bit-by-bit three-out-of-five majority to reconstruct the message.

Each cell also has a reverse setup channel that the mobile units can use to communicate with the base station. They use this channel to send 48-bit groups, again repeated five times to overcome noise and fades. Since everyone in the cell shares one reverse setup channel, the mobile units must wait for the channel to become free. Every eleventh bit of the forward setup channel that the base station broadcasts is a busy/idle bit that gives the state of the reverse setup channel. A mobile unit with a message to send must wait for the bit to switch from busy to idle, and then send a request to use the reverse setup channel. When the bit switches back to busy, the mobile unit can begin sending its message.

An example of the setup channels in use is when a cellphone powers on. The mobile unit measures the power of the forward setup channels it receives and picks the cell with the strongest power. It then uses the reverse setup channel to send its ID number to that base station. The base station alerts the system controller that the phone is available and in which cell it is located. When the phone is idling, this process repeats every minute.

As the name implies, the setup channels are used for distributing a few system-related signals and numbers, but the base station may have longer messages to send to specific mobile units. This traffic would consume the setup channel, and since each message is meant for one mobile unit, the voice channel is the natural place to put them. Although the voice channels are busy transmitting FM audio, there is some room for limited messaging.

The voice channels can carry short digital messages using the blank-and-burst process. To do this, the transmitter turns off the audio signal in the channel, which is the blank, and sends digital data for approximately 50 milliseconds, forming the burst. Each burst contains about 500 bits, giving a raw bit rate of 10 kbps. But as with the setup channels, there is significant repetition and overhead, so the data rate is only 1.2 kbps during the burst.

The advantage of using blank-and-burst is that the mobile unit does not have to wait for the reverse channel to be free, and the user will not notice that 0.05 seconds is missing from the conversation. Also, the blank-and-burst does not have to be announced in advance through the forward setup channel. The digital encoding scheme used by AMPS has a strong frequency component at 8 kHz, so the base station or the mobile unit can start a message with a few alternating bits to create a wave at this frequency, which acts as the signal to the receiver that a digital burst is coming.[3]

These messages are not the texting that would become popular over a decade later. The 1.2 kbps rate is just within a 50 millisecond burst, yielding 1.2 kbps × .05 seconds = 60 bits. If five blank-and-bursts take place every second, then the overall bitrate is still only 300 bps. The signaling between the base station and the mobile unit that goes on in the background may be important to the system, but the prime feature is, of course, to carry conversations.

The call setup sequence involves extensive back and forth between the mobile unit and the system controller. Upon receiving a call from the wired phone network, the system controller sends a system-wide page for the mobile unit using the forward setup channels of the base stations. The mobile unit receives the page and runs a scan of the setup channels to find the one with the highest received power. After waiting for the idle bit to appear in that cell site's forward setup channel, the mobile unit sends its ID number to the base station on the reverse setup channel, and the base station in turn alerts the system controller of the mobile unit's status. The system controller selects a voice channel and sends that assignment to the base station which passes it to the mobile unit. The mobile unit tunes to the assigned channel, upon which the base station is broadcasting the supervisory audio tone. The mobile unit receives and retransmits this tone back to the base station. Once the base station detects the supervisory audio tone coming back, it signals the system controller that the connection is valid and the call can commence. The system controller sends a digital command through the voice channel for the mobile unit to ring. When the user answers, the mobile unit sends a signal through the voice channel and the system begins to transmit the phone call.

A call originating from a mobile unit follows a similar setup procedure, although without the system initialization steps. Since the mobile unit is active, it is registered with the system and is already assigned to a cell. The mobile unit waits for the idle bit on the forward setup channel and then uses the reverse setup channel to send its ID number and the phone number to dial. The base station sends the information to the system controller, which assigns a voice channel and calls the phone number in the wired telephone system. The mobile unit tunes to the assigned channel and the call can begin.

Putting calls through between the mobile unit and the wired phone system fulfills one aspect of a cellular phone system, but there is another defining characteristic. When mobile phone systems used the radio broadcasting model, a mobile unit could move throughout the city and maintain contact with the base station through the same channel. Lowering the power and creating cells permits frequency reuse, which increases capacity, but mobile units can move between the cells. The systems must deal with the traveling mobile units in a way that keeps the calls connected and remains invisible to the user.

Transferring a call from one cell to another is a *handoff*, which takes place for power considerations. Every few seconds during a call, the system evaluates the power received by the base station from the mobile unit and compares it to the power received by surrounding base stations. Phones in the analog system broadcast with constant power, so the system could use the received power at the base stations as an indication of the distance to the mobile units. The base station that is carrying the call should be receiving the highest power from the mobile unit. If that is not the case, then the mobile unit has probably moved closer to another base station and the call should be based in the other cell.

The system controller performs the handoff by sending messages through the base station. First the system controller sends a message for the new base station to open a channel and for the old base station to stop broadcasting on its channel. The system controller also sends a message for the base station to pass to the mobile unit containing the new channel information. The mobile unit turns off its communication on the old channel and sends a disconnect message. It then switches to the new voice channel and begins to receive and retransmit the supervisory audio tone. When the system controller receives the disconnect message followed by a message that the new base station is receiving the supervisory audio tone, the handoff is complete. The entire process should occur in approximately 0.2 seconds.

In practice, the handoff is a time of vulnerability for the call, where it could be lost by the system. Handoffs presumably take place when the mobile unit is at the boundary between two cells and is therefore not receiving a strong signal from either base station. Due to fast fades, the power levels of both cells' signals could be varying quickly and widely, dipping beneath the threshold needed to maintain a connection and then rising back to an acceptable level. A misread of the power levels could cause a handoff to a cell with a weaker average received signal level. Or the received signal from the second base station could be going through a fade just as the system controller turns off the call at the first base station.

As a way to alleviate, although not eliminate, this problem, the system accumulates an average value for the received power. When the average power measured at the new base station reaches some level, usually four to ten times the power measured at the mobile unit's assigned cell, the system initiates a handoff. Including these delays, the handoff time in practice was typically around ten seconds.[4]

Other Analog Standards

The analog era of cellular phones is characterized by a proliferation of standards, although their basic operation was usually similar to AMPS. Frequency allocations varied between countries, and there were also decisions to be made such as channel bandwidth, mobile unit transmit power, and what sort of digital data transfer capability to include. All of the analog cellphones, however, operated as FM receivers and transmitters.

Besides AMPS, another widely used standard was NMT-450, the Nordic Mobile Telephone standard operating at around 450 MHz. The reverse link (mobile-to-base) was at 453 to 457.5 MHz, while the forward link (base-to-mobile) was 463 to 467.5 MHz. The standard used 25 kHz per channel, yielding 180 channels in the allotted 4.5 MHz. This is already significantly lower capacity than the 833 channels in AMPS, and with less bandwidth per channel, although AMPS had a comparatively spacious 25 MHz allocation. The standard also allowed for 225 channels using 12.5 kHz each, but with an accompanying degradation in audio quality. Even when another frequency band was added around 900 MHz (the NMT-900 standard), the impetus for a next generation replacement standard is easy to understand.

Using a smaller channel bandwidth than AMPS also means that the transmitted audio frequency range is limited. Rather than placing the supervisory audio tone above the conversation's frequencies, the supervisory audio tone for NMT-450 is at either 3945, 4000 or 4055 Hz. This is inside the audio signal's frequency range, so a filter removes those frequencies (4 kHz ± 55 Hz) from the conversation. The steady supervisory audio tone, called the Ø-signal in NMT-450, was broadcast instead of that frequency block, without the user noticing the missing 110 Hz. The standard also had a blank-and-burst capability to send digital data through the voice channels. The burst length was 200 milliseconds with a data bit rate of 600 bps, half that of AMPS.[5] The NMT-450 standard was designed to make the most of a relatively small frequency allocation, and was more compact and modest in its parameters than AMPS.

The UK's TACS, Total Access Communications System, had parameters that place it midway between NMT-450 and AMPS in performance. TACS used one thousand channels of 25 kHz, with the channel number later increased to 1,640. The TACS standard found success worldwide, sometimes in modified form. Japan, for example, used variations called J-TACS and N-TACS.[6] These replaced NTT's MCS standard which had also been a modification of AMPS using 25 kHz channels. The analog Japanese standards gave lower quality service than their counterparts abroad and were plagued with various problems.

The digital data rate for control signals were sent at the low rate of 300 bps, which experiences more noise than higher bit rates.[7]

By the late 1970's and early 1980's the pieces were in place to launch commercial cellular phone systems. Those pieces included the technology within the phones, as well as the creation of standards to set up and run the system. With those elements, the cellular phone could proceed to the next stage in its history.

5

The Analog Cellular Phone

After decades of planning and testing, the cellular phone finally emerged as a consumer product in the 1980's. This was the first generation of cellular phones, using frequency modulation to transmit and receive messages. Each mobile unit, the cellular phone, took the role of an FM receiver and transmitter. The basic principle had the cellular system acting like a band of radio stations, but with the system assigning the frequencies and tuning the receivers, rather than making the user turn a dial. Once all the available channels were in use, no more calls were possible. The second generation with its digital technology would address these and other shortcomings. But at the time the system was a huge step forward in radio and telephone development.

The early history of the cellular phone's introduction is mixed with expectation and uncertainty. Cellular phone systems are expensive to create and maintain, and some companies did not see a market larger than a few affluent car phone users. Others did see the potential and started moving early to establish a place in the industry. This left the governing bodies, such as the FCC, to distribute the available spectrum to service providers, performing a similar function as allowing stations into the AM and FM radio bands. But cellular service providers need the entire cellular band, or a large portion, to make a profit. Governments would be giving a few companies, perhaps as little as two, complete control over a market's cellular band. In their zeal for a controlled distribution process, the FCC was slow and careful, and probably became too deliberate.

The First Systems Reach the Market

Despite the position of AT&T's Bell Labs as the originator and first developer of cellular phone technology, the first cellular phone system to reach the public was in Japan. On December 3, 1979, a system called Mobile Control Station (MCS), started in Tokyo, and would later spread to Osaka and other urban areas. While AMPS at the time used 832 channels of 30 kHz each, MCS allowed 600 channels of 25 kHz. Also like AMPS, the mobile units were large and heavy at 7 kgs, installed into automobiles.[1] A big difference between the two standards is that MCS worked poorly. NTT may have been too eager to get the systems to the market, so while AT&T and Motorola were still conducting large-scale trials that would yield significant improvements, MCS was operating on the streets of Japan. The voice quality was low and dropped calls were common.[2] Approximately 80,000 subscribers joined annually through the 1980's and into the 1990's, representing a minuscule part of Japan's population of over one hundred million.[3] The turn-around, as will be discussed later, came in the late 1990's with the annual new subscription rate rising to five million. But returning to the 1980's, while the cellular phone was languishing in Japan, European systems were finding more success.

The first European cellular phone system started in the Nordic countries.[4] The process began in 1969 when the Nordic Mobile Telephone Group met to create an international cellular phone standard. International to them meant a system that would work among the interconnected Nordic countries, although other countries could adopt the standard. Part of the motivation came from deep-pocketed Saudi Arabia, which placed an order for a mobile phone system in the 1970's.[5] The result was the Nordic Mobile Telephone standard operating around 450 MHz (NMT-450). The standard offered 180 channels of 25 kHz, or 225 channels of 12.5 kHz each.[6]

Commercial operation of NMT-450 began in Finland in 1982, and the other Nordic countries soon joined, making NMT-450 the first cellular standard to work across a border. By 1987, 2 percent of the population in the Nordic countries was using cellular phones.[7] Two decades later cellphone penetration would be above 100 percent, meaning that the number of cellphones exceeds the number of people. But for the era of car phones and the early, hefty handsets, 2 percent adoption indicated success.

Other countries that had not developed their own systems soon took up the NMT standard. European countries such as the Netherlands and Spain, and around the world countries such as the aforementioned Saudi Arabia took up NMT. The addition of NMT-900 arrived in 1986, opening new spectrum around 900 MHz. This offered an additional one thousand channels of 25 kHz each, or 1999 channels of 12.5 kHz.[8] Meanwhile, as NMT was developing, its main European competitor emerged in the UK.

The British cellular phone business sprang from the Thatcherite privatization and deregulation of the early 1980's. The first step was to take the phone monopoly away from the General Post Office and set up British Telecom as a corporation to run the phone business. Another company, Mercury Communications, was given access to the phone market to act as competition.[9] The binary competition model also applied to the cellular phone systems. The government created two 25-year cellular licenses and gave them to Vodaphone and Cellnet. These were new, independent companies, although British Telecom had some ownership in Cellnet. Operational systems from both companies began in January of 1985,[10] using technology adapted for Britain.

The British market had needs that did not quite fit with AMPS or NMT, prompting the development of the TACS standard. Several countries, particularly in Europe, were already using NMT-450 in the early 1980's and that may have seemed like a natural choice for Britain. But the British regulators were looking for more capacity than NMT-450 offered. Instead, they went to Motorola, which modified AMPS to create TACS. Like the American spectrum allocation, Britain also set aside 50 MHz, divided into a reverse band and a forward band of 25 MHz each. But they sliced the bands into smaller channels. Rather than the 832 channels of 30 kHz each used by AMPS, TACS offers 1000 channels of 25 kHz. Enhanced TACS, E-TACS, introduced in 1987 expanded the channel number to 1640,[11] These advancements helped make TACS competitive in the marketplace of analog cellular phone standards.

Like NMT, TACS left its home to be adopted by many countries worldwide. In Japan, Daini Denden, a competitor of NTT, introduced J-TACS in 1989, a version of TACS to be used with the relatively small Handy Phone, which was itself a version of Motorola's UK TACS handset. In 1991 Daini Denden and another NTT competitor, Nippon Indou Tsushin, started offering N-TACS, with 1200 channels of 12.5 kHz each.[12]

Europe came to be covered by a set of incompatible cellular phone standards. France developed its own standard, called Radiocomm 2000, with cellular systems opening in 1985. The German standard was C-Netz, with service starting in West Germany in 1986 and expanding to East Germany in 1990. A notable feature of C-Netz was that this system used ID cards that the user could move from phone to phone, like the popular SIM cards of a decade later.[13] Italy also had an entry in the cellular phone analog standards marketplace called Radio Telephone Mobile System. With these various standards in place throughout Europe, travelers between countries had to change cellphones when they crossed borders. Partly in the name of European unity, development began in the mid–1980's on the international standard that would become GSM.

The Lengthy American Frequency Distribution

The FCC announced the definite allocation of spectrum for cellular phone usage in 1981. Cellular systems would use 40 MHz, divided into 20 MHz for the forward link (base-to-mobile) and 20 MHz for the reverse link (mobile-to-base). Splitting 20 MHz into 30 kHz pieces gives 666 channels. The FCC subsequently added an additional 5 MHz to each link, yielding a less interesting 832 channels.[14] Divided among two service providers, each system has 416 channels. Reserving 21 channels for control messages leaves 395 voice traffic channels per system. Assuming a frequency reuse factor of seven, each cell would therefore have 56 or 57 voice channels. For urban cells, this is probably not enough to satisfy capacity demands. In rural use with large cells, this number may not provide enough revenue to sustain the system. Second generation systems would improve the situation by adding more capacity for a given bandwidth, but at the beginning the cellular phone did not seem to be the promising business that it would become. Whatever its revenue-potential might be, the FCC had devoted spectrum to cellular phone systems, and had to distribute that spectrum to companies that would build and operate the systems.

The FCC set about distributing spectrum license-by-license and market-by-market, leading to a lengthy and methodical process that would delay the implementation of cellular phone systems in much of the USA by several years. This was done, however, with the best of intentions. Rather than give the spectrum to a small handful of large corporations, all applicants were welcome. But they would all have to prove their worthiness in every city. Set-asides were also in place for small companies and newcomers to the telecommunications business, which would be another source of contention.

There were many licenses to distribute, with 305 Metropolitan Statistical Areas and 428 Rural Statistical Areas. Each market's frequency allocations were divided into two bands, with Band A going to a company not in the wired telephone business and Band B going to an established telephone company. This gives 610 urban licenses and 856 rural licenses. The distribution would be in rounds of 30 markets, in order from largest to smallest. If more than one application arrived for a market, an administrative law judge would decide the recipient.[15] Applications for the first 30 markets, which were also the most populous, were due June 7, 1982.

The first round of allocations was orderly, although with more activity than the FCC had expected. The thirty largest markets brought 55 Band A applications and 135 Band B applications. A trend emerged wherein the smaller markets had more competition than their larger counterparts, perhaps indicating an intimidation factor. Chicago, for example, had only two applicants, while Tampa had eleven.[16]

The applications themselves, meaning the physical paper submitted, were massive. The requirements had been vague, so applicants put in whatever they thought could be relevant such as business plans, technical details, maps of terrain, and anything else that might make the applications seem substantial. AT&T applied in 29 markets with a seemingly voluminous 57,600 pages. Yet Graphic Scanning, a pager company, put in 30 applications containing an unreadable 1.5 million pages. After the first set of submissions, the FCC then accepted petitions by the applicants rebutting their competitors, adding more paperwork.

FCC judges decided some spectrum distributions, but agreements between applicants settled most markets. The first to reach a settlement were the Band

B applicants. AT&T would take 23 markets and GTE would have the other seven. They then withdrew their competing applications for each market. Negotiations also settled some of the Band A markets without the FCC's involvement.

In one compromise, several non-wireline companies agreed to share the Baltimore/Washington market, but not to merge or otherwise give up their individual autonomy. Instead they created the brand name of Cellular One to present to the consumers. The name was so well-liked that they licensed it to other systems, and Cellular One became a nationally prominent cellular service provider although there was no Cellular One company.[17] Meanwhile, as the cellular phone was coming into fruition, the company that had provided most of the impetus for its development abruptly left the market.

Despite the resources it had expended in developing the cellular phone, AT&T made the regrettable decision to leave the field in 1984. This took place at the time of the Department of Justice mandated break-up but was not required, it was a move initiated by AT&T itself. A study that AT&T had commissioned estimated that in the year 2000 the cellular phone market would have less than one million subscribers.[18] Given the high expected costs of building and running a system, the profit such a user base would provide did not seem indispensable to a giant corporation like AT&T. So like parents sending a grown child into the world, they passed on the cellular phone to others.

AT&T's estimate was, of course, a gross miscalculation. The cellular phone would move from cars to hand-helds and subsequently explode in popularity, rendering the predicted number of subscribers low by a factor of one hundred. The move to digital technology increased the capacity, and therefore the revenue potential, of a given slice of spectrum and introduced new digital services to sell. By the early 1990's, it was clear that the cellular phone business was one that AT&T could not sit out, and it re-entered the business in 1993 by buying McCaw Communications for over $10 billion dollars and renaming it AT&T Wireless. The prodigal parents had returned to reclaim whatever they could.

MCI also spent some time in the cellular phone business and made a decision to exit that seems ill-advised in hindsight. In the early 1980's MCI was experiencing extreme highs and lows. A $5.8 billion anti-trust lawsuit MCI had filed against AT&T reached a verdict in 1980, with MCI awarded $1.8 billion. This was a boost to MCI's fortunes, but AT&T appealed and got a new trial. The result was also a verdict in MCI's favor, but with a reduced award of $113.3 million. No longer awash in money, MCI had to sell its risky, money-losing holdings, which included cellular phone spectrum.[19] The hard times became harder, at least partly due to competition from Sprint, the other communications player trying to take market share from AT&T. Acquired by WorldCom in 1998 for $30 billion, MCI set on an ambitious plan of growth through acquisitions. But the expansion proved too ambitious. MCI entered bankruptcy in 2002, and was bought by Verizon for $6.7 billion in 2005.[20]

Another company that made a brief appearance on the cellular scene was Metromedia. The media giant originated when future media magnate and one of Bill Gates' predecessors as the richest individual in America, John Kluge, bought a small radio station in the 1940's. He later acquired the remains of the defunct DuMont television network, along with other television stations, and amassed a string of independent stations across the country. They were mostly small stations in the UHF band that found a niche broadcasting reruns and old movies.

When the cellular phone was about to reach the marketplace, Kluge decided that Metromedia would enter that business. To finance the move, Metromedia sold its television stations to Australian media mogul Rupert Murdoch, who used them to start the Fox network. With this new capital, Metromedia won spectrum and started offering service in various markets, but Kluge then made the decision to leave the business. This was the bleak period in the cellular phone's history, when profits were scarce and expenses were high. Metromedia sold its cellular holdings to Southwestern Bell in 1986 for approximately $1.65 billion.[21] The price worked out to $45 per covered population, which seemed high, although by 1990 the price for cellular spectrum would be around $100 per population.

Western Union also made an appearance in the cellular phone business, losing a big opportunity for life-saving revenue. With the decline of the telegraph, the venerable company was looking for new markets. In the 1970's they spent over a billion dollars on a national system that would let people instantly send letters through electronic terminals. The idea may have been prescient, but at the time it went nowhere. Paging had been a successful, if small, moneymaker, so Western Union made the decision to apply for cellular phone spectrum. It won several markets with millions of potential users, but when the company hit hard times, the decision came to sell everything. Western Union sold its cellular phone spectrum in 1985, giving away what would later turn out to be billions in revenue.[22] This became apparent quickly. For example, the LA market sold for $9.6 million, and the buyers subsequently sold it again four months later for $30 million. Unable to stop the decline, Western Union went into bankruptcy in 1994, and emerged as a smaller company focused on niche services such as international money transfers.

An American cellular phone system finally commenced commercial operation in Chicago in October of 1983, with a symbolic call to the grandson of Alexander Graham Bell in Germany. Subscribing was not cheap. Ameritech offered service with a $3,000 initial cost for equipment installation, then an additional $45 per month subscription fee, and then an airtime charge of 40 cents per daytime minute (from seven in the morning to seven in the evening) and 24 cents per nighttime minute.[23] Motorola introduced the DynaTAC 8000X, a portable phone for non-automotive cellular communications, with a list price of $3,9995 in March of 1984.[24] Oki Electric sold its own version of the briefcase phone for a more modest $2,995.[25] Given the high price, most consumers leased the equipment on a monthly basis.

The cellular phones that emerged were clearly for those with money to burn or with an employer covering the expense. A typical contract with U.S. West, which offered service in Seattle and Denver, included a base charge of $19.95 and then $180 for 300 minutes, both per month.[26] Any long-distance calls would produce a double billing to pay for the cellular system usage and then pay for accessing the long-distance network. Particularly intimidating was that, unlike European systems, the system charged the user for incoming calls. There was no way around this since the partitioning of the American phone network left the cellular system with no way of accessing the wired system's records and billing the caller.

There was a small respite in the cost as the equipment lost its novelty. The price, which began at around $3,000 decreased to $1,500 by 1985, and fell further when RadioShack began offering the equipment for $1,000 through its 7,000 branch stores. Cellular One in the Baltimore/Washington area encouraged leasing of the equipment for $99 per month, including sixty minutes of talk time and the option to buy after three years. And the technology advanced as well. Motorola offered one model for $3,145 that could put the user on speaker and could honk the horn or blink the lights to signal an incoming call.[27]

Despite the expense, a viable business was emerging. Illinois Bell's previous, non-cellular, wireless system had only 950 subscribers, and even that low number was too much for the system. Upon making a call, a user would have to wait, perhaps up to 30 minutes, for one of the few channels to be free for the call to go through. The new system, which split the Chicago area into 12 cells, could accommodate hundreds of simultaneous users. Ameritech estimated that the average subscriber would spend $2,000 a year on service, and in 1984 the number of subscribers crossed 6,000.[28] Yet while the cellular phone business had promise, it was not yet the fount of money that it would become.

When combined with the expense of building and running the system, and the price pressure of competition, the cellular business started out far from profitable. The other service provider in Chicago was Metromedia, which began service in January of 1985. Metromedia offered the first three months of service free, causing 2,000 of Ameritech's 12,000 subscribers to switch over. The success was more than expected, and Metromedia had to spend one million dollars to upgrade its system and add capacity for the new users. Many users, however, switched back after the trial period, pulled over by Ameritech's counter-offer of a $250 credit and free call-waiting and call-forwarding.[29] The title of an article in the June 25, 1985 edition of the *Wall Street Journal* summarized the mood: "Cellular Phone Companies Call Business a Tough One, With Profits Years Away." Despite this bleak assessment, competition for cellular phone licenses only became more intense.

After completing the first round of the spectrum distribution, and after applications for rounds two and three were already accepted, in April of 1984 the FCC announced that the spectrum distribution would be done with lotteries. They had clearly been overwhelmed by the response, and following the careful and deliberate selection system would delay the spectrum allocation for years. A random selection format simplified the process at both ends. From the FCC's perspective, the lengthy applications would no longer have to be read and processed. Also, the FCC could pick ten winners for each license in order, so that if one winner could not build a system, the next one would get the chance.

Even more significant than the FCC's role was the effect the procedural change had on those submitting applications. Rather than spending $100,000 to $200,000 per application, they could get an application in for $2,000.[30] Nearly anyone could apply for cellular phone spectrum, including individuals and companies with no connection to the industry. With this easier application process, the pursuit of cellular spectrum left the small world of wireless communications companies and entered the general population.

Investment schemes emerged, seeking to get as many chances in the lotteries as possible. American National Cellular, Inc., charged $10,000 to apply in two markets, and another $5,000 charge if one of them won. A competitor, the Cellular Corporation, charged $5,000 to apply in each market, with an additional $10,000 charge for winning applications. These businesses needed volume, both for revenue and to increase the number of lottery wins. American National Cellular produced an infomercial hosted by 1970's television personality Mike Douglas, and sent 1,000 sales agents armed with the videotape into the public to find investors.[31] Other companies advertised with flyers left under windshield wipers. All of these moneymaking opportunities involved manipulating the parameters of the spectrum distribution.

According to the rules of the lottery, each applicant got one chance in the selection mix, which the lottery companies countered by investor pooling plans. In a typical arrangement, each investor had a 50.01 percent share of the application for one market. The company split the other 49.99 percent among the other investors so that no investor had more than a 1 percent share in any two applications. This arrangement may not have adhered to the intent of the FCC's rules, but it was legal. In general throughout the spectrum allocation, any rule the FCC established was met by an army of lawyers and schemers who could find a way around it.

Unsurprisingly, the investor-driven system came under criticism since it encouraged speculation by private investors who may not be familiar with the industry. Most applicants planned to resell any spectrum won, rather than try to build a system, so the spectrum lottery became simply a standard cash-prize lottery. The fees charged were another point of contention, as some in the industry estimated that the standardized applications should actually cost no more than $2,500. Unlike the large and specialized applications at the start of the FCC's spectrum allocations, the applications for the lottery were about 50 pages, consisting of an engineering study. Consulting companies created a few standard engineering studies for each market. The lottery grouping companies bought these standard studies and then used them for all the applications, with a large mark-up. The companies justified their higher fees with the marketing and the level of assistance they would provide as compared to investors filing on their own.[32]

The other significant complaint was the promised return for what was, at the time, an investment into a business with unknown potential. The controversial figure, used in the Mike Douglas presentation and others was that spectrum would soon sell for $20 per population.[33] This was ten times less than the actual sales prices of the 1990's, but nobody knew this at the time, when sales were being made for less than ten dollars per population. Finally, any lottery is gambling, not an investment. The Cellular Corporation tried to mitigate the risk somewhat by giving lottery losers small shares of other markets, but a fraction of 1 percent share in a few licenses seemed like a small consolation.

As the lotteries took place, the complaints accumulated. The state of Arizona sued American National Cellular for fraud and misrepresentation and its chairman left the country. In November of 1985, the Federal Trade Commission shut down the company.[34] Considering that their inflated projections of the future price of cellular spectrum would turn out to actually be low, many customers would probably have preferred that the company had been left operating to submit their applications. But another business, called the General Cellular Corporation also took in thousands of applications. When they were shut down, investigators found that they had filed a few applications, but thrown most in the trash and spent the money.[35]

As the spectrum allocations continued, the unknown future of the cellular phone business fueled a mixture of indifference and intense interest. By 1986, the FCC had distributed the first 90 markets, with 200 Metropolitan Statistical Areas, and all of the Rural Statistical Areas still open. About 400,000 subscribers were using cellular phones in the U.S., generating annual revenues of $700 million. Yet the expense of building and operating the system made the prospect less attractive, and several large corporations such as AT&T, MCI, Western Union and Metromedia had abandoned the field. A consulting company performed an analysis of markets 91 to 305 and estimated that 80 percent would not be able to support two cellular providers, and 20 percent would not be able to support even one cellular system.[36] Digital technology would change the parameters of these types of analysis, but that advancement would come later. While the large corporations were skittish, speculation among newcomers only intensified.

The spectrum lottery became a get-rich-quick scheme, and the number of applications skyrocketed. A Dallas businessman spent $5 million to get

licenses in seven markets, which he sold for $34 million without building any-
thing. Dentists, truck drivers and accountants won spectrum. While the first
round of 30 markets had generated 185 applications, the final round of the Metropolitan Statistical Areas in April of 1988 had 300,000 applications.[37] To handle the lottery, the FCC brought out the air-blown plastic ball mixer that had
been used to pick draft numbers during the Vietnam War. As to who was buying the spectrum, some companies were still interested.

While many corporations were cooling to the cellular phone business,
McCaw Communications was taking the opposite approach, going deeply into
debt to accumulate spectrum. The company's origins are in the late 1960's,
when Craig McCaw ran his late father's small cable television company from
his college dormitory room. Using borrowed money, the company expanded
and by 1980 was a large cable television and paging company in the North-
west.[38] At that time Craig McCaw made the decision to enter the nascent cellular phone industry, and would use the business style he had developed, which
included complete dedication to the goal and a lot of financial leveraging. To
raise money, the cable television assets were sold to Virginia businessman Jack
Kemp Cook in 1986 for $755 million. McCaw then teamed with financier
Michael Milken to sell $600 million in bonds and raise more capital. All of this
money went into extensive acquisitions.

McCaw representatives crossed the nation, making deals large and small
to buy whatever spectrum was available, and in their eagerness frequently set
the new highest price. They bought MCI's spectrum in 1985, which covered 7
million people, for $156 million, representing $22 per population. By 1988
McCaw was paying approximately $80 per population. In 1989, McCaw made
the rare move of selling spectrum covering 6.1 million people for $1.2 billion,
but then used the money to finance a $1.9 billion purchase of half of the New
York City license.[39] In December of that year, McCaw bough LIN, a competitor in the spectrum amalgamation chase, for a price that worked out to $320
per population. This seemed excessive, but it gave them valuable licenses,
including the other half of the New York City license. The result of these deals
was to take the company from nowhere in the cellular industry to an extensive
network with a nationwide presence. The system McCaw built was so attractive that AT&T bought it in 1993 for $11.5 billion, plus the assumption of sev-
eral billion dollars of McCaw debt.[40] Besides McCaw, other consolidation was
taking place in the industry.

The A/B system that the FCC had set up to give new and small companies
an entrance into the market was dimming. Band A was for non-wireline companies and Band B was for the large, cash-rich telephone companies. The break
came in 1985, when Pacific Telesis, one of the regional offshoots of the Bell System, put in a bid to buy CCI, a company that owned Band A licenses in a few
California markets. The FCC ruled that it would allow the sale, with the new
restriction being that a company could not own two licenses in the same mar-

ket.[41] The other regional Bell companies soon followed and bought their own Band A companies. For example, Bell South bought MCCA and Graphic Scanning, and Bell Atlantic bought Metro Mobile.

By the late 1980's the cellular phone business was established as an industry, with service available in most cities of the developed world. The FCC's ungainly distribution process reached its conclusion. Spectrum had eventually found its way to companies that intended to build working systems.

Not only an American phenomenon, cellular systems were common, if mismatched between countries, in Europe. The developing world was largely absent from the new technology, and would have to wait for more development until the systems became feasible.

As is the case with all consumer electronics, development not only continued but also accelerated as the market grew. Most significantly the mobile unit left the realm of the car phone and become a handset. Having reached success, the flaws in capacity and capability became apparent, leading the industry to completely reinvent the cellular phone. Much of the technology behind the cellphone would have to be redone in the digital realm.

6

Digital Technology

The nearly universal transition of signals to digital representation in the last decades of the twentieth century is one of the most important trends in the history of communications. Rather than represent the information with a continuously varying quantity, such as frequency, the new systems would use a flood of elementary binary numbers. This steady sequence is a *bit stream*, which emerges from a voice encoder at the rate of 64,000 bits-per-second (64 kbps). This is a lot of bits, but the processing power that a small mobile unit can carry operates on those digital numbers fast enough for audio use. And compression techniques for digital audio signals emerged in the 1970's and 1980's that could significantly reduce that 64 kbps rate. By the 1990's, the technology had reached the point that the change could be made, and the demands on the existing systems reached a level that necessitated the switch.

This chapter examines what digital numbers are and how they fit into communications. This involves the introduction of several new and useful concepts. As will be seen, moving from an analog system to a digital system adds complexity but offers many advantages.

Finite-State Digits

Unlike an analog signal, a digital number is restricted to a small set of values, which are also called states. The most common type of digital number is the *bit*, which can take only two states. Most writings call the two states "0" and "1," although Chapter One used "-1" and "+1" for convenience in the examples. Any two names are usable, such as "A" and "B." Digital electronics generally represents the states with voltages, such as "0 Volts" and "1.8 Volts." Wireless transmissions often use the phase of a wave as the state, such as "0 degrees" and "180 degrees." Besides the names and representation, the number of states is also not limited.

More general than the bit, a digital number is a *symbol*, which can contain any number of discrete states. Nineteenth century French telegrapher Jean-Maurice-Emile Baudot conceived a five-level system to improve telegraphy efficiency. By the time the French Telegraphy Service adopted the system in 1977 it was too late for the telegraph, but Baudot's legacy lives on in the unit *baud*, which denotes symbols-per-second.[1]

The symbols are still usually translated into bits for comparison of different systems. A four-state symbol, for example, can represent the binary numbers 00, 01, 10 and 11, so it is equivalent to two bits. A one thousand Baud stream, meaning one thousand symbols-per-second, would then be equivalent to a bit stream of 4,000 bits-per-second. An eight-level symbol contains the information of three bits. The relation is that the number of bits represented by a symbol is the base-two logarithm of the number of states.*

Digital numbers offer two main benefits over analog signals for communication. First, computers use digital numbers, so digital communications can use algorithms for features like error-correction and compression. Second, the small number of states allows the receiver to exactly duplicate the transmitted number. If a transmitter sends either -5 Volts or +5 Volts to represent "0" or "1," for example, and the receiver measures -3.9 Volts, it can assume a value of "0." For the analog case, this would be distortion, so the received signal is always an approximation of the transmitted signal. On the digital side, while there may be distortion in transforming an analog signal such as voice to a digital stream, once the bit stream is ready it can move through the system with no distortion. And if noise corrupts some of the bits, error-correction algorithms can return the bit stream to its exact original state.

Channel Encoding and Coding Gain

Some of the computational processing that digital numbers make possible is error detection and correction through the inclusion of extra bits. This is *channel encoding*, since the processor assigns a digital number to the message for transmission through the communication channel. A simple example is to use a parity bit, where the last bit of each 8-bit group is set so that the sum is even. If one of the seven bits switches between transmission and reception, the parity bit indicates a discrepancy. Which of the seven bits switched is undetermined, so this is an error-detection scheme, without error-correction. If two bits in the group switch, then the parity bit is correct and the scheme fails. A parity-bit error detection scheme is therefore useful for communica-

---

*For N states, the number of bits, b, that a symbol represents is $b = log_2 N$, which is equivalent to writing $2^b = N$. For example, 4 bits give $2^4 = 16$ states, or 16 states represent $log_2 16 = 4$ bits. If a calculator only has base-10 logarithms, the conversion to base-2 logarithms is $log_2 N = log_{10} N / log_{10} 2$.

tion channels in which the odds of a bit switching are low, and the probability of two bits switching in a seven-bit group is low enough to ignore.

Error detection, such as parity bits, works for computer modems, but is not enough protection from noise for wireless channels. When the modem detects an error, it sends a message to re-transmit the bit group. For wireless systems, those re-transmits would be common enough to slow the communication significantly. Instead, digital radio communications turns to groups of bits that can correct their own errors.

Error-correction schemes add more bits to the data so that they can not only detect errors but also correct them. As an example of an error correction method, consider two data bits encoded into four-bit numbers:

Data Bits	Encoded Bit Group
00	0000
01	0110
10	1011
11	1101

Assume a received number of 0101, which does not match any of the encoded bit groups. It is, however, closest to 1101 since only one bit is different. The other encoded bit groups require two or three bit switches to become 0101, so the decoder can assume that the data bits sent were 11. This channel encoding method can therefore correct one bit error per group. Practical error detection and correction techniques are more elaborate than this simple example. But they generally follow the same principle of spacing the symbols within the binary numbers so that a bit-switched number remains closer to the original symbol than to any of the other symbols.

One common error-correction method in digital communications is the Bose-Chaudhuri-Hocquenhem algorithm. Setting up this algorithm to detect and correct one error in a 127-bit group requires using 7 bits for the error-correction, so the group contains 120 data bits. But to correct up to 10 errors out of 127 bits requires 63 bits, so only 64 data bits in the group are data.[2] The forward control channel in AMPS used this method at the cost of adding 12 extra bits to every 28 data bits.[3]

Error-correction requires non-data bits that reduce the data rate, but are nonetheless usually necessary, with their effect quantified as *coding gain*. A communication link that produces one bit error for every hundred received bits may, for example, experience one bit error in the message out of every one hundred thousand bits after error-correction, as if an amplifier had been added to the signal path. Cellphones generally split the bit stream into sub-streams of varying importance and apply different algorithms to each stream. Some bit groups may get no error correction, while others get many error correction bits and have high coding gain.

Digital communication also lets cellular systems deal with fast fades and noise spikes through *interleaving*, in which the transmitter sends the digital

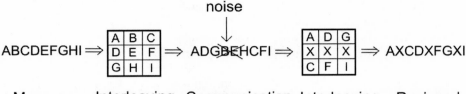

Figure 14: Interleaving changes the order of the message before transmission, distributing groups of errors throughout the received message.

numbers out of order. The shuffling can take place at the level of bits or with groups of bits. In a typical method, called block interleaving, the bits or groups are written into the rows of a block and then read out from the columns. The receiver reverses the process to put the bits into the correct order. A burst of noise or a fast fade between the transmitter and receiver might eliminate several bits, but the incorrect bits would be spread throughout the de-interleaved bit stream. Since each group of bits contains fewer errors, the error correction can operate successfully.

Sampling and Audio Compression

The first step in the digital communications process is to convert the audio signal into a stream of digital numbers. The popular method of accomplishing this is to have the electronics measure the amplitude of the analog signal at fixed instants in time. These recordings of the signal level are *samples*, and the speed at which they occur is the sampling rate. Sampling a wave only once in a period is not enough to avoid ambiguity. The wave must be sampled at least twice per period. The sampling rate must therefore be at least twice that of the highest frequency in the signal. For audio signals of up to 4 kHz, the sampling rate should therefore be 8,000 samples-per-second, or one sample every 125 microseconds. But the sampling rate alone does not determine the size of the bit stream.

The encoder converts each sample into a few bits, which rapidly increases the bit rate. To allow 256 amplitude levels requires eight bits, so each sample takes the form of an eight-bit number. Multiplied by the sampling rate gives a bit rate of 8,000 samples/second × 8 bits/sample = 64 kbps. Adding error correction bits further increases this rate to over 100 kbps. These bit rates were too high for the bandwidth and technology available in the late 1980's and early 1990's. Fortunately, compression techniques were coming into fruition just at that time which could reduce these bit rates by a factor of five or more.

Research into compressing voice began in the analog era with attempts to extract the most vital information from an audio signal. The basic idea was to pass the voice through approximately ten parallel filters to produce a few representative tones. Some other signals, such as an indicator of whether the speaker is saying a consonant or a vowel, were also necessary. The few tones and signals then went over the communications channel, and the receiver used them to reconstruct the voice. This procedure originated at Bell Labs in the 1930's and produced some workable communications links in World War II.[4] Research into voice compression continued along this path until the rise of digital electronics in the 1960's, when compression research shifted to the newer technology.

The basis for digital voice compression is the notion that sounds generated by human speech are predictable, at least on the millisecond scale. This means that if a computer has amplitudes of the previous several samples, then it can predict the next few samples with fair accuracy. As with much of modern technology, the method emerged in World War II. The problem then was to hit a plane with artillery taking into account the motion of the plane and the delay between firing the gun and the shell reaching the target. This created the field that would underlie the modern cellphone.

Speech compression in the digital domain uses the techniques of *linear prediction*. This starts with the examination of a sequence of numbers: x_1, x_2, x_3, etc. Each number could represent a plane's position in the original artillery problem, or the amplitudes of samples in voice encoding. Linear prediction assumes that the next number in a sequence is a linear combination of the previous several numbers. So x_N would be

$$x_N = a_1 x_{N-1} + a_2 x_{N-2} + a_3 x_{N-3} + ...,$$

with a_1, a_2, a_3, etc., being the prediction coefficients that define the sequence. The encoder takes in several milliseconds of speech and calculates the coefficients, which it then transmits along with the first few numbers of the sequence in place of the sampled speech. With the coefficients, early linear predictive encoders also sent signals indicating the general pitch and volume, among other quantities. The decoder then uses the coefficients and other numbers to reconstruct the sequence of amplitude samples.

Linear prediction voice encoding entered use in the 1970's, but was still primitive. In 1976 the Department of Defense adopted LPC-10, a linear prediction voice encoding standard that used ten coefficients and consumed only 2.4 kbps. The speech was rough but understandable. On the commercial market, Texas Instruments introduced a toy called "Speak and Spell" in 1978 that would say a word and the user would then spell it on the keyboard. It used linear predictive coding to store words in the small electronic memories available at the time.[5] The rough, highly modulated speech entered the popular conception of how artificial speech would sound.

Despite the progress in compression techniques, the reproduced voice was low-quality and robotic. The linear prediction formulas lose accuracy quickly as the decoded sequence drifts away from the original audio sequence. The process starts over at the start of the next time segment, and the two sequences proceed to separate again until they re-align at the beginning of the segment after that.

The origin of the low voice quality was the separation that develops between the decoded and the original sequences, and that error had to be much smaller to compete with the telephone. One way to improve quality is to use short time segments for the encoding, so that the sequences do not have a chance to separate significantly before being re-aligned. This requires the encoder to calculate and send the prediction coefficients more often, which reduces the compression of the bit stream. The choice was between quality and

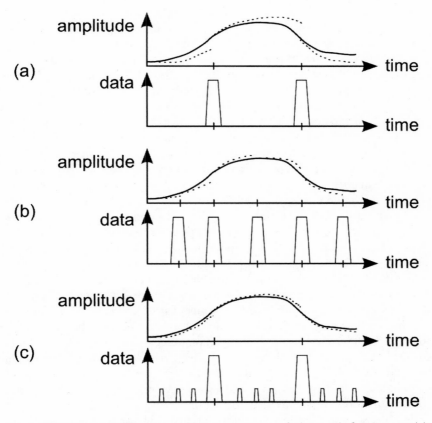

Figure 15: Linear prediction becomes less accurate as each time period progresses (a); using smaller time periods increases accuracy but requires more data (b); a compromise is to use the same linear prediction coefficients over the longer time periods and to send periodic corrections (c).

compression, but for products aimed at consumers accustomed to the tele-phone, no choice is possible. Cellphones must have both. Fortunately a com-promise emerged between the short and long time segments.

The voice encoding strategy that works is to keep the time intervals rela-tively long and periodically send correction messages within each interval. In this scheme, the same coefficients apply for the entire interval, so there is drift, but the corrections do not let the drift accumulate. Since the corrections are smaller than the new-interval information, this method improves audio qual-ity while still maintaining a good level of compression.

In GSM cellphones, this voice encoding method is called Regular Pulse Excited Long Term Prediction (RPE-LTP). The regular pulse excitation referred to in the name is the series of impulses that periodically readjust the decoder. The encoder takes in 20 milliseconds of audio, which at the rate of one sam-ple every 125 microseconds corresponds to 160 samples. Assuming 256 audio levels, this audio sequence uses 160 samples × 8 bits/sample = 1280 bits. The encoder calculates predictive coefficients for the sequence totaling 72 bits which are valid for the entire 20 milliseconds. In addition, the encoder provides 47 bits every 5 milliseconds as the correction impulses. In total, the encoder pro-duces 260 bits over each 20 millisecond period, which is a bitrate of 13 kbps, a five-fold compression of the original 64 kbps stream.

A similar method used by the second generation CDMA–based standard (called 2G CDMA here) is Code Excited Linear Prediction (CELP). As with RPE-LTP, the encoder calculates and sends the predictive coefficients once per time interval, and depends on periodic corrections within the interval to main-tain audio quality. The difference is that rather than send the correction terms themselves, the CELP encoder sends an index number for the most closely matching pre-defined correction terms. The collection of standard corrections is the codebook, and each index number points to one code.* The decoder receives the code, looks up the corresponding correction terms in the codebook, and uses those as the regular pulse excitations. Sending the code rather than the correction terms reduces the bitrate, but at the cost of more computation.

A CELP encoder must not only calculate the correction terms, it has to compare them with hundreds or thousands of pre-defined terms to find the best match. The original demonstration of this technique in the early 1980's consumed 150 seconds on a Cray-I supercomputer for each second of audio to encode.[6] While expensive, those examples were necessary since researchers in the field had to be convinced this method would not lower audio quality. A CELP encoder loses some information since the codes are almost always not an exact match with the needed correction terms, but the difference is not noticeable. Showing how quickly computational power advanced, by the 1990's

---

*This "code" is different from the "code" of Code-Division Multiple Access (CDMA). Both codes are long binary numbers, but they are different numbers with different uses.

a cellphone could make the calculations with a delay of only a few milliseconds.

Specific bitrate numbers help to clarify the difference between the CELP and RPE-LTP encoders. Both operate on a 20 millisecond segment of audio data which contains 160 samples and would use 1280 bits if uncompressed. The CELP encoder produces 71 bits for the predictive coefficients and the first few points in the sequence, which is not much savings over the 72 bits created by the RPE-LTP encoder. The main difference is in the correction terms. By sending only the index pointing to a sequence of correction pulses, the CELP encoder sends only 88 additional bits every 20 milliseconds, which is a significant savings when compared to the RPE-LTP encoder's 188 correction bits. The CELP encoder sends a total of 159 bits every 20 milliseconds, corresponding to a bitrate of 7.95 kbps. The compression ratio over the original 64 kbps stream is therefore approximately eight, which is an improvement over the RPE-LTP encoder's five-fold compression.

The Encoding Path

A summary of the encoding that transforms an audio signal into a digital bit stream ready for transmission may be beneficial at this point. The process starts with the audio signal coming from the microphone and passing through a filter that removes frequency components above approximately 4 kHz, so that the signal is ready for sampling. An analog-to-digital converter then samples the signal 8,000 times per second, and represents the magnitude of each sample with an 8-bit digital number. This 64 kbps stream goes to the encoder, which in the GSM case transforms it into a 13 kbps stream. After the voice

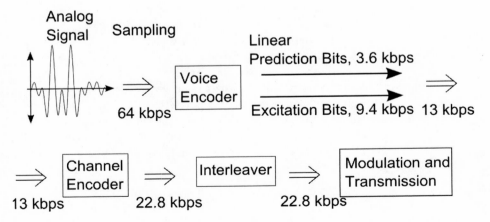

Figure 16: The encoding sequence in a GSM cellphone transforms a stream of 64 kbps into a stream of 22.8 kbps, including error-correction bits.

encoder is the channel encoder, which prepares the data for transmission across the communications channel. This means adding error-correction bits, moving the bitrate up to 22.8 kbps (still for GSM). That stream of bits then goes to an interleaver, which shuffles the bit sequence to minimize the effects of sequential bit errors. The interleaving does not affect the bitrate, so the stream of bits at 22.8 kbps is ready for modulation and transmission.

Digital Modulation

While the data may be digital, radio waves and antennas work in the realm of analog signals. This is an important distinction: the difference between analog and digital cellphones is in the electronics before the transmitter and after the receiver. The waves leaving the cellphone antenna or arriving from the base station are all sinusoidal. This is not to be confused with *puncturing*, which digital phones practice to conserve power in periods of low audio activity. During puncturing, the cellphone turns on the transmitter, sends a stream of hundreds or thousands of bits, and then turns the transmitter back off. So the transmission during puncturing is in bursts, but each burst is not digital modulation.

Digital modulation modifies a sinusoidal wave to carry digital information, and like analog modulation, there are several different modulation methods. The schemes generally involve switching one of the wave parameters, which are the amplitude, the frequency and the phase, between a discrete set of values. Since a wave parameter can take more than two levels, each wave is not a bit, but more generally a symbol. Recall, for example, that a four-level symbol represents two bits since the levels could correspond to "00," "01," "10," or "11." The transmitter sends a wave with one set of parameters to signify a symbol, then switches the parameters and sends another wave as the next symbol. Following the terminology of telegraphy, the switching methods are called *shift-keying*.

An important consideration to stress again is that the symbols carrying the digital information are in the form of analog waves. As an example, a digital cellphone using the 2G CDMA standard transmits 1.2288 mega-baud (million symbols-per-second) using a carrier wave with a frequency of approximately 1.92 GHz. The symbol rate corresponds to one symbol every 0.8 microseconds, which is fast, but the carrier wave period is a much faster 0.5 nanoseconds. This means that the transmitter broadcasts approximately 1600 wave periods in a single symbol. So even fast digital communication consists of long, steady sine waves.*

---

*There is a technology that uses nanosecond-scale bursts to represent individual digital symbols called Ultra Wide-Band. As the name implies, the fast wave impulses consumes a wide bandwidth. A typical system may use more than 500 MHz, which does not fit in the cellular phone bands. Ultra Wide-Band systems find most of their use in high frequency bands well above most wireless communications, and for low-power, short-range communication.

Amplitude shift-keying assigns a wave amplitude to each of the digital states. All of the problems of amplitude modulation in analog radio also apply to amplitude shift-keying. Noise and fast fades directly distort the wave's amplitude between transmission and reception. Also, as described in Chapter One, creating an efficient power amplifier for a signal with a widely changing average power is difficult. For these reasons amplitude shift-keying has generally not been used for second generation cellular phone systems. It is making an appearance in third generation systems for times when reception quality is high.

Frequency shift-keying, the digital version of analog frequency modulation, uses different frequencies to represent the digital states. As an example, computer modems of the 1980's used this type of modulation. For Bell System Series 108 modems, the frequencies 1070 Hz and 1270 Hz represented the binary states going in one direction, while 2025 Hz and 2225 Hz represented the two states going the other way. By using two different sets of frequencies, the system allowed full duplex operation, with both sides sending and receiving simultaneously. As with frequency modulation, while the instantaneous frequency remains within a narrow band, the total waveform over several bits can have a wide range of frequencies. This type of modulation has uses in wireless, but is far behind in popularity to the third type of modulation.

In binary phase shift-keying, the wave switches in phase by zero or 180 degrees. Recall that a sine wave only has a phase shift when compared to another wave. So comparing the modulated wave with a reference wave and finding no phase difference denotes one binary state, while finding a relative phase shift of 180 degrees signifies the other state. Also remember that a 180 degree phase shift of a sine wave is equivalent to switching between a positive and negative sign. The transmitter can therefore perform the modulation by multiplying a reference wave by the data stream of +1 and -1 values.

To demodulate, the receiver multiplies the incoming wave by the reference wave and sums over one bit period. This procedure measures the phase difference between the two waves, since summing the product of two sine waves with no phase difference always produces a positive number and doing the same for sine waves with a 180 degree phase difference always gives a negative number. But if the incoming wave and the reference wave have some other phase shift between them, such as 90 degrees, then the demodulation will not be as clear. Finding the right phase for the reference wave is the complication that renders this simple method more difficult.

For binary phase shift-keying to work, the receiver's reference sine wave must be synchronized with the incoming wave. Synchronizing the oscillators in the transmitter and receiver will not work, since there is an unknown and continuously changing propagation time between the two antennas. Ideally, if the propagation time is exactly one microsecond, for example, the receiver's sine wave generator would adjust to match the transmitter's generator with a delay of exactly one microsecond. But for mobile communications the distance between the two antennas is perpetually changing, as is the required delay in the receiver's reference wave generator. A wave with a frequency of one giga-hertz, for example, changes phase by 180 degrees with every 15 centimeters of distance between the antennas. The phase of the wave at the receiver is there-fore unpredictable, rendering the relative measure of the phase difference with the receiver's oscillator meaningless.

To overcome this difference, some systems send a steady, unmodulated wave along with the modulated wave to act as a reference for the receiver. The demodulator is then comparing the phase of the modulated wave with the incoming reference wave rather than its own oscillator. This works but adds the complication of transmitting and receiving the second wave. Another alter-native comes from the realization that while the phase measurement yields an arbitrary number, the phase switching is an unambiguous event.

Differential binary phase shift-keying is a variant that uses the phase shifts to carry the information, thereby doing away with the need to track the exact phase of the wave. As an example, a system might switch the modulated wave's phase to indicate a +1, and keep it the same to represent a -1. At the receiver, the demodulator can measure the phase difference between the incoming wave and its own oscillator. The measured quantity varies unpredictably, but the sudden 180 degree phase shifts will be clear. This addition brings binary phase shift-keying into the realm of practicality, but there is one more twist that car-ries it from acceptable to good.

QPSK sends two bits at once, using the orthogonality of sine and cosine waves to create two separate communications channels in the same frequen-cies. This is like two binary phase shift-keying modulators running at once, one using a sine wave and the other using a cosine wave. The sine and cosine waves are in quadrature, meaning that multiplying a cosine wave with a sine wave and summing the product over at least one period gives zero. So the two communication channels, though sharing frequencies, do not influence each other. The bits modulated by the sine wave form the in-phase stream, and those modulated by the cosine wave form the quadrature stream. At the receiving end, the demodulator multiplies the incoming wave by both a sine wave and a cosine wave to retrieve the in-phase and quadrature bit streams, respectively. QPSK therefore doubles the communication rate possible over a channel with no bandwidth penalty.

It is apparent that QPSK could stand for *quadrature phase shift-keying*, since it uses two waves in quadrature. For the case described, it could also stand for *quaternary phase shift-keying*, since the modulator creates two waves which can each take two states, giving four possible states. The states are the possible combinations of positive and negative sine and cosine waves. Alternatively, using trigonometric identities, the states are phase shifted versions of one sine wave, which provides another possible meaning for QPSK, that of quadriphase shift-keying:

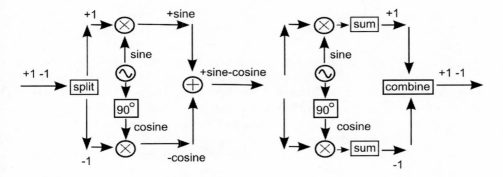

Figure 17: The modulation and demodulation procedures for QPSK, performed on two sample bits.

States as Two Waves	States as One Wave
sin x + cos x	$\sqrt{2}$sin $(x + 45°)$
-sin x + cos x	$\sqrt{2}$sin $(x + 135°)$
-sin x - cos x	$\sqrt{2}$sin $(x + 225°)$
sin x - cos x	$\sqrt{2}$sin $(x + 315°)$

As with binary phase shift-keying, QPSK has a differential form that lets the demodulation work without a synchronized oscillator in the receiver. This is, appropriately, DQPSK, which uses a 180 degree shift in the phase to indicate one of the bit levels. If there is no shift, then the demodulator outputs the other bit level. The American version of GSM used this method for digital modulation, while GSM itself used yet another variant.

Changing the shape of the bit representations leads to GSM's modulation method, *minimum shift-keying*. In minimum shift-keying the bits pass through a filter that shapes them into more gradual transitions. The voltage of a +1 bit, for example, may start at zero, climb gradually to a peak voltage at the middle of the bit period and then gradually diminish to zero volts at the end of the bit period. A -1 bit would follow the same progression, although with a reversal in sign, so that the peak voltage is negative.

In return for the extra complication of shaping the bits, minimum shift-keying offers some significant benefits. The effect of the bit shaping is to create smooth transitions in the transmitted waves, which is in contrast to the abrupt 180-degree phase switches in binary phase shift-keying. As discussed in Chapter One, the Fourier series of fast events contain more frequency terms than slow events, meaning that a fast transition uses more bandwidth. Minimum shift-keying therefore is more spectrally efficient than binary shift-keying. Also, since the continual phase shifts are measurable events, reference wave synchronization is not a problem.

Listed here have been some of the widely used digital modulation methods, and the question may arise of which one is better. The answer is, of course, dependent on the specifics of the communication system and the environment. Amplitude modulation, for example, was quickly dismissed above as not suitable for mobile applications because it offers no immunity to noise and fast fading effects. Yet in cases where the signal-to-noise ratio is large, AM offers a way to significantly increase the data rate. The symbols of QPSK have four values, which is enough levels to send two bits. Adding amplitude levels to further increase the number of levels is quadrature amplitude modulation. For example, if the sine and cosine waves can take on two amplitudes as well as the two phases, then each symbol has sixteen possible states, which is equivalent to four bits. The varieties of digital modulation are numerous. Unlike analog modulation, where FM is clearly better suited to cellular phones than AM, there is no definitive answer to the question in digital modulation.

The Bandwidth of Digital Modulation

Working in the digital realm does not bring a reprieve from the scarcity of spectrum, leading to the question of how much bandwidth the digital modulation schemes consume. The answer comes in three parts. First is the number of symbols that the communication link can carry in a second. The next detail is the number of bits that each symbol can represent. Taken together, the symbol rate times the number of bits-per-symbol gives the bit rate in bits-per-second. One more factor to consider after that is how much data each bit contains, or more accurately, how many transmitted bits make up one data bit. Later sections will examine the last step. For now, consider the first two parts of the question.

Approximating the digital stream as an analog wave can offer some understanding of the bandwidth used. Assume a digital stream of one thousand symbols per second, and that the symbols are two-level bits that alternate (+1, -1, +1, -1, etc.). Then approximate the alternating bits with a sine wave. One pair of +1 and -1 makes up one period of the sine wave, giving a frequency of 500 Hz. As discussed in Chapter One, multiplying a carrier wave of frequency F Hz by this sine wave creates two waves of frequencies $(F-500)$ Hz and $(F+500)$ Hz. The total bandwidth is therefore one kilohertz. This example describes amplitude modulation, which is equivalent to amplitude shift-keying, but similar analyses and results apply to frequency and phase modulation.

The first answer to the bandwidth question is that the symbol rate in symbols-per-second is approximately equal to the channel bandwidth in hertz. The next part of defining the bandwidth is to determine how many different levels the parameter such as phase or frequency can assume, which sets how many bits a symbol can represent.

The noise in the communication channel enters the bandwidth calculations since noise limits the resolution of the symbol levels. As a straightforward example, consider again amplitude shift-keying, in which a wave takes on multiple amplitudes to denote the symbol states. Assume a maximum sig-

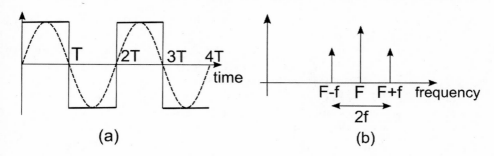

(a) (b)

Figure 18: A stream of alternating bits with period T and bit rate R = 1/T approximated by a sine wave of frequency f = ¹/₂R (a); after modulation by a carrier wave of frequency F, the bandwidth is 2f (b).

nal power of S, and also assume the presence of noise with power that randomly fluctuates between zero and N. The power that the receiver could measure is between zero and $S + N$, and the number of resolvable amplitudes is then $(S + N)/N$, or equivalently $1 + S/N$. By remaining within this limit, even with the addition of noise the received power remains closer to the transmitted state than any of the other symbol levels.

With the number of possible symbol states determined, the bit-rate soon follows. The number of symbol states represent $\log_2(1 + S/N)$ bits, so the bitrate in bits-per-second is this expression multiplied by the symbols-per-second. Since there is approximate equality between the symbol rate and the bandwidth, W, the expression becomes

$$\text{bitrate} = W \times \log_2(1 + S/N).$$

This equation is a fundamental leg of communication theory and determines the limitations of all digital communications systems. Its formulation originated in the first decades of the twentieth century using the simple reasoning given above, but it is commonly called the *Shannon capacity equation* after Bell Labs researcher Claude Shannon, who published a mathematical proof applicable to all digital communications in 1949.[7] The equation gives the theoretical maximum bit rate possible in a communication channel for a given bandwidth and signal-to-noise-ratio.

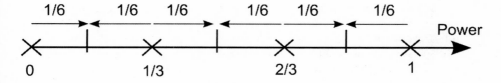

Figure 19: A maximum signal level of one and a maximum variation due to noise of ¹/₃(+/- ¹/₆) yields four usable signal levels.

Due to practical limitations, most communication systems operate at a fraction of the maximum rate. The GSM standard, for example, uses channel bandwidths of 200 kHz. Assuming a signal-to-noise ratio of two, the maximum capacity is 317 kbps. A more common signal-to-noise ratio of ten gives 691 kpbs as the maximum possible rate. But the actual bit-rate that GSM uses for the channel is a more modest 270 kbps. The third generation of cellular phones improved the situation by giving the system the capability to quickly reevaluate the reception quality and adjust the bit rate rather than stay at one bit rate for all environments.

There remains one more aspect to bandwidth in digital communications that is fundamentally important to digital phones, which becomes apparent from a slight rewriting of the Shannon capacity equation. Solving for the bandwidth gives a new equation:

$$W = \text{bitrate}/\log_2(1 + S/N).$$

The message of this equation is that for a target bit-rate, using a large bandwidth can offset the effects of a low signal-to-noise ratio. Even a noisy channel is therefore useable if the transmitter uses a large enough bandwidth. Or put another way, using a bandwidth that is larger than the data rate gives a wide signal-to-noise margin. This is the principle behind a scheme that is now commonly used in wireless communication.

Spread-Spectrum Communications and Processing Gain

A simple way to spread the spectrum of a message is to repeat the data bits several times. A data link may, for example, operate at one kbps, or one bit every millisecond. If the transmitter uses that one millisecond period to send one thousand copies of the bit, then the transmission rate becomes one Mbps. Assuming a two-level symbol so that each symbol represents one bit, the transmitter has spread the bandwidth from one kilohertz to one megahertz. An early example was in the AMPS standard, in which the transmitter repeated each 40-bit group five times, and the receiver decided the value of the data bits using a three-out-of-five majority.[8]

The repetition mitigates the effects of noise spikes and fast fades, but spreading also has benefits for long-lasting noise sources. Here a jammer or interferer overpowers a range of frequencies over many bit-periods. A strong interferer of 200 kHz bandwidth, for example, would completely eliminate several 30 kHz channels in an analog system. The 1.25 MHz channels of a spread-spectrum digital system, however, would be less affected.

The boost that spread-spectrum offers to data reception is termed *processing gain*, as if the data were being amplified. The signal amplification is only conceptual, with the meaning clarified by defining the terms involved. For analog communications, the measure of quality for the received waves is the signal-to-noise ratio, S/N. In digital communications, the equivalent to signal power, S, is the energy-per-bit, E_b, and the noise is a noise density N_o, with units of watts-per-hertz. So the ratio E_b/N_o is the digital equivalent of S/N. A high E_b/N_o generally results in few misread bits since the noise only rarely reaches a high enough level to obscure the bits.

Processing gain originates in the lowered effect of noise density on a wide-bandwidth channel. Continuing to examine the terms involved, energy-per-bit is the total signal power divided by the number of bits-per-second, $E_b = S/R$. The noise density is the total noise divided by the bandwidth, $N_o = N/W$. Putting these two definitions together shows that

$$E_b/N_o = S/N \times W/R.$$

The last term in this equation, the bandwidth divided by the bit-rate, is the processing gain, which acts like an amplifier for the signal-to-noise ratio. The 2G CDMA standard, for example, uses 1.25 MHz to send a data stream of 19.2 kbps, giving a processing gain of 64. To achieve the spread, the transmitter sends 64 bits for every one data bit.

For clarity, engineers often call the bits that go to the modulator for transmission *chips* in order to separate them from data bits. In the example, the transmitter converts each bit into 64 chips and then uses those chips to modulate the sinusoidal waves for transmission. The communication link can then tolerate a noise level that is 64 times higher than if only one chip represented one bit. While this offers benefits for a single user, it does nothing to alleviate the problem of limited bandwidth, and actually seems to make matters worse.

This is the same problem that FM radio, which used 200 kHz for each channel rather than AM radio's 10 kHz, faced in the 1930's. The solution then was to use the newly available, and largely empty, higher frequencies above one megahertz. This way out was not available to cellular phones. Governments around the world allocated about 20 MHz to cellular phones, placing the onus on technology developers to find a way to fit more high-bandwidth users into that spectrum.

Inter-Symbol Interference

To complete the discussion of problems in digital communications before dealing with the solutions, the different paths that the radio waves can take between a transmitter and a receiver introduce complications. As discussed earlier to explain fast fades, the waves reaching the receiver from different paths can be out of phase, leading to cancellation. If the waves arrive at the receiver antenna in phase, then there is no cancellation and their powers add constructively to form a larger signal. This is the opposite of a fade and would seem to be a welcome phenomenon. A closer examination, however, reveals another problem to overcome.

Inter-symbol interference occurs when delayed versions of the bit-stream reach the receiver and overlap with each other. Recall that radio waves travel at 3×10^8 m/second, which is fast, but the time periods involved with digital transmission are small. A rate of one mega-symbol per second means that each symbol lasts one microsecond, during which a radio wave can travel 300 meters. One wave may travel directly from the transmitter to the receiver, while another wave may take a path 900 meters longer. The receiver then detects two competing bit streams, which is really the same bit stream but with a three-bit offset. In practice, a cellphone in an urban environment will probably receive several delayed copies of the same wave, with relative amplitudes between the copies and the delay times all varying significantly and quickly. Digital cellphones commonly use two methods to overcome this problem.

One method of untangling inter-symbol interference is for the transmitter to send, at regular intervals, a pre-set pattern of symbols that the receiver can use to separate the different incoming streams. The receiver does this with a device after the demodulator called an *equalizer*. The equalizer compares the demodulator output with the known pattern to find the time offsets between the various bit streams, and then it applies the right delays to the streams so that they line up in time. This needs to be done often since the delay times can change in the millisecond time-frame. The GSM standard uses this method, with the middle of each group of 148 bits being a standard sequence of 26 bits used for equalization.

Spread-spectrum systems use a similar method to untangle the competing received bit-streams, although without needing the extra sequence of bits. As described, such a system translates a single data bit into many chips, such as a ratio of one bit to 64 chips. Rather than simply copying the bit 64 times, the transmitter uses pre-defined 64-chip sequences to denote each data bit. The receiver also has the 64-chip sequences in its memory, and uses them to pick out the bit streams from the many incoming waves. The process is explained more fully in the context of CDMA–based systems.

While the preceding may imply that inter-symbol interference is always bad, some systems use the mechanisms involved to increase the data rate. A MIMO (Multiple Input/Multiple Output) system divides the bit stream into smaller streams and broadcasts each using a separate antenna. If the antennas are far enough apart, the transmitted waves will take different paths to reach the receiver and therefore arrive with different delays. The receiver uses the bit patterns as a reference to separate the streams, demodulate and process them, and then merge the smaller bit streams into one fast stream. If there is no multipath, so that the bit streams arrive at the same time with no delays, then the receiver has no way to separate them and the communication link breaks down.

Multiple Access Methods

Digital cellular phone systems acutely feel the limits of bandwidth, prompting a need for new methods to efficiently use the available spectrum. The motivation behind moving from the first generation analog systems to the second generation digital systems was to increase capacity and to allow digital data communication. The two goals seem to be contradictory, and spread-spectrum transmission appears to exacerbate the difficulty. The 25 MHz AMPS band divided into 30 kHz–wide segments yielded 832 channels, so when each user gets 1.25 MHz, would there only be room for 20 users?

Fitting multiple users into a limited spectrum is the multiple access problem, for which three solutions emerged. These are in addition to the concept of the cellular system itself, which increases capacity by dividing the mobile units into spatially separated regions to allow frequency reuse. The increase in capacity that the cellular concept provides is significant, but not nearly enough, prompting the development of these three multiple access methods.

The following section briefly describes the first two methods, based on separation in frequency and time. The third method, where the users are separated by codes, is the basis of some second generation cellular phones and all third generation cellular phones. This method will therefore be described in more detail both due to the importance it has in the history of cellular phones and for the digital communications concepts it contains.

Frequency division multiple access (FDMA) gives each user a different frequency, as is done for radio and television. FDMA was also the multiple access method for the FM-based analog cellular phone standards. The only significant difference between an analog cellular phone and a radio was that the system would control the channel selection, rather than the user having to tune a dial. Like radio, each transmitter gets its own channel, and is free to use that channel as it sees fit. There is strong motivation to use as much transmit power as possible in order to overcome noise and fading. Powerful transmissions are a drain on the battery, but as long as they do not overlap into neighboring channels, the strong waves are not a problem for the system.

The cellular phone industry briefly considered FDMA as a basis for digital systems since it would offer continuity with the existing analog systems. Service providers could upgrade their analog FDMA systems to a digital FDMA system easily and quickly, at least relative to the other options. By the time the digital stream exits the modulator, it is an analog signal. If parameters such as channel width remain the same, the base station could therefore broadcast the digital streams with much of the same equipment used for the analog signals.

While attractive in some ways, FDMA–based digital system did not emerge. An FDMA–based system would be simpler and less expensive to set up, but would not increase capacity or make room for more digital services.

The advantages of using the other multiple access methods were large enough to make the more expensive transition worthwhile.

A system using Time Division Multiple Access (TDMA) places several users in the same channel, but separated into different time slots. This technique followed the digital voice compression enhancements of the 1970's and 1980's. A voice encoder could take in a few milliseconds of speech and reduce it to a few hundred bits that could be sent over a channel in a fraction of a millisecond. Between those bursts of data, the channel is free for others to use. To get a sufficiently high bit-rate the channels have to be wider than an analog's 30 kHz channels, but the time division makes up the difference in bandwidth.

In a typical setup, that of GSM, each frequency channel is 200 kHz wide (actually 180 kHz with a 10 kHz guard band on either side), and divided into eight time slots. Using the 30 kHz AMPS channels, only 200 kHz/30 kHz/channel = 6.7 channels could fit into a frequency space that wide, so moving to eight users offers some capacity improvements. And there are other attractive features to a TDMA system that the next chapter discusses in more detail. First, however, another method of solving the multiple access problem is worthy of discussion.

Code division multiple access (CDMA) puts several users in the same frequency band and at the same time, with separation achieved through codes. The Walsh codes of Chapter One offer a way to accomplish this feat. For example, a system may use 64-bit Walsh codes and assign each user one Walsh code. Call the Walsh code for user X by the name W_X. The channel encoder replaces each bit of X's data stream, consisting of +1 or -1, with $+W_X$ or $-W_X$. So each data bit transforms into 64 chips for transmission. The transmitter then sends the stream of chips into the channel, where it coexists with the chips sent by all the other users.

The receiver picks up a wave, call it M, and performs the operation $M \otimes W_X$. Due to the orthogonality of the Walsh codes, all the components of M made up of other Walsh codes yield a result of zero from this operation. The component of M meant for user X results in +1 or -1, returning the original data bits. This sequence briefly explains the idea of CDMA, although more details are needed to understand a CDMA–based cellular phone system.

The implementation of CDMA in cellular phones is more general than the Walsh Codes, as it depends on the receiver and transmitter using synchronized noise to encrypt and decrypt the signal. The transmitter multiplies the data by the noise before sending, so that the transmission appears to be just noise. A receiver that takes in these waves and sums over any period of time would get a result of zero. If, however, the receiver multiplies the incoming waves by its own copy of the noise source, then the result would not be zero. The peaks of both the waves and the noise would align so that after multiplication the positive peaks remain positive and the negative peaks become positive, allowing an average value to emerge over each bit-period. Any other parts of the waves, including messages encrypted with other noise sources, still average to zero.

In practice, noise sources cannot be exactly reproduced in two locations. The term *random* is reserved in a technical context for the outcome of an unpredictable event, and noise is, by definition, random. As such, a noise source on one side of a communication channel cannot be duplicated on the other side. Instead, communication systems use signals that are reproducible but have no pattern. This is *pseudonoise* (PN), and the device that produces it is a PN generator. A PN bit stream can perform the same function as the Walsh codes, provided the bit stream is noise-like enough. The property of how much a sequence of bits resembles noise may seem vague, but it is an exact and measurable quantity. The first step in understanding this quantity is to introduce a way to compare digital numbers.

The *correlation* of two sequences is a measure of the similarity between them, and is found with the $\otimes$ operator. Two different Walsh codes have a correlation of zero, meaning that $W_n \otimes W_m = 0$ when n $\neq$ m. Two copies of the same Walsh code have either perfect correlation, $W_n \otimes W_n = 1$, or perfect anticorrelation, $W_n \otimes -W_n = -1$. Looking beyond the Walsh codes, any two binary sequences have a correlation that falls somewhere within the range of -1 to +1, and it indicates the extent of overlap between their Walsh code components.

As discussed in Chapter One, any binary sequence can be understood as a sum of Walsh codes. For example, two binary sequences called a and b, both four bits long, contain some combination of the four-bit Walsh codes,

$$a = a_1 W_1 + a_2 W_2 + a_3 W_3 + a_4 W_4,$$

$$b = b_1 W_1 + b_2 W_2 + b_3 W_3 + b_4 W_4,$$

with a_n and b_n, $n = 1,2,3,4$, being the multipliers for each Walsh code. Then the correlation between the two numbers is

$$a \otimes b = (a_1 W_1 + a_2 W_2 + a_3 W_3 + a_4 W_4) \otimes (b_1 W_1 + b_2 W_2 + b_3 W_3 + b_4 W_4),$$

$$= (a_1 b_1) + (a_2 b_2) + (a_3 b_3) + (a_4 b_4).$$

Two numbers therefore have a correlation of zero when they do not share any Walsh codes. To use the terminology of Chapter One, numbers with zero correlation are orthogonal. At the other extreme, if both numbers contain only the same Walsh code, for example $a_2 = b_2 = 1$ with the other coefficients all zero, then the correlation is one. Equivalently, the correlation is -1 if $a_2 = 1$ and $b_2 = -1$. While this analysis is for two different binary numbers, it also applies for one number.

The *autocorrelation* of a bit sequence is the correlation between that bit sequence and shifted versions of itself. Consider, for example, a one hundred bit binary number a. With no bit shift, the autocorrelation is one, since $a \otimes a = 1$. Then shift each bit over by one place to the right, with the bit on the right end wrapping around to become the new first bit. Call the new number $a_{shift+1}$, and the autocorrelation for that shift is $a \otimes a_{shift+1}$. Repeating the shift produces one hundred correlation numbers before the number is back to its original position.

The autocorrelation of a bit sequence indicates its predictability. The linear prediction methods described previously for voice encoding, for example, are dependent on the relatively high autocorrelation of bit sequences representing voice. If the autocorrelation results for a long digital number are near zero, then its shifted versions are nearly orthogonal and can provide the codes for a CDMA–based system. Each user within the system can run the same PN generator with a unique offset to create the different codes.

The Rise of Spread-Spectrum Communications

Having introduced the relevant concepts, a three-part technical definition of a spread-spectrum communication system is now possible. Firstly, and most obviously, the bandwidths of the transmissions are considerably larger than the bandwidth of the messages they contain. FM radio has this characteristic, using large frequency channels for 10 kHz–wide audio signals, but a spread-spectrum system adds two other defining properties. The transmitter modulates the message with a pseudo-random signal, so that the transmission appears to be noise. And thirdly, the receiver picks its message out of the noise by performing a correlation with its own copy of the pseudo-random signal. Given the noise-like quality of the broadcasts, it may be unsurprising that the early developments in spread-spectrum communication were for secure military applications.

The first spread-spectrum systems saw limited use in World War II on the German side. The earliest known publication of the spread-spectrum concepts was a patent given to the German phone company Telefunken in 1935, and a working system saw use a few years later during the war. This was before digital PN generators, so the transmitter and receiver each had disks with identical jagged edges. A motor would spin the disks while a sensor brushing along the edges converted the bumps into voltage to create the pseudo-random signal. To keep the spinning disks on both sides of the communication link synchronized, the transmitter also broadcast two tones at a fixed multiple of the spin rate. The German army used this equipment to transmit from Greece across the Mediterranean to Libya in order to send messages to Rommel's army.[9] The system offered security, but was cumbersome.

After the war, development continued in classified military projects. Engineers at Sylvania solidified many of the concepts of spread-spectrum communications while working on a radar contract in the late 1940's. In particular, they identified that spread-spectrum links offered processing gain. The goal of the work was to create a radar system that could withstand jamming, and with processing gain, the receiver could find the weak radar waves even in the presence of a stronger signal. Since, in the case of radar, the transmitter is also the receiver, the system avoided the problem of synchronizing random sources. They could use true noise sources, such as the small voltage fluctuations across a vacuum tube. While the specifics were classified, some of the general conclusions concerning spread-spectrum communications found their way into the radio engineering world so that by the 1950's it was a promising field of research.

More breakthroughs in the field came during an Army contract for a secure wireless teletype system. Called F9C, development took place first at the Massachusetts Institute of Technology and then at Sylvania during much of the 1950's. As a step forward, this was a digital system, using frequency shift-keying to send 45 bps over 10 kHz of bandwidth. Unfortunately, the digital PN generator was a cumbersome and complicated machine, larger than a typical household refrigerator, which would mix several long digital numbers together to create low-correlation codes. But the system worked, with field trials beginning in 1954. One problem that quickly became apparent was that of multipath propagation.

The F9C developers' answer to the multipath problem was the *rake receiver*. Probably named after the garden implement, this device sends the incoming waves into parallel correlators, each using a different delay on the PN code. The rake receiver could process each arriving wave separately and add the results. The transmitter periodically sent a short pulse, and the receiver would measure the arrival time for the incoming copies of the pulse and assign the delays to the rake receiver paths. The F9C system saw use in Europe and the Pacific region during the late 1950's and early 1960's.[10]

Many of the elements of a spread-spectrum communication system that would find use in cellular phones were established by 1960. The concepts, such as jammer rejection and processing gain, had escaped the boundaries of classified material into the general engineering community. The rake receiver was in use and effectively alleviating the problem of multi-path propagation. One other development is significant enough to warrant mention here, that of the shift-register PN generator.

A PN generator produces a sequence of bits with low autocorrelation, meaning low correlation between shifted versions of itself. Since a PN generator is deterministic, it typically involves loops that create a repeating sequence of bits. The number of bits in a cycle, however, can be large. The 2G CDMA standard, for example, uses a PN generator that produces 1.2288 million bits-per-second, yet the pattern only repeats every 41 days. The low autocorrelation ensures that the output appears noise-like and that shifted versions of the sequence are orthogonal. A base station can therefore send messages to multiple mobile units using the same PN generator, but with different shifts. The first digital PN generators were large and complicated circuits, but a breakthrough introduced the conceptually simple circuits used today.

The modern PN generator uses rings of shift-registers to create its bit sequence. A shift-register is a simple electronic component that holds a bit until it receives a command to shift, at which point it sends the bit to its output and accepts a new bit from its input. At each shift, the bits move one position over in the chain. The shift-register at the end of the chain sends its bit to the PN generator output, and it also sends a copy of its bit back to the first shift-register, forming a loop that produces repeating sequences of bits. Such a simple arrangement would only produce as many digits as registers, and a CDMA system needs PN sequences that are at least millions of digits long. To add complexity and increase the code length, PN generators include operations between the shift-registers. Those operations form the characteristics of the modern PN generator.

The idea for simple, shift-register based PN generators seems to have originated at the Jet Propulsion Laboratory in Pasadena in 1953.[11] As with many engineering advancements that are necessary and possible with the current equipment and conceptual development, this device may have originated in several places simultaneously. The secrecy of military projects also adds to the difficulty in tracing the history. Whatever its exact origin, by the late 1950's, this type of PN generator had entered the standard set of spread-spectrum communications tools.

Another method of creating spread-spectrum communications links, frequency-hopping, also has a role in the world of wireless communications. With this method, the transmitter broadcasts for a while using one carrier frequency,

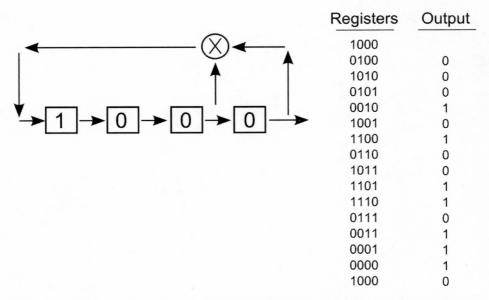

Registers	Output
1000	
0100	0
1010	0
0101	0
0010	1
1001	0
1100	1
0110	0
1011	0
1101	1
1110	1
0111	0
0011	1
0001	1
0000	1
1000	0

Figure 20: A simple PN generator made up of four shift-registers and one operator, producing a repeating sequence of 15 bits with an autocorrelation of $-1/8$.

then switches to another frequency and continues broadcasting. The switching rate may vary from a few to millions of times in a second, depending on the system. So while the broadcast may not be particularly wide-band during one of the broadcast intervals, over a period of a second or more it appears to take up a large swath of frequencies.

As an example, a signal with a bandwidth of one kilohertz may switch frequency one thousand times per second over a band of one megahertz. If the switching pattern is evenly distributed, so that the broadcast visits each one kilohertz slot in the band exactly once in every second, then the average broadcast power, measured over the entire band for at least one second, will appear to be evenly spread and one thousand times lower than the actual transmission power. But a receiver that switches frequency along with the transmitter would measure the full broadcast power, creating an effect similar to processing gain. Other users could also be operating in the same band and switching among the frequencies. If the broadcasts do not fall on the same one kilohertz slots at the same time, or if the overlap is small, they will all seem to consume the entire one megahertz band, yet not interfere with each other.

The same protection against noise and interference applies with this spread-spectrum method as with the PN-based method, as does the security benefits. An interfering signal a few kilohertz in bandwidth would only eliminate a few slots in the frequency-hopping band, leading to some millisecond-long holes distributed through the main signal. A receiver trying to eavesdrop into the communication link would also come up with only noise unless it had the exact frequency-switching pattern so that it could follow the signal. This spread-spectrum technique came under examination in World War II, including from one unlikely source.

Among those who worked on aspects of frequency-hopping systems was silent screen siren Hedy Lamarr.[12] While married to a munitions manufacturer in Vienna in the 1930's, Lamarr became acquainted with the basic ideas of radio-controlled bombs and the problem of jamming. During the war, while in the Hollywood milieu, she made the acquaintance of George Antheil, a composer dealing in the avant-garde and technological. His composition, "Ballet Mechanique," was for an orchestra of player pianos, all controlled by rolls of slotted paper. Lamarr's idea was to control the frequency-switching in a radio control system with similar slotted paper rolls. A bomb or torpedo would have an unwinding roll synchronized to an identical one in the transmitter, creating a secure communication channel. A patent was granted in 1942, but the army apparently never implemented the idea, and it became obsolete in the digital era. It was an interesting invention, but trivia questions that occasionally appear along the lines of "which movie star invented the technology behind the modern cellphone" are exaggerating.

Frequency-hopping spread spectrum has a place in many digital communications systems. The Bluetooth standard, for example, which allows cellular phones to communicate with headsets or other peripherals, uses frequency-hopping to spread the users' signals in order to reduce interference. GSM also has an optional frequency-hopping mode that system providers can invoke if needed. In both cases, Bluetooth and GSM, the frequency-hopping rate is approximately one thousand times slower than the bit rate. These standards therefore only partially experience the benefits of spread-spectrum communications. To fully utilize spread-spectrum, the hopping rate should be faster than the bit rate. Or the system can turn to code-based spreading techniques such as CDMA.

Cellular phone CDMA implementations typically use both Walsh codes and PN generators. A transmitter in the 2G CDMA standard multiplies data bits by both a Walsh code and two PN streams to serve different purposes. In the forward link (base-to-mobile), Walsh codes separate the user channels, so each user gets an assignment of one Walsh code. Rather than send a data bit, the base station transmits the Walsh code. The Walsh codes are relatively short and have some regularity to them, so the PN streams make the transmission more noise-like in order to reduce interference between users. One of the PN streams addresses each user, adding to the code separation provided by the Walsh codes, and breaking up the regular bit patterns. The other PN stream addresses all the users within a cell.

The mobile units in a cell apply all of their codes in sequence to retrieve the data. First, all the cellphones in a cell share the offset for one of the PN codes, which they apply to pick their base station's waves out of the background noise and the waves from other base stations. Then each cellphone applies its own offset with the second PN stream to extract its own part of the incoming waves.

Then the cellphone can apply its Walsh code to produce the data stream. The second PN code and the Walsh codes perform largely the same function, but are both necessary, as explained in the next chapter. In short, a cellphone occasionally needs to read from more than one communication channel.

With all of the applied codes, the 19.2 kbps data stream expands to 1.2288 Mcps (mega-chips-per-second), which then travels over 1.25 MHz channels, bringing the benefits of spread spectrum communications. Reception of the message is possible even at low power, allowing for large cells. Alternatively, the cells can be small and use lower transmitting power.

The capacity of a CDMA–based system is potentially higher than one based on FDMA or TDMA. One advantage is that CDMA does not have frequency reuse restrictions. In the FDMA–based standard of AMPS, the FCC split the 25 MHz spectrum among two service providers, giving 12.5 MHz for each system, which further divides into 416 channels of 30 kHz each. Assuming clusters of seven cells, each cell then has 416 channels/cluster / 7 cells/cluster = 59 channels/cell available channels. TDMA–based digital systems offer some capacity increase but the effective channel width is nearly the same as AMPS.

In the GSM standard, for example, each channel is 200 kHz wide, but split into eight time slots. As a result each user has the equivalent of approximately a 25 kHz channel.

In a CDMA–based system, however, the channels are 1.25 MHz. The 12.5 MHz spectrum would divide into ten channels, but practical limitations produce nine channels. Since the PN codes separate the messages sent to each mobile unit, none of the frequency reuse restrictions apply. Waves intercepted from adjacent cells at the same frequency do not interfere with the communications since the codes are different. If four of the 64 Walsh codes are reserved for system overhead purposes like paging and control, then each of the nine channels can serve approximately 60 users, resulting in 60 users/channel × 9 channels = 540 available channels in a cell. The capacity is therefore about ten times higher than that of the other systems. But before CDMA–based systems were in operation and this could be shown in practice, the capacity increase was a subject of contention.

The capacity limit in a CDMA–based system is not a fixed number, but varies with system conditions. With FDMA and TDMA based systems, once the system controller assigns a user a frequency channel and a time slot, the mobile unit owns that channel and can broadcast at whatever power is necessary. High power helps the system to overcome noise and fades. When all of the channels are taken, the system is full. In a CDMA–based system, each mobile unit's transmitted wave appears as noise to the other phones, lowering the E_b / N_o of their received waves by raising N_o. A mobile unit could use a high E_b, but that energy adds to the N_o seen by the other mobile units. The processing gain allows for the E_b / N_o to be low, but at some point it is too low and the bit errors are frequent enough to interrupt the call. The phones are therefore all encouraged to keep their transmitted powers as low as possible in order to keep the noise level down.

The system can still increase capacity when full by lowering the transmitted power of each phone through puncturing. As described at the start of this chapter, the chip rate remains 1.2288 Mcps, but the transmitter periodically switches on and off. The number of bits that get through the system drops, and the audio quality or rate of data transfer is lower. But the average transmitted power, and therefore the noise seen by the other units, also drops. So the system can accommodate more users, although at the cost of slower data transfer rates. As an alternative explanation, puncturing adds a layer of TDMA over the CDMA system. The cellphones take turns transmitting in order to share the channels.

Another advantage of CDMA–based systems is the use of rake receivers to not only eliminate inter-symbol interference but to also allow the mobile units to communicate with multiple base stations simultaneously. Recall that each path of the rake receiver is a correlator using a different PN code to extract the data bits from the received chips. Besides using the different correlators to process delayed versions of the waves coming from one base station, some of the correlators could be applying an entirely different PN code corresponding to a communication link with another base station. This creates a stronger signal, and allows mobile units to make smoother hand-offs.

Despite the theoretical benefits, CDMA faced practical challenges when implemented into a cellular phone system. The PN generators throughout the entire system, including all the base stations and all the mobile units must be synchronized to within a fraction of a microsecond for the system to work. Without synchronization, the receivers will not have the right code needed to extract signals from the noise. Fortunately, the Global Positioning System (GPS) was just becoming operational when CDMA–based cellular systems were in development. The base stations could synchronize using the GPS signal, and the mobile units could synchronize with the base stations.

Another challenge is power control, which determines system capacity. As described, a high ambient noise level, N_o, lowers the capacity or could even render the system completely unusable. The primary source of noise is the mobile units themselves, so the system controller must tightly control their power levels.

One obstacle to power control is the near/far problem. The base station by necessity must transmit to the distant mobile units with high power, which could overwhelm the weaker transmissions to the nearby mobile units. And the transmissions from the nearby mobile units could mask the weak waves arriving from the distant mobile units. To correct this, the system must continuously measure the received power at both the base station and the mobile units and make adjustments. If the received power level is significantly more than what is needed, the base station instructs the phone to lower its transmitting power. Adjustment instructions in the first CDMA–based system were sent 800 times per second, so the system could respond quickly to a changing environment to keep the noise level down and the capacity up. Later systems would increase that adjustment rate to over 1000 times per second.

While digital technology adds complexity to communications, the advantages are too great to ignore. By converting the analog signal into a stream of digital numbers, the system has more to transmit, but can make use of powerful digital techniques. The technology developed in the mid-decades of the twentieth century and was reaching fruition as the cellular phone appeared in the early 1980's. The final necessary steps in fields such as audio compression and integrated circuit manufacturing arrived as the cellular phone was ready to become digital. But the added power of digital processing also introduced variation in the ways to achieve the benefits. While analog systems all followed the FM transmitter/receiver model, digital systems could be fundamentally different from each other and still operate well.

7

Digital Standards

Concepts of digital communication may hold some interest by themselves, but they only become useful to cellphones when implemented as standards. These digital standards are at base similar to the analog standards discussed in Chapter Four, since they are sets of rules that companies follow to create compatible equipment and systems. The largest difference, besides the technology, was that the business had expanded greatly since the first generation of cellular phones introduced around 1980. By the early 1990's the initial predictions about the cellphone's future were clearly too modest. Enormous revenue and prestige were at stake, bringing intense competition.

The competition in the 1990's was largely between two digital cellular phone standards: GSM and 2G CDMA. Development and implementation of GSM began first, motivated by the incompatible standards across Europe. GSM (Groupe Special Mobile) planned GSM (Global System for Mobile Communication) as a universal standard that could unify European communications while improving capacity and performance. Since digital technology allowed for compression of audio signals, each user only needed a channel for a fraction of the time, allowing time-sharing, which is the basis of TDMA. The industry in the USA soon followed Europe's lead, but then another contender emerged, a standard based on CDMA.

Some knowledge of the standards in question is necessary to understand the struggle between them in the 1990's, and that is the aim of this chapter. A basic rundown of what a GSM and a 2G CDMA cellphone do is in order. And at the risk of spoiling the ending of the next chapter, CDMA prevails and becomes the basis for the third generation standards, so the following descriptions dwell on the details of the 2G CDMA standard more fully than the others.

The GSM Standard

The task for the creators of GSM in the 1980's was to fit a digital system into the available spectrum. At the time, this was 50 MHz divided into two parts, the reverse link (mobile-to-base) at 890 to 915 MHz and the forward link (base-to-mobile) at 935 to 960 MHz. Each part is 25 MHz, which further divides into 124 channels of 200 kHz each.[1] This part of the multiple access method is FDMA, which is similar to analog systems.

Besides frequency segmentation, GSM uses TDMA to increase capacity by separating the users into time slots. Each channel is made up of 4.615 millisecond frames, and each frame contains eight slots of 0.577 milliseconds. A user assigned to the first slot of the reverse link could transmit during that time, and then wait until the first slot of the next frame to transmit again. On the forward-link channel, the same user would have the fourth slot. The three-slot stagger lets the cellphone switch between transmission and reception. The mobile unit can still receive the base station's signal between assigned time slots and measure the received power level, but due to encryption it cannot read the data in the other slots.

Various overhead functions reduce the data rate, but it is still significantly higher than what analog systems could achieve. With switching time and other delays, the data bursts are 0.546 milliseconds long, so 0.031 milliseconds (about 5 percent) of each slot is unused. Looking more closely at the time slots, the message consists of 148 bits, including 3 buffer bits at the start and at the end.

The raw bitrate of 148 bits per 0.546 milliseconds is about 270 kbps, but not all of the 148 bits are data. There are two data segments of 58 bits (57 bits are data and 1 bit signals whether the data is voice or messaging), and a 26-bit segment between the two that the mobile unit and base station use for timing synchronization and equalization. An interleaver shuffles the 57 bit data segments, so the two data segments of any time slot are not sequential. Excluding the 26-bit fixed pattern and the two voice/messaging indicator bits, each time slot only contains 114 data bits, and since there are 216 frames per second, the usable bit rate for each user is 114 bits/frame × 216 frames/second = 24.6 kbps. Furthermore, of those bits, many are error-correction bits. While this rate is low when compared with later standards, it is sufficient to carry the 22.8 kbps stream of encoded voice and yield higher quality than many analog systems.

In addition to equalization based on the middle bit sequence of each time slot, a GSM system can also combat multipath problems with frequency hopping. When the system activates this feature, the channel switches frequency after every frame, yielding 217.6 frequency hops in a second. While fast on the human scale, the time between frequency hops is enough to send approximately four million periods of the carrier wave, so from the perspective of the electronics, the system is hardly dynamic.

The frequencies follow a pattern of up to 64 hops before returning to the same channel and repeating the sequence, so the frequency changes are also not sufficiently random to create the noise-like appearance of frequency-hopping spread-spectrum communications. Of those 64 channels, it is hoped that only a small number suffer from significant intersymbol interference. Rather than one user being stuck in a poor channel, all of the users spend a little time in the bad channel and most of their time in the other, presumably better, channels.

Audio signals travel through a GSM system on traffic channels with varying bit rates. The 4.615 millisecond frames are in groups of 26, with 24 frames for traffic and 2 frames for system information. The voice rate is 13 kbps, although this becomes 22.8 kbps with error correction, and non-voice data, which can tolerate some small delays, has rates of 9.6 kbps, 4.8 kbps, or 2.4 kbps when operating at full rate. There is also a half-rate mode with all of the numbers halved. The half-rate mode increases capacity by giving each user fewer time slots, such as a slot every second or third frame, at the expense of lowered voice quality and slower data transmission. Even when operating at full rate, the transmitter can shut off for a few frames when voice activity is low to save battery power and free the slots for other users.

The messages, whether voice or data, follow a straightforward path to transmission. First the transmitter adds error correction bits to the data stream. Then it interleaves the 57-bit data groups to counter noise spikes and fast fades. A PN code then enters usage, but to encrypt the bits, not to spread the spectrum. Each chip replaces one data bit. After this the modulator divides the bits into in-phase and quadrature streams to modulate the transmitted sine wave and cosine wave, respectively.

In addition to the data in the traffic channel, there are also control channels used for system messages. There are several control channels that perform various functions, although a few give an idea of their general usage. The broadcast control channel, for example, sends the cell ID number and system information, or dummy bits if there is not enough data to send. The base station broadcasts this channel continuously, and the mobile units use it to measure reception power. Upon making contact, the mobile units then use another channel, the synchronization channel, to align frames and time slots with the base station. Another channel, the common paging channel addresses all the mobile units with notices of an incoming call. Since the control channels are continuously running, and the voice channels send digital messages even when the user is not talking, the supervisory audio tone of the analog standards is unnecessary.

The capacity of GSM is higher than AMPS, largely due to the benefits of digital technology. While AMPS fits 6.67 users, each taking 30 kHz, into a 200 kHz channel, GSM places eight users into the same channel. This gives a modest capacity increase of $8/6.67 = 1.2$. The significant difference is in the more tolerant reception requirements.

A benefit of digital communications is that some reception requirements are more lenient. AMPS mandates a minimum signal-to-noise ratio of 63 due to the limitations of FM in the 30 kHz channel widths. GSM, by contrast, uses a variant of QPSK called GMSK that requires a signal-to-noise ratio of only 8.* At this signal-to-noise ratio, the bit error rate is 10^{-4}, meaning that on average one received bit out of ten thousand is incorrect, which is sufficient for the error-correction to work without slowing the communication link. The lower signal-to-noise requirement allows the frequency reuse factor, which is 7 in AMPS, to be 3 in GSM, since some overlap of a signal into surrounding cells is tolerable. The number of channels available in a cell is therefore the number of channels used by the service provider divided by three. Taking this into account the capacity of GSM is 2.8 times larger than AMPS in the same spectrum.[2]

Other TDMA–Based Standards

Besides usage as a standard in itself, GSM formed the basis of other standards. This is similar to the variants of AMPS such as TACS and J-AMPS, which were standards created to meet local needs while making use of the research that went into AMPS. While that first generation work came from the USA, the GSM variants looked to Europe for direction. This includes the USA, which was lagging in digital cellular phone development.

The Cellular Telephone Industry Association picked TDMA as the basis for the digital successor to AMPS. The standard took the name IS-54, and became IS-136 when updated in 1994. The names D-AMPS and American TDMA also appear in some writings, as does U.S. Digital Cellular (USDC) and North American Digital Cellular (NADC). Whatever the name, this standard's goal was to make the transition from AMPS to a digital system as easy as possible.

D-AMPS replaced much of AMPS with digital technology, while maintaining other aspects without change. The standard used the same 30 kHz channels as AMPS, but split them into three time slots. This gave each user the equivalent of only 10 kHz, rather than GSM's 25 kHz. To make up some of the difference, IS-54 used an encoding and error correction scheme with 20 percent of the bits as overhead, rather than GSM's 30 percent. The standard was estimated to surpass capacity of AMPS by a factor of 3.5 to 6.3. While the higher capacity and voice quality is an improvement over AMPS, the low data rate would be a liability by the late 1990's.

A standard close to IS-54 came onto the Japanese market with even more stringent bandwidth limitations. The standard is PDC, which usually stands

---

The technical literature invariably uses the logarithmic scale for power levels. In that scale, the decrease from 63 to 8 becomes a drop from 18 dB to 9 dB.

for Personal Digital Cellular, but Pacific Digital Cellular also sometimes appears. PDC went further than IS-54 by using the 25 kHz channels of the analog standard JTACS, divided into 3 slots. The narrower channels would yield an estimated increase in capacity over AMPS of 4.2 to 7.6. Like IS-54, however, PDC proved to be deficient when i-mode, with internet access, reached popularity in the late 1990's. The 9.6 kbps data rate was suitable only for text-based web browsing, prompting another revision of the systems.

The clear advantage of these GSM variants is that they work within the defined analog system channels. While the performance, measured by data rate, may not be as high as in GSM, service operators could make the switch to digital with relatively little expense. An alternative to these standards was an untried, but ultimately successful, CDMA–based standard.

The 2G CDMA Standard

The first issue to broach when discussing the second generation CDMA–based standard is what name to use. The simple name "CDMA" was often applied to the standard, although this is too vague to be accurate. The standard uses CDMA, like a particular make of automobile uses an internal combustion engine. Since there was only one standard using CDMA in the mid to late 1990's, there was no ambiguity. When CDMA standards began to proliferate some confusion was inevitable. Australia's Telstra, for example, used CDMA as the marketed name of their second generation system. When they shut down that system in favor of a third generation system called Next-G in 2007, CDMA came to be associated with the obsolescent past. But in actuality, Next-G is another CDMA–based system.

Within the industry, the commonly used name is the serial designation IS-95, with IS standing for Interim Standard. The interim status eventually ended and the designation became TIA/EIA-95 (Telecommunication Industry Association/Electronic Industries Alliance), although the name IS-95 has survived, probably due to habit. The name put on the standard for the public was "cdmaOne." For clarity, the name used here is 2G CDMA.

This standard uses spread-spectrum techniques, and therefore allocates spectrum into wide frequency blocks. The AMPS spectrum of 824 to 849 MHz for the reverse link and 869 to 894 MHz for the forward link was still in place, but divided into 1.25 MHz frequency segments. Each 2G CDMA channel therefore consumed 42 AMPS channels. The data stream of 9.6 kbps becomes 19.2 kbps with error correction bits, and then transmits with 64 chips used to represent one bit, yielding a chip rate of 1.2288 Mcps. The chips that encode a particular bit come from both Walsh codes and PN generators.

The Walsh codes have different roles in the forward and reverse link, and in both cases form only a part of the CDMA process. In the forward link, for example, the base station assigns each user one of 64 Walsh codes, while reserving some for control channels. This separates the users, but is inadequate in two respects. First, there is more separation needed, such as between users in different cells. Also, at 64 bits the Walsh codes are too short to make the transmitted signal sufficiently noise-like. For these reasons, 2G CDMA adds two more PN generators to the message preparation.

One PN stream is the short code, which despite its name is a sequence 32,768 chips long. At a rate of 1.2288 Mcps, the short code repeats every 26.67 milliseconds, so in time it is quite short. The first use of the short code is to differentiate between cell sites. All of the short code PN generators in the system are identical and synchronized, but each cell uses different delayed versions of the chip stream. By using the same short PN code offset, all of the mobile units in the cell can pass the base station's waves through the first level of decryption. Waves from other cells, with different short PN offsets, continue to appear as background noise. The system therefore uses the short PN codes to render the waves from different base stations to be orthogonal to each other. And this code also serves another important purpose.

In quadrature modulation as introduced in Chapter Six, the bit stream splits into two parts, an in-phase stream and a quadrature stream. The modulator multiplies the in-phase stream with a sine wave and the quadrature stream with a cosine wave to produce two orthogonal waves for transmission. The 2G CDMA standards adds an extra digital step. After creating the in-phase and quadrature streams, but before modulation, both streams are multiplied by the short PN code with different delays. This creates two bit streams that are orthogonal in the digital domain even before modulation. The orthogonality of the short PN code helps the communication link by separating cell sites and also by separating the in-phase and quadrature streams. But it is too short to create an adequately noise-like signal for spread-spectrum communications, and requires the help of another code.

The long PN code does the work of making the signal appear to be noise and is true to its name by being lengthy. Even at a rate of 1.2288 Mcps, the long code repeats only every 41 days. This code renders the digital stream closely noise-like, which is vital to CDMA–based systems. Each communication link needs to use a different noise source, however, so the long code needs modification. To separate the users, the transmitter uses the mobile unit's Electronic Serial Number as a mask for the long PN code generator's output, meaning that the long PN code passes though more operations involving multiplication with the bits of the Electronic Serial Number. The mask renders the long PN code specific to each mobile unit, so even if the mobile unit uses an unassigned Walsh code, it will not be able to decrypt the message. But not all of the channels need this level of separation.

Out of the channels available within each frequency segment, several exist only for system messages and setup purposes. The simplest is the pilot channel, which the base station broadcasts continuously as a power and timing reference. The data is a stream of +1 bits, encoded using Walsh code zero, which is itself made up of 64 chips all set to +1. The base station splits that stream of chips into the in-phase and quadrature streams, multiplies those streams with short PN codes using the settings for that cell and then broadcasts the resulting signal. Since the long code with the Electronic Serial Number mask is not used, any mobile unit in the cell can read this channel.

The cellphones use the pilot channel to gauge the signal strength of nearby base stations and to synchronize the internal clock and the PN generators in the cellphone with those in the base stations. Another channel, the sync code channel contains general information such as ID numbers for the cell, system and network, and the system time. This channel uses Walsh code 32 and then the short PN code. Again, the long PN codes are not used, so this channel is available to all phones in range. Paging channels can be Walsh codes 1 through 7, depending on the system, and send information such as notification of an incoming call to specific mobile units. In this case, the base station does apply the long PN code with the Electronic Serial Number mask, then the Walsh code, and finally the short PN code before transmission. These channels send occasional system information, but of greater interest are the traffic channels.

The path that data follows through the forward traffic channel, broadcast by the base station and received by the mobile unit, is the most elaborate. The data stream starts at variable rates depending on voice activity and system settings, with a maximum setting of 9.6 kbps. Adding error correction bits increases the rate to 19.2 kbps and block interleaving then mixes the order of the bit groups. At this point the bit stream multiplies with the long PN code that has the electronic serial number mask, but the rate remains at 19.2 kbps since only one out of every 64 bits from the long PN code generator are used. The transmitter next replaces 800 bits per second with power control bits that tell the mobile unit whether to increase or decrease transmission power. After that each bit is replaced with the 64 chips of the assigned traffic channel Walsh code, finally yielding the rate of 1.2288 Mcps. That stream splits into an in-phase stream and a quadrature stream, which are each operated on by versions of the short PN code. They then go to be mixed with sine and cosine waves for transmission as analog waves. During this chain of events, the spectrum was spread once, but the principle of CDMA was applied three times with three different codes.

The mobile unit extracts the message from the received wave in reverse order from the transmission, with each step stripping away one layer of encryption. The first step is for the receiver to demodulate the analog waves through multiplication by sine and cosine waves, producing two noise-like chip streams. Those streams contain all the digital transmissions in that frequency block from all sources both inside and outside the cell. Performing digital multiplication with the short PN codes removes everything except digital messages sent by one base station. But all the messages to all the users in that cell and frequency block are still present in noise form. Correlating with the mobile unit's assigned Walsh code finally strips away all interference from the stream and leaves only the message meant for that user. The stream still appears to be noise, which one more multiplication, performed with the long PN code, transforms into the data. The transmission and reception path just described form the forward link, which is only one half of the conversation.

The reverse link follows a different procedure since the mobile unit has a different, and more challenging, broadcasting environment when compared to the base station. First, the channel encoder adds more error-correction bits, moving the 9.6 kbps data stream to 28.8 kbps, rather than the 19.2 kbps of the forward link. The data stream then goes to a Walsh code block, but not to replace every bit with 64 chips. Instead, the block takes in six bits at a time and uses that six-digit binary number as the index to pick a Walsh code, which goes to the output. Since 64 chips replace each 6 bits, the 28.8 kbps data stream becomes a 307.2 kcps stream. This is part of the spreading, and a subsequent block does the rest by replacing each chip with four chips from the long PN code, creating a noise-like chip stream with a rate of 1.2288 Mcps. After this, the stream is split into an in-phase stream and a quadrature stream, mixed with copies of the short PN code and sent to modulate the sinusoidal waves for transmission. A half-chip delay in the path of the quadrature stream offsets the two outputs so they do not both switch at once. Whereas the for-

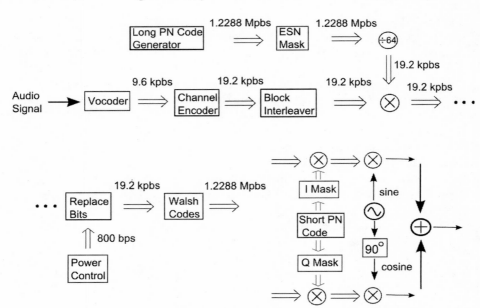

Figure 21: The transmit procedure for the forward link (base station to mobile unit) in the 2G CDMA standard.

ward link used QPSK for modulation, the reverse link therefore uses Offset-QPSK.

The first job of a cellular phone system is to accept new mobile units. Given the nature of cellular phones, a new entrant can appear anywhere and at any time, so the base stations and the new mobile units engage in a procedure of back-and-forth messaging. Upon powering up, a cellphone may have no information about the surrounding system. This includes the timing needed to synchronize PN generators, without which no communication is possible. Therefore all it can do is measure the received power of any available pilot channels from nearby cells. Recall that the data stream of the pilot channel is just one bit, +1, repeated endlessly and spread using the short PN code with the cell's ID number as a mask. The mobile unit picks the pilot channel with the strongest received power and synchronizes its internal PN generator with the incoming stream. The mobile unit then switches to the sync code channel which contains cell and system information, including the system time and the short PN offset for that cell.

The mobile unit's messages back to the base station go through the access channel, but it first has to make contact. Using the received power to make an estimate of the required transmit power, the mobile unit sends a message through the access channel and waits for a reply. If there is no acknowledgement, the handset sends the message again with a higher power, and repeats the process until a message from the base station appears. Once contact is established in both directions, communication can begin.

While in operation, the mobile unit monitors the paging channels for messages such as a notification of an incoming call. Upon receiving or placing a call, the system controller assigns a Walsh code to the phone and a call can commence. All the while, the cellphone also measures the power of any received pilot channels, searching for powerful signals. If a pilot channel from another cell has more than twice the received power of the current cell, the mobile unit switches to the other cell.

System planning for 2G CDMA is done with the realization that users can share frequencies, which makes the concept of a cell more general. Unlike an AMPS system, with clusters of seven cells, which lowers the number of channels available in any cell by a factor of seven, all channels are available to all users. Rather than being a problem, same-frequency transmissions from adjacent cells is encouraged. A mobile unit can be in contact with multiple base stations simultaneously.

The rake receiver, introduced to spread-spectrum communications in the 1950's, found a use in 2G CDMA to not only communicate through multiple propagation paths, but also to be in simultaneous contact with multiple base stations. The receiver first demodulates the incoming waves using sine and cosine waves, creating the in-phase and quadrature chip streams. The rake receiver divides the streams into four separate correlators, which apply the short PN codes to remove the base station encoding. The receiver then recombines the streams into one strong stream and applies the assigned Walsh code and long PN code and extracts the data.

The cellphone rake receiver has four parallel receivers, one of which is perpetually searching incoming waves to find strong signals, which it then assigns to the other three receivers. One advantage of the rake receiver is to reduce the effects of fading. If one link is in a fade, there may still be enough power in the other two links for adequate demodulation. And the rake receiver also has benefits for making handoffs easier and less prone to dropped calls.

Being in communication with multiple base stations allows the mobile units to make soft handoffs, in which the transition between cells is gradual. This is in contrast with a hard handoff, where the phone must drop a call in the old cell and pick it up in the new cell. The switch in a hard handoff is a vulnerable point where a call is most likely to be dropped. A soft handoff lessens the problems involved so there are fewer dropped calls.

Even a CDMA–based system, however, uses hard handoffs in some situations. The rake receiver is located in the receiver chain after demodulation, so all the base stations in communication must be using the same frequency channel. A cell may be in one channel but entering a cell where that channel is full, requiring a switch without the rake receiver, which is a hard handoff. In the late 1990's most cellphones also had to be able to switch between digital and analog operation, which was also a hard handoff. Analog systems have been almost completely replaced, so such handoffs are now rare.

One other aspect of a 2G CDMA system vital to understanding its operation is power control. As explained earlier, a CDMA–based communication link appears as noise to receivers without the right code. Users joining a cell therefore raise the noise level, as does high-power broadcasting by existing users. At some point the noise level becomes high enough that some of the communication links cease to function. A clear goal of the system is therefore to keep the transmit powers of the mobile units as low as possible. But low power transmission introduces an added risk of dropping a call since the broadcast environment is continuously changing. A mobile unit may have to quickly increase power for a few milliseconds to overcome a fade, but should then quickly return to low power operation afterward.

The handset finds a power level for broadcasting with two methods. First is the approximate procedure used during handset initialization, in which the phone sends messages through the access channel with higher and higher powers until a reply comes back. Once the handset and base station have two-way contact, tighter power control takes place. The base station measures the mobile unit's E_b / N_o level 800 times per second and uses this information to decide on an appropriate transmitting power level. Then, as the base station prepares data for the forward channel, it removes one bit and replaces it with a power control bit. This bit instructs the phone to either raise or lower its power by 25 percent. With a power control bit sent every 1.25 milliseconds, the base station can maintain tight control on the mobile units in its cell.

The two main digital cellphone standards, one based on TDMA and the other working with CDMA, emerged in the early 1990's, leaving the industry with a choice to make. The TDMA system, GSM, had an earlier launch and built and insurmountable lead. Yet by gradual validation through usage, CDMA proved to be valuable for cellular phones. The rivalry between the two systems through the 1990's is one of the most interesting stories in modern communications.

8

The Digital Cellphone

While the cellular phone was making its first appearance on the markets during the 1980's, the industry was already planning the next stage in its evolution. The technology marched forward, increasing the capabilities of the cellular phones and decreasing their size. They shifted from being mobile units, meaning car phones, to handsets that people carried everywhere. The cellular phone became the cellphone. The business world was waking up to the enormous revenue potential in the field, and the market was also taking notice of the cellphone.

More capacity and more data transmission were on the way, even if the details of how those improvements would happen remained a mystery. Up to this point in the history, data meant voice messaging, but with the digital era dawning, a clear delineation between voice and data emerges. Data began as text messaging in the mid–1990's, and within a few years included pictures, audio, and internet access. All of these data transfers are more demanding than the 300 baud symbol rate that AMPS delivered during data trials in 1984.[1]

The only way to allow more data transfer would be to give each user more bandwidth, which seems contrary to the goal of adding more capacity. As described in Chapter Seven, completely revamping the systems to use digital technology meets both requirements. Another motivation propelling changes, particularly in Europe, was to replace the incompatible systems with one international standard. Nordic NMT, British TACS, French Radiocomm 2000, German C-450, Italian Radio Telephone Mobile System and other analog systems operated in Europe, rendering cellphones country-specific. Some of those systems, such as Radiocomm 2000 and C-450, were not successful for various reasons, such as poor service and low capacity. In comparison, the American standard, AMPS, performed well, so the drive to replace it was not as strong as in Europe.[2]

The planning for GSM began early, while the assorted European analog

114

standards were just beginning to appear. Representatives of eleven countries met in Stockholm in 1982 to plan a European-wide system, and the organization took the name Groupe Spécial Mobile (GSM).[3] The acronym transferred to the standard the group created, although the meaning became the grander Global System for Communication. A trial of a GSM–based system was conducted in Paris in 1988 using 300 kHz frequency segments divided into ten time slots each. The results were poor, prompting a change in the parameters to 200 kHz segments of eight time slots, and the system then worked well.[4] GSM service started in 1992, and by 1996 had reached 103 countries, so it really had become a global standard.[5] While Europe was making a clear and ambitious drive to improve the cellphone, the situation in the USA was unclear.

Competing Standards for Digital Cellular in the USA

Creating a digital standard in the USA is as much a tale of business and politics as of technology. Unlike in Europe, where the GSM standard had consensus from the start, American companies tested and championed different technologies. As expected, the technology that each company found to be superior tended to match its holdings in patents and experience. Motorola, for example, had extensive experience in AMPS, and so was in the FDMA half. Swedish-based Ericsson was deeply involved in GSM development, and fell in the TDMA half. A third half, that of CDMA, emerged later from Qualcomm, which was founded by engineers who had experience implementing CDMA–based satellite links. But when discussions began in the late 1980's, there were only two choices.

The first task facing regulatory bodies was whether to base the planned standard on FDMA or TDMA, and trials of both showed mixed results. FDMA had the advantage of translating well from AMPS, allowing for a quicker and easier transition. AT&T demonstrated a digital FDMA–based system in Chicago in 1987 using 10 kHz channels, and encoding the voice at a rate of 8.3 kbps. Since the system performed well, when Motorola conducted a follow-up trial in Santa Ana, California, they decided to push the parameters further toward higher capacity. The equipment encoded the voice at 6.2 kbps and transmitted using frequency segments of only 7.5 kHz. This was apparently too compact for the current technology, since the system performed poorly with low audio quality.[6]

On the other side, Ericsson set up a TDMA–based demonstration system in Los Angeles. The plan had been to use 30 kHz frequency segments divided into three slots, but they could not get it working in time. Instead, they used two time slots, equivalent to 15 kHz channels, which allowed a voice encoding rate of 13 kbps. With these unambitious parameters, the system performed well, with good audio quality. The comparison may not have been equal, but the impression of the superiority of TDMA had been made.[7]

The Cellular and Telecommunications Industry Association settled the matter at a conference in Denver in August of 1987. Every member company got one vote, regardless of size or experience. Sixteen votes, including AT&T and Motorola, went to FDMA, while TDMA received 32 votes from companies such as Ericsson and Northern Telecom. With TDMA chosen, the development could begin, and the results of the European GSM trials helped in determining what would work. By 1989 the standard was ready and available under the serial number IS-54, later revised as IS-136. D-AMPS (Digital AMPS), USDC (United States Digital Cellular) and NADC (North American Digital Cellular) are commonly used names for IS-136. While the industry was moving ahead with a TDMA–based standard, another technology, CDMA, was building support. Championing this approach was a new company that would ride the eventual acceptance and success of CDMA to the upper levels of the industry.

The Qualcomm story began when a trio of professors formed a consulting company, Linkabit, in 1968. The small concern soon grew into a company bidding for government contracts in fields such as digital satellite communications. The applications included using what were then exotic spread-spectrum techniques such as CDMA. The company's advancement continued, but expansion can be difficult, and the competition for large government contracts is intense. Looking for more growth and advancement, the management thought they found a solution.

The much larger communications company M/A-COM bought Linkabit in 1980, bringing a large amount of capital and resources. But as often happens, the plans of the buyers did not match those of the sellers. Dissatisfied that the larger company was letting the new Linkabit division wilt, several employees, including the founders, left to create a new company. That company was Qualcomm, founded in 1985 with no specific product to sell other than the experience of its few employees.

Qualcomm's first big moneymaker was satellite communications for trucking. Qualcomm's involvement started with a $250,000 contract from Omninet to study the technology, but the association continued until the two companies merged in 1988. The communications system, under the name OmniTracs, began service that year.

Due to the constraints of communicating with a satellite, the data rate of OmniTracs was necessarily low. The satellites were in geostationary orbit at 35,000 kilometers away from the Earth's surface, rather than the low-earth orbits of approximately 1,000 kilometers used by later satellite phone systems with hand-held mobile units. The transmission rate from the satellite to the mobile unit was 10 kbps, although only 5 kbps of that was data and the rest were error correction bits. The reverse link was even slower at only 132 bps, of which only 44 bps were data. The modulation method was 16-level frequency shift-keying, meaning each symbol represented four bits, so the transmission rate was really only 33 baud. Yet to overcome the loss from the enormous propagation distance, the transmitter spread that small rate over one megahertz, yielding a processing gain in the thousands.[8] Despite the low data rates, the system provided a vital service and faced little competition. With this steady source of revenue, Qualcomm could face the expense of entering the cellular phone business.

The proposal to use CDMA for digital cellular phone systems came in 1988, which was both too late and too early. It was too late because the industry had already decided to base digital cellular phones on TDMA. And to demonstrate a trial system by then, work should have commenced years earlier. But the technology needed for such a system was only beginning to become available.

The military and satellite systems had been using CDMA for decades, but at the time it was probably not feasible for a commercial telephone system. Critics were well-aware of the challenges described in previous chapters, which include exact synchronization throughout the system and careful power control of all the mobile units. So Qualcomm's top people took to the road, giving spirited presentations proclaiming the potential that CDMA offered cellular phones, and Qualcomm found some support for its plans. This irked some in the industry who did not believe CDMA could work and backed TDMA. As one technology columnist wrote in 1994: "CDMA is based on statistical mathematics that not one person in a thousand can comprehend, none of them in the investment banking community. Its roots lie in military systems—the folks that buy $500 toilet seats."[9]

CDMA–based systems offered the promise of better performance, but the resources involved made a commitment risky, particularly when compared with D-AMPS. One of the selling points of D-AMPS was that it used the same channels as AMPS, so a service provider could keep the AMPS system running while gradually switching more and more channels to D-AMPS. A CDMA–based system, however, would swallow 42 AMPS channels for each of its channels. Considering frequency reuse restrictions, each AMPS cell had approximately 57 voice channels and one control channel, so switching to a CDMA–based system could not be done gradually. And the performance of such a system in practical operation, as opposed to theoretical operation, was unproven. So potential customers, the service providers, were reticent to make a commitment until CDMA had been shown to work in a real, commercial system.

While the industry proceeded with D-AMPS, they did not shut the door on CDMA. Qualcomm was free to develop the technology alone and to sell it directly to service providers. One early partner was Pacific Telesys (also called PacTel, which later became part of SBC, then Cingular, and then AT&T Mobility), which was interested since the Los Angeles system had reached full capacity.[10] Qualcomm requested $200,000 from PacTel to study CDMA, but PacTel instead offered one million dollars to set up a demonstration in six months.[11]

The first demonstration of a CDMA–based cellular phone system took place on November 3, 1989, in San Diego. PacTel had allowed Qualcomm to put equipment into their base stations to set up the system. The 1.25 MHz frequency segments that became part of the standard originated here, since that was the spectrum that PacTel was willing to give up for the trial system. The Global Positioning System was only partially completed at the time, so the start of the demonstration had to wait for the satellites to be overhead. Handsets were not available at that point in the development, so the mobile unit was a van outfitted with racks of electronic equipment and monitors. Participants could watch the communication links to the nearby base stations on the monitors. With the rake receiver in use, the mobile unit would link to three base stations at the same time, and as the van moved, the links would transition between base stations. A more advanced trial was conducted in 1991, also in San Diego, with antennas placed in the area to broadcast noise in order to simulate a system operating with a heavy user load. The trials were a success, showing a capacity ten times that of AMPS.

Development of a CDMA–based cellular phone system continued through the early 1990's, gradually finding potential customers. Meanwhile, in January of 1992 the board of the Cellular and Telecommunications Industry Association unanimously endorsed TDMA as the basis of digital cellular phone systems in the USA. This recommendation did not follow the European example of being an inviolate command. European regulators had allocated spectrum and assigned it to GSM operation, while the American frequency allocations did not require a specific standard. The PCS band, created by the FCC in the early 1990's, would be only for digital cellular communications, but providers could use any of the available digital standards. This allowed some companies to pursue CDMA–based or D-AMPS systems.

The first CDMA–based cellular phone systems began to appear in the mid–1990's. Qualcomm continued to run tests and demonstrations, setting up trial systems in the District of Columbia, as well as in Germany and Switzerland in 1992. Performance was good, and the systems showed promise, so eventually Qualcomm was able to acquire some commitments for CDMA–based systems. In 1995 PCS PrimeCo, AirTouch Communications, and Sprint Technology Ventures announced CDMA deployment plans. More significantly, commercial service began that year in Hong Kong and then in Los Angeles.

While these first CDMA–based systems were working through their initial technical problems, GSM systems had been operational around the world for several years. And cellular companies in the USA, particularly McCaw Communications, which became AT&T Wireless in 1993, were investing heavily in D-AMPS. China went with GSM in 1995, deciding that CDMA was not ready. This move guaranteed that GSM would always have a higher number of worldwide subscribers than 2G CDMA, and by a wide margin. The previously mentioned skeptical technology columnist wrote a follow-up column in 1996 pointing out these difficulties. The title was clear: "CDMA: Blazing a Trail of Broken Dreams."[12]

An early area of growth for CDMA–based systems, which would serve as a successful proving ground for the new technology, was South Korea. This emerged from a joint development deal made in May of 1991 between Qualcomm and the Electronics and Telecommunications Research Institute, a Korean industrial association. The origins of the deal were in the late 1980's, when the South Korean cellular phone industry was completely run by foreign companies, leaving domestic companies eager to find an entrance into the field.

In August of 1990, Qualcomm proposed CDMA development as a way for South Korea to find a place in the industry. Under the agreement of 1991, Qualcomm would receive royalty payments for the use of CDMA–based systems in South Korea, but would donate 20 percent back to the Electronics and Telecommunications Research Institute.[13] Service began in a few locations in South Korea in January of 1996, and was available throughout the country in April. The service proved to be popular, with over one million subscribers by the end of the year.[14]

By the turn of the century, working systems had demonstrated CDMA's advantages and the industry recognized that CDMA would form a part of future cellular phone standards. Yet since the demand for capacity and services was still accumulating, GSM could offer a competitive advantage in many situations. The American digital standard, however, revealed its weaknesses sooner. While 2G CDMA and GSM systems could access the internet, send e-mail, photographs and other data services, D-AMPS could not handle more than voice and some text messaging.

As consumers came to expect more services from their cellphones beyond being merely phones, the restrictions of D-AMPS became liabilities. In the year 2000, Verizon's CDMA–based system had the most subscribers and the largest coverage area in the continental USA. Next was Cingular, with a smaller subscriber base and coverage, and systems based largely on GSM, but also with some D-AMPS systems. In 2001, Cingular decided to move completely to GSM and drop D-AMPS. In third place was AT&T Wireless, which used the D-AMPS systems that McCaw had built. It began transitioning to GSM in 2000, but was too late to stop the decline and was bought by Cingular in 2004.[15]

The ultimate victory for CDMA came when the European Technological Standards Institute chose it as the basis for the next version of GSM. This would be the third generation of cellphones meant to improve the ability of the mobile units to download non-voice data. At a meeting in 1998, several possible standards were proposed, all of them based on CDMA. But this situation would not necessarily be a boon for Qualcomm since the proposals bypassed many of Qualcomm's patents. Qualcomm representatives also attended, but their presentation was scheduled last and the meeting adjourned before their turn.[16] While Qualcomm had found ways to make CDMA work for a cellular phone system, most of the defining principles had emerged from mid–20th century military projects. There is room for companies to find other ways. In addition, the patents Qualcomm had acquired in the late 1980's to early 1990's would soon be reaching the end of their twenty-year life spans.

The PCS Spectrum Auction

As the importance of cellular phones, and the promise of portable wireless communications, became apparent, new available spectrum materialized. The process began in Europe with preparations for the upcoming GSM networks. Governments created a new frequency band called Personal Communications Network, solely for GSM systems. The American FCC soon followed with its own new allocation for the promised digital systems.

Announced at a White House press conference in July of 1993, Personal Communications Services (PCS) would be exclusively for digital service. The frequencies of the PCS band are approximately twice that of cellular, which has both positive and negative aspects. Antenna size is proportional to wavelength, so as the frequency doubles, the wavelength halves, and handset antennas could be half the size of those on previous models. On the less beneficial side, the loss an electromagnetic wave experiences as it propagates over terrain rises with frequency, so PCS would be shorter range and have smaller cells. The base stations would therefore be more numerous and closer together, adding to the system expense.

Despite these ambitious goals, a decade later PCS service was the same as that offered in the cellular band, which had by then converted to digital technology. The benefit of creating the PCS band was that it offered more bandwidth for cellular phone service. Of course, this was not known at the time. Cellular phone service was still analog, so PCS was something different.

The PCS band consists of two parts, 1850 MHz to 1910 MHz for the reverse link (mobile-to-base) and 1930 MHz to 1990 MHz for the forward link (base-to-mobile), so there was 60 MHz to allocate. This is slightly less than the two 75 MHz bands in the European allocation, but still wide when compared to the 25 MHz cellular band. As with the spectrum allocation of the 1980's, the FCC's plan was to have two service providers in each market, although with some new features added to the distribution process.

The FCC split the PCS band into six blocks, lettered A through F. In the 51 large service areas, called Major Trading Areas, the band had A and B blocks, each with 30 MHz. Blocks C through F were for the 493 smaller Basic Trading Areas, with block C set aside for small businesses. At 30 MHz each, the C blocks were valuable frequency bands with significant revenue potential, a point understood by everyone involved in the industry by that time.

One unambiguous result of the previous cellular phone spectrum distribution was dissatisfaction by the FCC and Congress. The plan had been to give the spectrum to companies that would use it to build working systems, and was handled in a fair manner that allowed small businesses a chance to enter the field. That fairness may have been part of the problem. Everyone who received spectrum, or their representative, submitted an application stating that they should be given spectrum because they planned to use it. Many of the small investors had no connection to the communications industry and clearly intended to sell their spectrum for a profit. The deal-making and the years-long distribution process delayed the construction of systems in many locations. So the FCC did not succeed in using the lucrative spectrum to increase government revenue or in getting working systems built efficiently.

To avoid the problems encountered with the 1980's spectrum lottery, the FCC turned to an auction to distribute the spectrum. The auction would either filter out speculators or make them hand over significant revenues to the treasury, so the government would come out ahead. And by skipping the small investors and selling directly to the companies with an investor-driven commitment to build systems, the intermediate deal-making step of the previous distribution could be avoided. The auction method of distribution also benefited the public, which would have PCS systems installed and working soon. As happened with the previous distribution, however, the process hit many snags.

The first auction, for the A and B blocks in the 51 Major Trading Areas, went smoothly. The auction began in December of 1993 and ended the following March. These blocks were meant for large corporations with heavy involvement in the wireless industry, so there were only three main bidders. One was AT&T, now firmly in the cellular phone business after leaving it for much of the 1980's. Another was PCS PrimeCo, a conglomerate formed by several companies, including AT&T spinoffs Bell Atlantic, Nynex and U.S. West. The third bidder was Sprint Telecommunications Venture, created by a group of companies that included long-distance telephone service provider Sprint. The auction raised seven billion dollars, which worked out to $15 per population covered.[17] While this orderly and efficient auction was taking place, a more eventful auction was also meandering its way to a conclusion.

The FCC handled the auction of the C blocks, for small businesses, at the same time as that for the A and B blocks, and generated considerably more interest. Over 400 companies registered for the auction,[18] with many pushing the boundaries of what could be considered a small business. One bidder was NextWave, created by the founder of Omninet, which had been crucial to Qualcomm's early success. The potential company found investors to commit $550 million.[19] Another *soi-disant* small company in the bidding was Go! Communications, with $100 million in capital and $700 million in loan commitments from investors. Besides the loose definition, the FCC also helped small businesses by allowing lenient payment terms. Winners would only have to produce 10 percent of a winning bid, with the rest paid over ten years. Bidding was by computer, a revolutionary way to run an auction in the early 1990's, and quickly became competitive as bids rose above the levels set by the A and B auctions.

In one case, the computer auction format proved to be a liability, with a large bid made by mistake, leading to extensive legal wrangling. Puerto Rico based PCS 2000 was a company bidding for the Norfolk, Virginia, license. The previous bid had been $16,369,313, and PCS 2000 meant to bid $18,006,000. An employee at Romulus Telecommunications, which PCS 2000 had hired to make bids, added an extra digit, putting in $180,006,000. Under the rules of the auction, this bid could not be fully withdrawn. PCS 2000 would have to pay the difference between that bid (reduced by various small business concessions to $135 million) and the winning bid. As is often the case, the cover-up was worse than the infraction. Romulus Communications tried to claim that the FCC had made the error, but with the transparent bidding process, this was clearly not the case.[20] The FCC imposed heavy fines due to the error and the misrepresentation, but later reduced the amount to $3.2 million. The bidding was not without snags, and the problems continued once the auction was over.

NextWave won many licenses, but did not have the money to pay its bids, and the FCC was unable to retrieve the spectrum. The licenses had been won with $4.8 billion, and NextWave's plan was to lease the spectrum to service providers. For example, it had a deal to sell MCI ten billion minutes of air time. Unfortunately, there was a dip in business interest in wireless around 1997, perhaps due to the distraction of the Internet stock bubble, and some of the investors dropped out. NextWave placed at least some of the blame with the FCC, which held up granting the licenses by nearly a year as it investigated NextWave's funding sources. Without enough value in its assets to cover the considerable liabilities, NextWave filed for bankruptcy in June of 1998.

The contract to buy the spectrum did not include a lien clause so the FCC could not simply take back the licenses, although it attempted to do so. In January of 2000, the FCC canceled NextWave's licenses and called for a new auction. In February, the bankruptcy court canceled the FCC's cancellation, giving the licenses back to NextWave. Then a federal appeals court ruling reversed the previous ruling, putting the licenses back under FCC control. The FCC held another auction for this spectrum, this time requiring full payment by the winning bidders at the conclusion. Verizon, Cingular and AT&T Wireless won the spectrum with $16 billion in bids.

But NextWave was not yet finished with its struggle to keep the spectrum. In June of 2001, the U.S. Court of Appeals for the District of Columbia ruled the FCC's seizure of the spectrum had been invalid. Finally, in January of 2003, the U.S. Supreme Court ruled that NextWave could keep the licenses even though it had defaulted on the payments. But without the cooperation of the FCC, NextWave would have a difficult time operating in the cellular phone field, so the two parties reached an agreement in 2004. NextWave would return some of the licenses to the FCC, sell others to raise capital, and keep some of the licenses for its own use.

The NexTel Route to Spectrum

While companies were scrambling to get a piece of the FCC's allocated cellular phone spectrum, another potential player was creating a new frequency band on its own. The idea came to Morgan O'Brien, a lawyer who had spent time at the FCC, to buy licenses in another frequency band and then use those frequencies for cellular phone systems.[21] The target was the Specialized Mobile Radio band meant for dispatch services such as taxis and delivery trucks, and situated at frequencies close to those used by AMPS. Using updated digital technology, the existing users could take up a small piece of the frequency band, leaving the rest for cellular phones.

While a good idea, there was a sizeable obstacle. The Specialized Mobile Radio spectrum was sliced into tiny pieces, usually with dozens of owners even within the same city. Buying enough licenses to create a nationwide cellular phone system meant negotiating thousands of sales.

O'Brien founded a company called FleetCall and spent the late 1980's assembling the needed spectrum. The plan was to create a system covering six large cities, and by the early 1990's the spectrum was ready, at a cost of $250 million to buy 1,600 licenses. While definitely a lot of money, the licenses covered approximately 60 million people. The $4 per population spent was a deep discount compared to the AMPS and PCS license deals. Service began in 1993 with the first fully digital system in the USA. That year the company also changed its name from the dispatch-sounding FleetCall to the more consumer-technology oriented Nextel.

The good idea behind Nextel proved to be difficult to achieve in practice as the service suffered from quality problems, but investors were still interested. While the phones may have needed work, the valuable spectrum could not be ignored. In 1993 Motorola, which funded many companies in the cellular phone industry as a way to sell equipment, put $1.8 billion into the company in return for stock. MCI, which had sold out of the cellular phone business ten years earlier, bought its way back in with a $1.3 billion purchase of Nextel stock in 1994. AT&T had similarly purchased a return to the industry a year earlier by acquiring McCaw Communications. Craig McCaw then put the money made by that deal to use by buying about 20 percent of Nextel.

Despite the initial problems, the Nextel product did manage to find success in the market. As a carry-over from the dispatch technology, a call could stay up with many users listening and using the push-to-talk feature to join the conversation. This proved popular with businesses, providing a niche for Nextel. The company had some success before being bought by Sprint in 2005.

The Satellite as a Base Station

While cellular phone systems were becoming common by the mid–1990's, they were still far from ubiquitous. In the USA about 24 million people, less than 10 percent of the population, were subscribed in 1994, and the overall rate for the Americas was only 3 percent. The situation was similar in Europe, where some countries, such as Finland and the United Kingdom, had subscription rates approaching or over 10 percent, but the overall rate for Europe was about 2 percent. Africa and Asia had negligible overall subscription rates. Except for the most developed countries, leaving the large cities meant losing coverage. Some companies saw the vast areas without service as an opportunity to create a world-wide phone service, which meant using a satellite-based system.

Satellite communications began in the 1960's as a way to bypass lengthy cables. The first satellite to be used for communications was the Earth's natural satellite, the moon. A link between Hawaii and the mainland in the early 1960's used the moon as a reflector. Each end of the link needed a 25 meter dish to overcome the enormous loss caused by the distance to the moon, which is 400,000 kilometers (for comparison, the diameter of the Earth at the equator is 12,756 kilometers).[22] Artificial satellites were an improvement since they are much closer to the Earth and can receive and re-transmit waves, rather than just reflect. The first was Telstar I, launched July 10, 1962, and put into low earth orbit since the Delta I rocket could not reach geostationary orbit. Transatlantic television broadcasts using the new satellite started days later. More satellites were soon in orbit, and AT&T proposed a communication system using 40 to 70 satellites in the late 1960's, but did not pursue the development. Three decades later, with the success of cellular phones as an impetus, this type of system finally saw implementation.

The first of the satellite phone systems, ready after a decade of expensive construction, was Iridium. Work began in 1987 by a consortium of several companies sharing the $5 billion price, with Motorola having the largest share of the investment and doing much of the development. The original plan was for 77 satellites, leading to the Iridium name since that is the atomic number of the element iridium. The number of satellites changed to 66 in 1992, but the organization kept the name Iridium.

Satellites started launching on May 5, 1997, from Vandenberg Air Force Base in California, and soon all 66 satellites and 5 spares were in orbit.[23] Geostationary orbit, at 35,768 kilometers, would be too far for hand-held units to contact, so the satellites were at a low earth orbit of 900 kilometers, rounding the Earth every three hours. The operation of the system was similar to that of a cellular phone system, but rather then the mobile unit moving between cells, the cells moved as the satellites passed overhead. Once the technical feat of building the system was done, service began November 1, 1998, and Iridium faced the more challenging task of selling subscriptions.

Iridium had significant marketing problems to overcome. One obstacle was the expense, with phones costing $3,000 and a service charge of $7 per minute, later reduced to a still hefty $2.50 per minute. To keep the expense of running the system from soaring too high, the designers had left limitations. Some regions in Europe, Africa and Asia were out of range, so the system was not truly global. Even more limiting, the handsets could not contact the satellites from indoors or from most urban areas.[24] And a still larger obstacle was the competition from the Earth-bound cellular phones.

In the intermediate decade while Iridium was in development, cellular phone systems had grown to cover more of the world. Not only was the developed world almost fully covered, but much of the developing world also had service. Places without even electricity had working cellular phone systems. Also, the GSM standard had replaced the numerous incompatible standards, so a single cellphone could work in over 100 countries. Perhaps most significantly, Iridium had a worldwide maximum capacity of 25,000 users, so the potential growth was limited from the start.[25] The planners did not, however, have to worry about reaching that limit.

The response of consumers to Iridium was disappointing, with subscriptions rates less than planned. A $180 million campaign launched the system, with advertisements in 37 airline in-flight magazines, business-oriented publications, and copious free publicity. The target market was traveling business executives, with an estimated size of approximately eight million, and Iridium received 1.5 million inquiries for information. Yet out of that number only 20,000 subscribed. When Iridium filed for bankruptcy on August 13, 1999, it had 55,000 subscribers, a fraction of the expected 400,000.[26] The new plan was to bring the satellites into a lower orbit and let them burn up in the atmosphere, but the Department of Defense saved part of the system for military use.

Iridium's story is an example that being the first to the market is not necessarily a guarantee of success, and is actually usually not a good place to be. The problem is that later competitors can learn from the pioneer's experiences and benefit from advances in technology. Saehan/Eiger Labs introduced the MP3 player, but Diamond's Rio then dominated the market, followed by Apple's iPod.[27] A survey of 66 industries conducted in the year 2000 concluded that first movers had only a 6 percent share of the American market.[28] An exception is when the first company is able to use its head start to create a patent portfolio that future competitors must license. A company that can quickly and significantly change the product to counter more advanced competition could also meet the challenge of being first, but the Iridium system was not amenable to change. In the case of satellite phones, while Iridium's follower had some advantages, it was still not able to reach commercial success.

The Globalstar satellite phone system had a life cycle similar to that of Iridium. In 1991, Loral teamed with Qualcomm to create a cellular phone system with 48 satellites. Loral produced the satellites and Qualcomm developed the handsets and overall system. Unlike Iridium phones, the Globalstar phones could use cellular systems when in range, then switch to the satellites in areas with no coverage. The satellites orbited at 1400 kilometers, and each satellite had 16 beams with each beam being a cell with 85 channels. As with Iridium, this was a cellar system with the cells passing over the user at a rate of approximately one per minute.[29] Also like Iridium, the commercial response was underwhelming. Service began in October 1999, soon after Iridium had filed for bankruptcy. The charge of $1.50 per minute was less than that of Iridium, but was still expensive when compared to regular cellular phone service. The result was a subscription rate approximately one third of what had been planned.[30]

With the downfall of Iridium and Globalstar, the satellite phone industry became dormant. TRW Space and Electronics Group and Teleglobe formed a venture in 1994 to develop a system called Odyssey, with 12 satellites in medium earth orbit. Interest in such a system evaporated and the project was abandoned in 1999. Cellular phone coverage continues to grow quickly, so the need for a satellite-based system has diminished further. A small market continues to exist for coverage in the oceans, deserts, and other sparsely populated areas.

Satellite phones found small niche markets, and their lack of success in the overall market is a sign of the rapid growth of the cellular phone. The 1990's saw the cellphone transform from an oddity to commonplace, and finally into ever-presence. The big story in the wireless field for the decade was not radio, television or satellite communications, but was instead the cellphone. And the success was so readily apparent that no one, including the public, governments or businesses, could not change to meet the new opportunities.

9

The Business Reaches Maturity

A sign of the changing nature of the cellular phone industry came to me one morning in February of 1999. It was probably the usual clear and pleasant morning in San Diego, and I would soon begin my work evaluating antenna radiation patterns. But there was a new twist, a fellow member of my group appeared at the door, with the kind of agitation and excitement that can look like glee. "Did you hear about the layoffs," he asked in a loud stage whisper. I had heard rumors, but nothing definite.

The announcement came soon after, the company was selling a division, but the layoffs were company-wide. Some people who had been with the company for years were shown the door. Others who had just joined and were still in temporary housing as they moved to the area also saw their jobs evaporate. The supervisor for my group called a meeting later in the day to tell us that we had been spared. But rumors continued and we spent the next few weeks wondering if we would soon have a lot more time to work on our resumes instead of on cellphones. Fortunately the further layoffs did not materialize. Months later the company sold our division, but by then I had transferred to another part of the company.

Meanwhile, everybody left in the company was engrossed by the rising stock price and the corporation's changing nature. When I had joined three years earlier, it was a technology innovator with a small company atmosphere. There were few management layers and contact with those at the top of the company was common. There were relatively few employees, and most were simply engineers who could work on many aspects of a project. Growth and success quickly transformed the small company into a large corporation. The job hierarchy grew dramatically, and new, specialized positions appeared that focused intently on one specific part of a project. Yet the rise in the company's fortunes, and that of the employees who owned stock, was dramatic. The message was clear: the cellular phone business was definitely a business.

The late 1990's was when the cellphone found consumer popularity. The once exotic electronic devices became ever-present in the developed countries, as nearly everyone seemed to have one. And in the developing world cellular systems presented a way to build communications infrastructure without the heavy investments of wired systems. The cellphone is now basically everywhere, and the industry that supports it channels enormous streams of revenue. At this stage of the history, the cellular phone reaches such a prominent place in our world that economic, business and societal factors are as much a part of the story as the technical aspects.

Nokia's Success with Manufacturing

While infrastructure and electronic components are important to a cellular phone system, the consumer only comes into contact with a few elements. One is the service provider who runs the system and bills the user periodically. In the past there may have been differences in supported features and coverage area, but the systems have been built up to the point of being identical for most users. The service itself should be mostly transparent, with the only indication that reaches the user being the monthly statement. Choosing a service provider has therefore become a cost-based decision. But the cellphones have a full range of styles and features, and compete in the marketplace for the public's attention. The manufacturers are therefore familiar and form, to a large extent, the public face of the industry. One company in particular, Nokia, has reached prominence through its cellphones.

Nokia's success in the cellular business in the late 1990's originated in management decisions made decades earlier. As mentioned in Chapter Three, the oil shock of 1973 prompted the company to shift focus from industrial products to electronics, and large development investment followed. By 1988, 59 percent of Nokia's revenue came from electronics, with industrial products such as forestry, rubber products and electrical cable making up the rest. Guiding Nokia during this time was CEO Kari Karaimo, who had followed the example of successful Asian countries by stressing technological advancement and global sales. His successor, Jorma Ollila, became CEO in February of 1992 and moved wireless phones to be Nokia's centerpiece.[1] Pretax profit was down 89 percent in 1991, caused in part by a collapse in sales to the disintegrated Soviet Union,[2] so management was keen to find a new direction for the company. Nokia was by then a giant corporation with 44,600 employees, and produced a significant portion of the USA's cellphones, although with little visibility.

After entering the cellphone markets under the names of other companies, Nokia finally struck out on their own in the mid–1990's. Nokia's role in the 1980's was as an Original Equipment Manufacturer for other companies who would then sell the cellphone under their own brands. Most of Nokia's American sales were under the Tandy brand and sold in Tandy's RadioShack stores, starting in 1985.[3] Nokia also manufactured cellphones sold under the names of IBM, Control Data, Northern Telecom, Hitachi, Olivetti, Ericsson, British Telecom, and others. To meet the demand, Nokia and Tandy opened a factory in South Korea, with each having a 50 percent stake.[4] Nokia's focus had always been on international markets, and through these joint projects they quietly extended into the cellphone industry of many countries including the USA.

Emerging from the background, Nokia began marketing its own cellphones worldwide in the 1990's, with its ascendancy to the top coming in the last few years of the decade. At the time Motorola was the dominant company in the business, having created much of the industry. Recall from previous chapters that Motorola had taken over early development from AT&T and created the AMPS standard in the USA and the TACS standard in the UK. To spur adoption, Motorola helped fund service provider companies worldwide. And Motorola phones, such as the small, lightweight StarTac, were popular sellers. The stumbling point came when Motorola clung to its analog technology a little too long. This provided the opening Nokia needed to introduce its digital phones in the American and Asian markets, leading to a 73 percent rise in sales from 1997 to 1998.[5] By the end of the decade, Nokia was entrenched at the top of the handset industry.

The story of Nokia in the late 1990's was not always one of success, with some markets remaining immune to the Nokia charm. One example was Japan, which may be ironic since many believe the company, with its phonetically simple name, to be Japanese. Nokia's 12 percent market share in 1995 fell to 5 percent in the year 2000, possibly due to the difference between the European and Japanese markets. European cellphones of the time weighed approximately 100 grams, and Nokia's Japanese cellphone weighed 92 grams. But Panasonic's handsets were 70 grams or less.[6] This was a loss for Nokia, since after a decade of moribund growth, the cellphone was finally catching on in Japan.

Japan Discovers the Cellphone

The creation of Docomo cleared the path for the explosive growth of cellular phones in Japan, even if no one knew it at the time. Nippon Telephone and Telegraph (NTT) had begun the cellular phone business with the world's first commercially available system in 1979, although the popularity did not materialize. International corporations, backed by their governments, were applying pressure in the 1980's for Japan to open its communications markets, requesting an AT&T–like breakup for NTT.[7] In response, NTT spun off its unspectacular mobile phone division in 1992. This was no great sacrifice given the state of the cellular phone business in Japan at the time.

By 1990, Japan had about one million subscribers, representing less than 1 percent of the population. While one million customers can be seen as a good market, the cellular phone business was high-cost, and NTT's monopoly broke in the late 1980's as Nippon Idou Tsushin and Daini Denden began offering cell phone service.[8] In addition, the Japanese economy remained static in the 1990's, so only about 80,000 new subscribers joined annually.[9] This was the state of the market that the division found, but it made the best of the situation in an impressive manner.

The new company took the name of Docomo, close to the Japanese phrase *"doko de mo,"* meaning "anywhere." With the success Docomo has enjoyed since then, its name is now firmly part of the Japanese lexicon.

The turnaround in the Japanese cellular market came when the companies providing service and equipment began to cater to the consumers' needs, rather than depending on the self-sacrificing Japanese to make the effort. One problem was the expense. Service providers charged 60,000 yen to open an account, perhaps to due tradition since a regular phone line cost 70,000 yen to activate. Subscribers also had to make a deposit on the cellphone, even though there would be a full replacement charge if they lost it. And the per-minute service charge was about three times higher than that in the USA.[10] The companies were doing nothing to counter the perception that the cellphone was a luxury product.

Perhaps taking a cue from the way the business was developing in Europe and North America, Docomo made an abrupt change to market the cellphone to the masses. They eliminated or reduced charges, lowering the costs of owning and operating a cellphone to a European or American level. This meant operating at a loss until business volume increased dramatically. The phones themselves also became more appealing to the Japanese, meaning they became smaller.

Manufacturers such as Hitachi, Fujitsu and Matsushita tried to make small, lightweight phones in the early 1990's, but had quality problems. They mostly passed the blame to the manufacturers of the components that go into the phones.[11] Whatever the problems were, by the mid–1990's they had been sorted out. Motorola's StarTAC phone was successful when it arrived, and other small phones soon followed. After 1995, the number of subscribers rose by five million per year. The cellphone was a success, but the real breakthrough was still to come.

The cellphone reached universality in Japan around the year 2000, driven at least in part by the introduction of i-mode service, which brought internet access. While 50 percent of the population of the USA was using the internet by the year 2000, the usage rate for the Japanese was only 15 percent.[12] With i-mode, a user could access the internet for only a monthly fee of 300 yen and an additional data transfer charge of 0.3 yen for each 128 bits.[13] These were not the first terminals to combine a handset and the internet, but they were easy for the general public to use. In 1999, the year Docomo introduced i-mode, the annual new subscription rate reached ten million.

Popularity in the Developing World

The cellphone is one high-tech gadget that found wide acceptance in countries not usually associated with advanced technology. In 1994, the continent of Africa contained about 7.5 million cellphones, which grew to 76.8 million by 2004. This is equivalent to an annual increase of 58 percent, a higher rate than even Asia's 34 percent average over that period.[14] Low cost cellphones and service were a necessity in Africa, and once they were available the market could grow. People living in villages with no plumbing and electricity could finance a cellphone for about $50 and get service for less than $2 a month. Lacking electrical lines in many of these areas, vendors with car batteries sell phone recharges, providing one small example of the economic activity spurred by cellular phones.

While the product may be affordable, the systems are still expensive to construct and operate outside of developed areas due to the lack of reliable infrastructure. The small and muddy roads prohibit bringing in heavy machinery, so companies must truck in the equipment piece-by-piece in a lengthy and laborious process. Each base station also needs its own electrical generator since electrical power, when available, is intermittent. Despite these difficulties, a wireless network is more economical than its wired counterpart. Copper wires are not only expensive to string and maintain, they are susceptible to theft. In a wireless system, by contrast, the service provider's equipment is all centrally located at the base station. And once a base station is in place, the system can add of subtracted users at almost no cost, so a wireless system is more flexible than a wired phone network.

Qualcomm Reaps the Rewards of Foresight

Returning to the story that opened this chapter, by the late 1990's Qualcomm found itself with a golden patent portfolio offset by a leaden set of investments. Such was the cost of developing CDMA technology alone while the rest of the industry pursued TDMA. Qualcomm's experience lay in technology research, but for CDMA–based systems to ever reach the market, someone would have to manufacture equipment and build the systems. And so, with OmniTracs, the satellite-based communication system for trucking, providing revenue, Qualcomm ventured into new business areas.

Much as Motorola had done a decade earlier, Qualcomm spent the 1990's building a CDMA–based cellular phone industry, either alone or with business partners. It joined with Northern Telecom to make CDMA infrastructure such as base stations and network equipment in December of 1994. No one was manufacturing CDMA–compatible cellphones, so Qualcomm teamed with Sony in the same year to design and manufacture handsets. Together they created Qualcomm Personal Electronics with Qualcomm and Sony having 51/49 percent ownership. Qualcomm Personal Electronics remained the only manufacturer of cellphones for CDMA–systems until 1997, when Nokia, Samsung and Motorola brought out their own models. When Sony left the North American cellphone manufacturing business in July of 1999, Qualcomm was left developing cellphones on its own.

Qualcomm also put money into service providers to help set up CDMA–based systems. Buying parts of cellular phone companies in Mexico, Chile, Australia, Russia and other places, Qualcomm created an extensive portfolio of international holdings. Taking on responsibility for all of these aspects of the industry had the desired effect, and 2G CDMA systems reached the market and gained acceptance. Yet upon achieving this milestone, these enterprises became a drag on the company.

Despite Qualcomm's eventual success in the industry, the stock price remained moribund. Even the 1998 decision by the European Telecommunications Standards Institute that the successor to GSM would be CDMA–based had no significant effect on Qualcomm's share price. Qualcomm's 1998 income had been a little over $3 billion, and assuming a typical price-to-earnings ratio of 15, the company's market capitalization could have been over $50 billion. Instead, the market capitalization was stuck below $5 billion. The problem was the loss from the various new enterprises.

Qualcomm's excursions into new fields had produced workable products, but it could not compete with the top companies in those specialized areas. The infrastructure division was the largest drain, requiring $800 million in annual revenue to run, but bringing in about half that amount. The phone manufacturing division earned $1.4 billion in 1999, but still did not turn a profit.[15] Qualcomm had reached an enviable position in the cellular phone industry by 1999, having developed the technology that would be the basis of future systems. But the financial industry did not yet take Qualcomm seriously as a profitable business. In the late 1990's stock market bubble, largely driven by the internet and communications, the low-performing Qualcomm stock was a stand-out.

The turnaround began in late 1998, as Qualcomm shed the unprofitable auxiliary businesses. First the portfolio of foreign phone companies was spun off as Leap Wireless in September of 1998. Then the big move came in February of 1999, when Qualcomm cut 700 employees in a cost-saving move and at the same time announced the sale of the infrastructure division to Ericsson. Qualcomm had experienced rapid growth, from 1,262 employees in 1993 to 11,200 in 1999, so the 700 positions represented about 6 percent of the company. The second large change was in December of the same year, when Qualcomm announced the sale of the handset division to Kyocera. The sale price was $500 million and a commitment to buy Qualcomm chips for the next five years.[16] The changes had the desired effect and the stock price began increasing.

The pent-up value in Qualcomm was suddenly released in 1999 as the stock price soared. Qualcomm's IPO had been on December 16, 1991, selling 20 percent of the company as four million shares at $16 each.[17] Over the following eight years the stock approximately tripled in price. Then in 1999, the price increased by a factor of ten from February to November. Qualcomm's $5 billion market capitalization finally reached the expected $50 billion. And the big surprise came at the end of the year.

An analyst at PaineWebber Group Inc. predicted the price would double again in a year, based on an expectation that licensing of CDMA would bring in $20 billion annually.[18] At twenty-eight years old, the analyst may not have had decades of experience to back up his claims, but he had already made a name in the stock-picking field with successful recommendations to buy NextWave and Ericsson before their large, and ultimately temporary, price breakthroughs. Reacting to the prediction, on December 29, 1999, the stock price rose by 31 percent, adding another fifteen billion dollars to Qualcomm's market capitalization. While these gains were spectacular, they were also short-lived. By mid–2000, Qualcomm's value was back to where it had been around October of 1999. The price was still about ten times higher than it had been two years previously, so shareholders had been well compensated for staying with Qualcomm.

Having reaching prominence, Qualcomm's main task has been to maintain its position. The 2G CDMA standard, along with GSM, has become obsolete in comparison with the third generation standards. But since all of the new standards are based on CDMA, Qualcomm can still realize revenue through licensing. Of the 732 patents that the Third Generation Partnership Project, which develops the successors to GSM, listed as essential in 2005, Qualcomm owned 279. With a similar name, but a different composition and development plan, is the Third Generation Partnership Project 2. This group has been developing CDMA2000, the follow-up to 2G CDMA, and of 527 essential patents, 340 are from Qualcomm.[19] And the company has been looking beyond its base of cellular phones into other aspects of the wireless communications industry.

Another venture is MediaFLO, for video downloads to handsets (FLO is for Forward Link Only). Qualcomm bought television channel 55 nationwide for $38 million in 2003, and has spent $800 million to develop the MediaFLO system, which Verizon launched in 2007. Competition is from the DVB-H service created by Crown Castle, which bought 5 MHz of spectrum around 1.6 GHz. Crown Castle paid only $12.6 million for that spectrum, but being at a higher frequency than channel 55's 716 to 722 MHz, these radio waves will experience more loss as they propagate over terrain.[20]

Consolidation of Companies

Cellular phone companies growing to mammoth size is not an exclusively American phenomenon, as demonstrated by looking at the situation in the UK.

The original companies when service began were Cellnet and Vodaphone. In 1989 the government added more spectrum and three companies received licenses: One2One, Microtel and Unitel. Before the systems even reached the public, One2One merged with Unitel and Microtel changed its name to Orange. One2One launched its service in April of 1994, and Orange did the same in September.[21] From that point the UK had four cellular phone companies, all providing nearly identical service.

When identical products are in the market, advertising tends to increase as the companies try to bypass rationality and appeal directly to emotion for differentiation. An early leader was Orange, with its ever-present "the future's Orange" campaign. The names and advertising were also shifting away from the technical to the emotional. While company names featuring the letter "X" or "Z" had moments of popularity, the letter "O" was in fashion at the time, perhaps due to its human feel. Besides Vodafone, the other companies were Orange, One2One and Cellnet, which changed its name to O2.

And the consolidation continued. In April of 1999, Deutsche Telecom bought One2One for £8.4 billion, making it part of T-mobile. Meanwhile, Vodafone merged with the American company AirTouch and the entire new company was bought by the German company Mannesmann. As part of the deal, Mannesmann sold Orange, which it owned by then, to France Telecom. While the number of trades may be confusing, the rationale behind them is efficiency in operation. The combined companies could provide the same service with less expenditure. This leads, ideally, to lower costs for the consumer and, more commonly, higher profits for the companies. And the pursuit of profits is a worldwide interest.

The cellular phone business in the USA, and the phone business in general, condensed through the 1990's into a few giant corporations. In the early 1980's when AT&T split into Pacific Telesis, Nynex, Bell Atlantic, Ameritech, U.S. West, Bell South, and South Western Bell, the consumer was supposed to benefit from the increased competition. Of those, Bell Atlantic and Nynex merged in 1996 to become the new Bell Atlantic, and then that company merged with GTE. Only three years later that company merged with Vodafone to become Verizon. Following another path, South Western Bell changed its name to SBC and bought Pacific Telesis in 1997, and then bought Ameritech in 1999. Finally, SBC merged with Bell South to become Cingular in 2000. The fragmentation of the businesses had been largely reversed over the course of less than a decade.

Fortunately for the consumer, price declines accompanied the consolidation. One big milestone came in 1998 when AT&T introduced the Digital One Rate, with flat rates such as $150 a month for 1,400 minutes.[22] This was an example of a company using its size to lower the price, since AT&T had national coverage and owned the long-distance telephone cables. The flat rate was simple and economical, and was particularly popular with business subscribers.[23]

The other service providers were compelled to follow by introducing their own flat rate. This is, at least partially, the fruit of the Department of Justice's break-up of AT&T. Prices fell due to both technological advances and competition. The competition was between a few large corporations, but it was having an effect. The upward trend of technology and downward plunge of prices were driving the cellphone into more hands.

The success of the cellular phone business at the end of the 1990's was enough to challenge the capacity of the networks. By 1998 the USA contained approximately 65,000 base stations, servicing 77 million users. This works out to a ratio of approximately 1200 users per base station, but the distribution of users is never even, so some cells had a light load while others were overloaded. Systems were operating at capacity, leading to busy signals when calls could not go through, and dropped calls when a user moved into an overloaded cell. To meet the new demand, AT&T and Sprint PCS spent $2 billion and $1.5 billion, respectively, upgrading their systems in the 1999 to 2000 period.[24] But this expenditure was not enough to save AT&T Wireless, which was transitioning from success to decline at the time.

In the space of a few years AT&T Wireless found itself first at the top of the cellular phone business, and then bringing up the rear. AT&T Wireless sprang into existence in 1993 when AT&T bought McCaw Communications for over $10 billion. By 1998, it was the largest cellular phone service provider in the USA, receiving recognition as having the best system and best customer service.[25] Up to that point, AT&T Wireless was a division of AT&T, so the two names could be used interchangeably. This situation ended in April of 2000 when AT&T Wireless had an Initial Public Offering and entered the stock market as a separate entity. In July 2001 the division formally spun off and launched as a new company. But by then the peak period was over and the stock price began dropping.

The decline of AT&T Wireless came from a quick shift of technology that left it outdated. The problem was the technology that AT&T had inherited from McCaw Communications. The system used D-AMPS, the digital replacement for AMPS that the Cellular Telephone Industry Association board had unanimously endorsed back in January of 1992. The technology, however, did not have the capabilities of GSM or 2G CDMA, like internet access and transferring photographs. A few years earlier, these features may have seemed like unnecessary luxuries, but by 2000, customers were expecting them. In that year AT&T Wireless began building a GSM system operating in parallel with its D-AMPS network, but was behind the competition.

In 2003, the USA had three large service providers. Verizon had built a CDMA–based network that covered almost the whole of the continental USA, and had a market share of 32.8 percent. In second place with a GSM network that covered most urban areas and highways was Cingular, with a 14.7 percent market share. Surprised to find itself in third place was AT&T Wireless, with a 12.8 percent market share. The mergers that created Cingular in 1999 and Verizon in 2000 moved AT&T Wireless to the back, and the less functional networks did not help.

As its fortunes declined, AT&T Wireless found itself in a position where everything seemed to getting worse. The previous reputation for excellent service was dissipating. A 2003 survey found that per 10,000 customers, AT&T Wireless had 3.39 complaints, while Cingular had 1.33 and Verizon had 0.76.[26] Finally, Cingular bought AT&T Wireless in 2004 for $41 billion. Cingular inherited some customers, equipment and employees with the acquisition, but most important was the AT&T name. Although Cingular was the larger company by a wide margin, there was little doubt that the new company, the largest cellular phone service provider in the USA, would take the name of AT&T Mobility.

Intellectual Property

As the cellular phone industry reached maturity, meaning tremendous revenues were at stake, legal performance came to equal design, manufacturing and marketing in importance. This is the realm of intellectual property, usually taking the form of patents. The cost of research and development of a new product can be much higher than the manufacturing cost. To continue expending such high resources on research, companies need to know that they can recoup their losses by charging more for their products than just the manufacturing costs.

This and previous chapters have given the example of Qualcomm, which expended significant resources over approximately a decade to develop technology that uses CDMA for cellular phone systems. The reward came when that technology reached popularity and the patents became valuable due to licensing revenue. According to Qualcomm's 2006 annual report, revenue included $4.8 billion in equipment and services and $2.8 billion in licensing and royalties. While great for Qualcomm, from the perspective of those paying the fees, the situation does not seem fortuitous. Why should anybody pay royalties and what is the right amount to pay? At times, some have even questioned the validity of intellectual property as a concept. So the ideas behind patenting are worth examining to better understand the current cellular phone industry.

The protection of intellectual property that exists today derives from European law of centuries past. Patents began in the fourteenth century as royal privileges given to inventors.[27] As is often the case with privileges, there was a potential for abuse which was soon well-realized. Queen Elizabeth I, for example, granted patents for basic necessities such as salt, vinegar and brushes, not to inventors, but to her subjects with connections, and also to those who owed her money as a way to raise revenue. There was outrage in Parliament, leading the Queen to voluntarily curtail the granting of patents. Soon after, the Statute of Monopolies, signed by King James I in 1623, took away most of the monarch's power to grant monopolies but kept patents for new products.

Patents lasted 14 years, and were meant to give incentive to invest and innovate. Further progress in British patent law brought the process into a centralized, though inefficient, bureaucracy. England, Scotland, Wales and Ireland had separate patent offices, so patents were difficult and expensive to obtain, and even when granted, patents were easy to challenge with vague arguments. As a corrective step, the Patent Law Amendment Act of 1852 established a single national patent office and simplified the application process. The cost of obtaining a patent dropped from several hundred pounds to a manageable £25.

The Patent Act of 1793, written by Thomas Jefferson, established patent law in the USA based on the British model. Unlike the modern system, the government would file patents but not examine them closely for worthiness or originality. Any disputes were left to the courts. Finally in 1836, Congress created the United States Patent Office to examine applications. The system worked adequately for over a century, until demand brought forth more change.

Until the 1980's, the ten federal circuit courts heard patent cases, and each court had applied different criteria. The 10th Circuit Court, for example, covering the Rocky Mountain area, was most likely to rule for the patent holder, so that was a popular venue for patent infringement cases.[28] Above the federal circuit courts, the United States Supreme Court has ultimate appeal power over patent disputes, but rarely hears patent cases. Judges, who had legal backgrounds, did not like to hear patent cases, with their technical minutia, and tended to dismiss the suits. Of cases that reached a ruling, only one in four found patent infringement. Filing patents was therefore not the high priority for companies that it is today, since they were so weak and malleable. But then a fundamental shift occurred in the law.

In 1982 Congress created the Court of Appeals for the Federal Circuit (CAFC) to hear cases in a small number of areas, including patent appeals. Congressional reports of the time show a strong influence from the economic conditions of the late 1970's. With industrial decline being acutely felt in many areas, and competition from other countries such as Japan becoming strong, Congress was open to the creation of laws that help business. The CAFC manifested this pro-business outlook by greatly increasing the strength of patents and the domain they covered.

While the circuit court judges may not have liked dealing with patent disputes, many of the CAFC judges are former patent attorneys who revel in the technical details. In 1978, the various appellate courts ruled for the patent holder in infringement cases approximately 40 percent of the time, while in 1982, the CAFC ruled for the patent holder in 80 percent of cases.[29] With this strengthening of patent protection, patents became increasingly valuable to technology companies. Companies brought more to be patented, and the government obliged by granting more patents.

The categories covered by patents greatly increased with court rulings in the 1990's, in particular to cover software and algorithms. The starting point for this expansion is *Diamond v. Diehr* of 1981, in which the Supreme Court faced a dispute concerning a patented algorithm. At issue was a rubber curing machine that depended on a computer-controlled algorithm. The Court upheld the patent, ruling that while software is not patentable, the complete machine described by the patent, including the algorithm, is patentable. The Court changed this in 1994, for a ruling on *in Re Appalat*. For that case, the Court upheld a patent on software that processed waveforms on an oscilloscope screen making them easier to read. Patents could then be granted for software and algorithms running on general computers. Although everyone knows that these are software patents, the wording of the patents is still for a machine, which is a computer with the program loaded. Another milestone was the 1988 case of *State Street Bank and Trust v. Signature Financial Group*, in which the court upheld a patent on State Street's flowcharts describing its investment strategy. Business methods and algorithms were therefore patentable.

The number of patents issued has increased, perhaps to the detriment of quality. Some note that the patent bureaucracy of the United States Patent and Trademark Office and the CAFC has a financial interest in increasing the number of patents.[30] The larger volume of granted patents is also a result of more activity from companies and patent lawyers. Advances that are obvious are not patentable, but the Patent Office is not in a position to declare something obvious, particularly when facing challenges from persistent patent lawyers. While these descriptions may leave the impression that the current patent system is a free-for-all, there are some curbs on patentability.

The development of patent law has not been an exclusive march to increase the power of patent applicants. The 2007 Supreme Court decision for *KSR v. Teleflex* re-introduced some limits on the range of patentable applications.[31] At issue was a patent Teleflex held for a system that combined two existing devices, a pedal controller and a throttle control. The court ruled that such a combination did not meet the requirement of non-obviousness, and therefore is not patentable. Yet patents are still granted for the combinations of previously known elements if their total is novel. The overall conclusion is that there is no overall conclusion. The merits of many patents can be argued for and against in many ways, and usually on a case-by-case basis.

The economic justification for patents is that they allow inventors to recoup investments by raising the costs for competitors to produce the same product. But those costs should not rise too far. To be more specific, a company spends D to develop and M to manufacture a new product. A competitor that copies the product could bypass the development stage and produce the product, only spending M. When the idea is patented, the competitor must also pay P, which could be royalties, legal fees and a patent infringement penalty, or an investment to develop a different product with a similar application. If $D >> P$, meaning that D is much larger than P, inventors are discouraged from developing new products, since other companies can sell the product and take the inventor's return on investment. At the other end of the scale, if $P >> D$, other companies are discouraged from trying to compete, leading to a monopoly situation and a lack of technological innovation. Both cases show a stifling of competition. In between is the point that an economist would call the optimum, since the general economy has the greatest chance of advancement.[32] At this point $P + M \approx D + M$, or by extension $P \approx D$. The laws of nature and business control D, but patent law controls the size of P by setting the breadth and duration of patents. In most countries the patent duration is twenty years, while the breadth is a subject of continuing debate.

To complicate the analysis, the costs of development are usually not clear, as the example of pharmaceutical patents show. New drug development takes 10 to 15 years and costs $800 million to $1.2 billion, and most drugs will not make it through the entire process to reach the market. One success story is fluoxetine, which pharmaceutical company Eli Lilly first sold in 1988 under the brand name Prozac. Sales reached $2.7 billion annually, making up one quarter of Eli Lilly's sales. Eli Lilly made back what it had expended to develop fluoxetine many times over, but the revenue was also needed to subsidize investments in drugs that did not reach the market. The patent expired in 2001, and generic drug maker Barr began selling fluoxetine as well, causing Barr's stock price to rise 50 percent from May to August of that year.[33] Barr had been handed free money derived from Eli Lilly's investments. But Eli Lilly had its period of monopoly and made a significant amount of money, after which society's best interest is served by introducing competition.

Patents in the electronics industry usually represent less investment than in the case of pharmaceutical products, but there is wide variance. Some ideas may consume an army of engineers working for years to realize. Others may come in a flash to a single employee who works out the details of implementation in a day or a week. Both cases generate the same level of patent protection. If a few significant patents are not forthcoming, a company can accumulate a large portfolio of smaller patents to improve its position in licensing negotiations.

As is usual with legal matters, lawsuits spurred the flood of patents that companies have been accumulating. The significant case occurred in the late 1980's, in which Motorola sued Nokia and Tandy for patent infringement. Nokia agreed to pay licensing fees in exchange for Motorola dropping the suit, and had learned a valuable lesson. In the 1980's filing patents was not a high priority for Nokia, which only filed around ten per year. After the lawsuit, Nokia implemented a reward system to encourage employees to file patents. The motivation worked, with Nokia filing 800 patent applications in 1998 and 1000 applications in 1999. Other companies in the field followed similar paths, with Ericsson filing 1,000 applications in 1999 and Motorola filling a voluminous 2,000 patent applications that same year.[34] Having obtained so many patents, companies are encouraged to use them.

Once patents are in place, companies face the choice of whether to license them from the holders and how much to pay. An analysis of the decision can start with quantifying the value of using the patented feature over using an alternative. This is a per-unit dollar amount, V, that companies rarely publicly disclose. The bargaining power between the two companies, denoted B, is another important factor. In this context, the bargaining power is a number between zero and one showing how much a company can get its way. If the patent owner, for example, would like to receive \$20 per unit, and the licensing company would like to pay \$10 per unit, then $B = 0.5$ means both companies have equal sway and the price would be \$15 per unit. One more factor to consider is the strength of the patent, S, which is also a number between zero and one. The price per unit, U, that a company would pay to license a patent's technology is therefore

$$U = V \times B \times S.$$

In these litigious times, the costs of court actions can be the primary consideration in licensing decisions. When considering negative court decisions, the per-unit patent value reveals other components:

$$V = F \times L + k,$$

in which F is the profit-per-unit, L is the fraction of sales lost to court injunctions, redesign time and other delays, and k is the per-unit redesign price. The new formula for the license price is

$$V = (F \times L + k) \times B \times S.$$

The royalty payouts made by Research In Motion, the producers of the Blackberry cellphone and texting device, serve as an example of the significance of these new terms. A jury ruled against that company in 2006, ordering a \$33.5 million penalty for patent infringement. Yet this established that $S = 1$, and that L would be high. Research In Motion therefore agreed to license the patents for \$612.5 million.

The process of determining payments remains variable, since the companies involved rarely specify their estimates of the cost terms. A 2007 survey examined jury decisions in patent infringement lawsuits in the USA, revealing some interesting trends. Among lawsuits brought between 1982 and 2005, only 58 reached a jury decision. Most cases reach a settlement before the ruling. The average royalty rate set by the decisions was 13.3 percent, meaning that the licensing company would have to pay 13.3 percent of the product price to the patent holder. Among cases involving electronics, the study found a mean royalty rate of 6.49 percent.[35] These rates may be higher than average since the ruling sets $S = 1$, putting the patent holder in an advantageous position.

The large patent portfolios both support and are fed by the system of cross-licensing between technology companies, perhaps to the detriment of the market. Companies sign agreements to share patents, with the portfolios measured not just by the significance of their contents, which is difficult to judge, but also by their sizes. If there is a mismatch in portfolios, an exchange of money makes up the difference. This system encourages companies to file many patents, which may be a waste of resources. Furthermore, companies can sign an agreement to trade patent rights rather than invest in research to create their own versions, further discouraging innovation.[36] And small companies without extensive patent portfolios have the obstacle of having to make large licensing payments.

Groups creating new standards must also find their way through the licensing thicket in order to make a usable standard. The danger is that after a standard is published and implemented into products, a company comes forward claiming to own parts of the technology used in the standard and demanding payment. The fact that a company followed the published standard is not a justification for patent infringement.

A seminal case involved a standard for computer memory chips.[37] The Joint Electron Device Engineering Council (JEDEC) spent the 1990's developing an industry standard for computer memory chips. Once the standard was done, memory chip manufacturers could follow the standard to make chips that would be compatible with existing computers. Meanwhile, Rambus, a company that had been part of JEDEC but later dropped out, had a 1990 patent for aspects of memory chips used in the standard. Throughout the 1990's, Rambus filed extensions to the patent to clarify claims, with many of the revised claims tracking the standards development. Finally, the standard was ready, products reached the market, and Rambus filed a suit against chip-maker Infineon in the year 2000, claiming that their JEDEC–compatible chips infringed on Rambus' patent. A jury ruled for Infineon and decided that Rambus had committed fraud by not disclosing the patents to the standards body, and ordered Rambus to pay Infineon's legal fees. The case then went to the Court of Appeals for the Federal Circuit, which reached a conclusion that would make the work of standards bodies more difficult. The CAFC reversed the previous ruling, finding that while Rambus had attempted to commit fraud by not disclosing the patents, no fraud was committed since Rambus had no legal obligation to disclose or publicize its patents. The case eventually settled with Infineon making royalty payments to Rambus.

The large number of patented features in a cellphone could have a noticeable effect on the price as the patent owners demand payment. Qualcomm, for example, claims that its royalty rate has stayed at around 5 percent of the wholesale phone price, even as the number of patents covered has grown.[38] Other companies make similar claims, and manufacturers that have to make several 5 percent payments find the costs quickly accumulating. Some estimates pre-

dict that 20 to 30 percent of future wireless mobility devices may be patent royalties.[39] The patent holders offer a simple solution for manufacturers: use just
our set of patents and you will save money. The manufacturers, of course, would
like to avoid this level of dependency on one or a small set of patent holders.

Third generation cellular phone standards involve hundreds of patents,
so these issues are important. There are two standards bodies, the Third Generation Partnership Project (3GPP), for a GSM successor, and 3GPP2 for a 2G
CDMA successor. A 2004 survey examined the ownership of 7,796 patents
declared as essential to one or the other or to both.[40] For 3GPP, 732 patents
were listed, although a committee set up by the survey authors narrowed this
down to 157 essential patents. Of these, Nokia owned 40, Ericsson owned 34,
Qualcomm owned 30, Motorola owned 11, and the rest were owned by others.
For 3GPP2, the study's committee determined 108 out of 527 patents to be
essential, and in this case Qualcomm owned 54, Nokia and Motorola both
owned 14. The large companies making cellphones have a stake in both streams,
but they also have a larger stake in one side or the other.

In developing the third generation cellular phone standard to follow GSM,
the European Telecommunications Standards Institute has requested that companies declare all essential patents, and agree to license those patents on Fair,
Reasonable and Non-Discriminatory terms. That concept is as vague as it
sounds. Furthermore, the Standards Institute does not have the power to rule
on patent disagreements, only the courts can do that, but it can design the standard without using the technology of an uncooperative company.[41]

With the economic potential of wireless communication recognized,
rivalry for that revenue is in full effect. And not only companies, but governments have interest in the competition as they try to steer as much of the industry as possible into their borders. With the expected growth of the wireless
market, that competition can only increase. But even more than the money
involved, cellphones have had profound effects on society and the individual.

10

Implications of Cellphones

On the morning of January 5, 1996, Yahya Ayyash, chief bomb-maker for Hamas, was handed a cellphone by an old college roommate. After a few seconds of conversation, he was killed when the phone exploded. Given Ayyash's profession, he may have appreciated the workmanship. The phone was one of the small models available at the time, and was fully operational while also containing a significant amount of explosives. It is generally believed that the cellphone was created by Israel's security service and reached Ayyash's friend indirectly through relatives. An airplane seen circling over the area may have sent the signal to detonate after confirming Ayyash's identity.[1] In that case, a cellphone held a clear danger. Yet the possibility that the cellphone is a slow killer holds more interest for the public.

Much of the miasma of threat arises from the mystery of the invisible. Holding a 0.2 watt light bulb near the body would probably not strike most people as a dangerous or damaging activity. But the electric and magnetic fields surrounding and emanating from cellphones lie outside the visible spectrum. And so people wonder what is coming out of their handsets.

Adding to the uneasy sense of the unknown is the mystery that surrounds tumors and cancer. A tumor does not come with an indicator of its origin, which leaves doctors, patients, and the public searching for possible causes. Even when such a cause seems to present itself, there is still a strong random quality. If smoking caused lung cancer, for example, everyone who smoked would get lung cancer, and yet many do not. Cause and effect is difficult to assign with cancer, so doctors instead deal with risk levels. All activities fall somewhere on the scale of risk, with a low risk indicating safety. But where the safe risk level lies is undefined.

Safety and Risk

The concept of safety does not have a technical or scientific definition, and there is no generally-applicable risk level that would trigger preventative actions. Society and politics instead determine a population's reaction to risk. An example is the automobile, which is the leading cause of death in the USA for people ages two to thirty four. On average, one person was killed and 70 people injured by an automobile every twelve minutes in 2006.[2] Advancements in safety features may lower these numbers, but they will probably remain at approximately the same level in the foreseeable future. Despite the risks, people like cars and like driving, and the automobile is too essential to modern society to remove or to significantly limit. Perhaps the cellphone is also in this category, but there is another slot it could fall into which is not so accommodating.

Some activities produce risks that have fallen out-of-fashion with society. The prime example in this case is smoking. Studies have shown an increased likelihood of lung disease in smokers. One study, for example, found that while less than one percent of the non-smoking population would die of lung cancer by age 75, a much larger 16 percent of life-long smokers would succumb to that disease.[3] In contrast to automobiles, smoking is the subject of many safety-motivated banning campaigns.

The difference may lie in the purpose and utility of the activities. Smoking is only done for personal enjoyment, while people can use automobiles for useful activities. Cellphones occupy space in both categories. They perform useful functions and people also spend a lot of time using them just for enjoyment. Some may argue that users should curtail the second type of usage, but that may be unnecessary if there is low risk. To better understand the arguments, the first step is to quantify the risks.

The usual quantifier that published studies give for risk is the *odds ratio*, which is the increase in the chances of an event occurring if some condition is met. As an example, the event could be lung disease, and the condition could be smoking. The number of smokers with lung disease to all smokers is a measure of the odds that a smoker would contract a disease. The ratio of non-smokers with lung disease to all non-smokers gives the odds for non-smokers. Dividing the first number by the second is the odds ratio. So if, for example, one out of ten smokers gets lung disease, while one out of one hundred non-smokers do, then the odds ratio is $0.1/0.01 = 10$. The chance that a smoker will develop lung disease is ten times higher than for a non-smoker in this example.

Numerous studies conducted over the past several decades have found lung disease odds ratios varying from 2 to 32 for long-term smokers, with most in the range of 8 to 16.[4] The wide spread of odds ratios shows that the data and results are often controversial. Perhaps someone in the study who smokes is more likely to be from a particular socioeconomic status, or live in a certain place, or have another quality that increases the incidence of lung disease. These are examples of confounding factors that affect the results. The field of epidemiology is devoted to creating and running studies that deal with confounding factors and produce usable odds ratios. But even if the odds ratio comes from a skilled epidemiologist, it does not contain all of the risk information.

The odds ratio considered with the number of cases, taken together, ascertain the risk. This is because a ratio applied to a small number will probably produce another small number. A 2004 article titled "Swedish Study Links Cellphones to Brain Tumors" provides an example.[5] The article reported on a study that found an odds ratio of 1.9 for a certain type of tumor among people using cellphones for at least ten years. Yet the incidence of that type of tumor among the general population is expected to be one in 100,000, or 0.001 percent. The increase of 1.9 would raise the rate of incidence to 0.0019 percent, a rate which is still small. The previously mentioned British smoking study, by contrast, found an odds ratio of 16 for smokers to die of lung cancer, which has a significant effect since approximately 1 percent of non-smokers die of lung cancer. A high odds ratio combined with an appreciable starting point produces real risk. By this definition, cellphones do not create a high risk.

Tumors and cancers along the side of the head are rare, so a high odds ratio, such as one hundred or higher, would have to be found to represent a risk that would motivate people to give up their phones. Given the extensive usage of the cellphone for over two decades, such a high odds ratio for disease would have probably been apparent. Yet epidemiological studies have produced modest odds ratios. This does not, however, settle the question of whether cellphones are safe. If one billion people are using cellular phones, then the extra 0.0009 percent of the previous study represents nine thousand people. Those thousands of people who develop this type of tumor may regret having used a cellphone. Among the uncertainty, unsubstantiated notions also govern people's reaction to the cellphone.

An example of a rumor affecting cellphone usage is at the gasoline pump where, according to the story, a spark could cause an explosion. A 2003 investigation of alleged incidents failed to produce a single case of this actually happening. The origins of such stories are murky, and citations tend to be far removed from the source material. One widely circulated story in the *Bangkok Post* from 1999 reported explosions at petrol stations in Indonesia and Australia. But those reports have since been discredited.[6]

Sparks do occasionally start fires at gasoline pumps. In a typical scenario, someone may leave the pump running and enter the car, and then exit to remove the nozzle. The action of clothing rubbing against the seats can create a static charge that causes a spark upon touching the pump handle, which could ignite gasoline fumes. Few things in life are impossible, and any device with a battery can yield a spark, but the chances of a cellphone producing a strong spark seem to be low enough not to worry about. Companies that run gasoline stations are aware of this, but continue to ban cellphones at their stations. Perhaps they do this as a legalistic precaution, or they may be seeking to keep waiting times low and believe that cellphone talkers move slowly.

The ban on operating cellphones in an airplane is also an example of safety concerns where there may be no realistic unsafe conditions. The chances of cellphones interfering with airplane navigation systems are small. A cellphone is no more likely to degrade an airplane's operation as it is to interfere with a television or a radio. Experience to date shows that this is the case.

Observant travelers will see that on most flights, while some passengers make a show out of turning off their cellphones, others do not bother. This is not to say there are no real safety concerns. An object like a cellphone could come out of someone's hand and fly across the cabin. Cellphones in an airplane could also overload the systems they pass over, since by being high above the ground, the mobile unit is not solidly in one cell. Instead it has approximately equal power links to several cells. So, as before, business reasoning and an aversion to any liability, no matter how small, motivates the ban. To the public, however, a drastic measure such as a ban reinforces the belief that cellphones have malevolent power. And the belief in danger can have powerful effects even when the chances of harm are small.

According to surveys, 4 percent of the UK's population believes they have Electromagnetic Hypersensitivity, and suffer real problems such as headaches from exposure to electric and magnetic fields. The knowledge that the human body has no known reception mechanism that can register radio-frequency energy is of little comfort to those in pain. In a study at the University of Essex,[7] researchers exposed forty-four Electromagnetic Hypersensitivity sufferers to either GSM-like waves or no fields. Only two out the forty-four could correctly tell when the fields were present. Conducting the same experiment with 144 subjects who did not have Electromagnetic Hypersensitivity found that five correctly identified the exposure times. Both results are in the expected range for random guessing by the subjects. The power of the mind is stronger than the fields that a cellphone could produce, and their psychological impact is a relevant factor.

As cellphones decrease in size and power, and they become a common part of life, their perceived threat may diminish. Unlike the substantial brick-style phones that existed up until the late 1990's, the slighter handsets seem more like small electrical devices, rather than portable radio stations. The cellphone has also lost its status as a new and exotic invention and has found acceptance. As with most novel developments, familiarity dulls the fear of the new. And besides psychological factors, cellphones have been losing broadcast power.

The amount of power that the cellphone puts out has steadily decreased as the technology develops. Since broadcast power drains the battery and limits talk-time, the motivation to lower power is clear. Furthermore, as explained in previous chapters, keeping the broadcast power as low as possible increases the system capacity. This last point does not apply to analog standards, so NMT, the Nordic standard, used a steady 1.5 watts for the transmit power, and the AMPS standard used a constant 0.6 watts. Those were the phones of the 1980's to mid–1990's, and the power only fell from that level.

With the switch to digital technology, the cellphone's transmitting power dropped precipitously and continues to fall. A GSM phone, for example, has a peak transmit power of two watts, but that is when the transmitter is active. Recall that GSM divides each channel into eight time slots of 0.577 milliseconds each, so the transmitter is only broadcasting one-eighth of the time. The average peak transmitting power of a GSM phone is therefore around 0.25 watts. A 2G CDMA cellphone transmits for longer than half of a millisecond, but with a peak power of approximately 0.2 watts. And that is at maximum power, used only when the link to the base station is weak. In most cases the system will keep the transmit power at the lowest possible level in order to extend the battery charge time.

As a final consideration, any transmitted power that is lost to the head or hand is wasted, so phone designers are motivated to create phones that send as much of the power outward as possible. There is some leeway in the design of the antenna and metallic structures in the phone body to direct the radiation. Despite the best intentions, some fields still impinge on the head and are worthy of further examination.

Biological Effects of Cellphone Fields

The primary effect people would like to know about is cancer, which is both lethal and mysterious. Cancer is the effect of mutated cells reproducing and spreading. A cancerous tumor starts with a phase called hyperplasia, which occurs when a cell experiences damage to its DNA, the plan that guides the cell's development and functioning. When a certain kind of damage occurs, the cell begins reproducing at an unusually high rate, forming a mass of cells. This is a tumor, which can remain harmless indefinitely. But if one of the produced cells is abnormal in shape and function and begins producing other mutated cells, then the tumor has entered dysplasia. Those cells no longer function in their usual role and become detrimental to the operation of the cells around them. If the tumor does not break the tissue and remains localized, it is *in situ* cancer, which can be removed whole. If the tumor does break the tissue and mutated cells enter the bloodstream, the cells can spread to other organs and interfere with their functioning. While this growth is occurring, the body's healing systems provide resistance, especially through apoptosis, which is a cell's tendency to destroy itself when damaged. Not only must cells mutate, but apoptosis must be somehow repressed for cancer to appear. So while the early stages, cells that could lead to cancer, are common, most do not progress to become cancer.

The origin of the cancer process, and the advancement from stage to stage could have many causes, and there is a large random component. Some stimuli may start the process with damage to the DNA, while others may increase the odds that a tumor will proceed from one stage to the next. A theory holds that chemicals called poly-aromatic hydrocarbons cause the increased incidence of cancer among smokers, since measurements of the blood and lung tissue of smokers have found elevated levels of DNA with these molecules attached.[8] Another possible origin of cancer is ionization through radiation, where the high energy transferred to an electron causes it to leave the DNA molecule. In both cases, an external stimulus changes the DNA, causing mutations that could lead to cancer. The fields from cellphones, however, are not in either category.

Cellphone radiation is non-ionizing, meaning that the odds of an electron leaving an atom due to a nearby transmitting cellphone antenna are vanishingly small. The important point to consider is that electromagnetic waves come in packets called photons. The energy in a single photon is so small it is measured in units called electron-volts, where one electron-volt is the energy required to move a single electron through an electric potential of one volt.* When a photon interacts with an electron, its energy can transfer into the kinetic energy of the electron.

If the outer electron of a typical atom gains approximately one electron-volt, it will have enough energy to escape the nucleus' positive electric charge, leaving behind an ionized atom.[9] The energy transfer must happen at once with a single photon because the electron does not hold onto the extra energy for long. The electron will probably re-emit the energy as a new photon almost instantaneously (less than 10^{-15} seconds). So two photons that have 0.5 electron-volts each would have to strike the electron almost exactly simultaneously, which is unlikely unless many photons are flowing around the atom, meaning the overall field strength is high. For photons with still less power, the number that must simultaneously strike an electron is higher, and the odds of this occurring are yet lower. So the energy in the photons of an electromagnetic wave determines if it will be able to ionize atoms and the number of photons is of secondary importance.

The energy in a photon is strictly determined by the frequency of the wave, with a higher frequency corresponding to more energy per photon.† X-rays, which are electromagnetic waves with frequencies around 10^{18} Hz, have approximately 4000 electron-volts in a photon. This is more than enough energy to ionize DNA, although the electrons in a tissue that must be removed to cause

---

*A power of one watt is equivalent to an energy transfer of approximately 6.25×10^{18} electron-volts per second.

†The formula is $E = h \times f$, with E the energy in electron-volts, f the frequency in hertz, and h Planck's constant with a value of 4.14×10^{-15} electron-volts per hertz.

cancer represent a small target, so even extended exposure to X-rays may not do harm. Ultra-violet light, at frequencies of about 10^{15} Hz has a photon energy of approximately 4 electron-volts, which is enough to ionize DNA, leading to the concern that long exposure to bright sunlight could increase the risk of skin cancer.

Electromagnetic waves used for radio communications have frequencies around one gigahertz, corresponding to photon energy of 0.000004 electron-volts (four micro-electron-volts). Increasing the amplitude of the electric field increases the number of photons, but their individual energy remains constant. These photons do not have enough energy to remove electrons, and are therefore non-ionizing radiation. This method for electric and magnetic fields to affect biological tissue is unlikely, but there are other processes to examine. An electric field could, for example, move ions within the tissue. But a close examination indicates that this, too, is unlikely.

At the cell walls within biological tissues, a complicated flow of charged atoms and molecules is constantly taking place. An electric field would, by definition, cause the charged bodies to move which might disrupt the processes. But a simple analysis shows cellphone fields would not cause any noticeable movement.

Chloride ions are among the most mobile ions in an aqueous solution at body temperature and are therefore a good example. Their mobility is 10^{-7} m²/volt × second.[10] The electric field strength immediately adjacent to a dipole transmitting 0.2 watts can be in the hundreds of volts-per-meter, but this decreases quickly with distance and material such as skin and tissue heavily attenuates the amplitude, so 100 V/m is a probable ceiling for values within the body. Multiplying this field magnitude by the mobility gives 100V/m $\times 10^{-7}$ m²/volt × second $= 10^{-5}$ m/second, which is the speed of the chloride ion moving in the electric field. Diminishing the movement is the changing amplitude of the field, which switches direction twice every nanosecond. The ion will therefore move less than 10^{-9} second $\times 10^{-5}$ m/second $= 10^{-14}$ m before reversing direction. This distance, approximately one thousand times less than an atomic radius, is so small it is unlikely to have any noticeable effect.

The one unambiguous, measurable effect of cellphone fields on biological tissue is heating, so this is the aspect that governing bodies examine. Researchers quantify exposure levels by the *specific absorption rate* (SAR) in watts per kilogram or, equivalently, milliwatts-per-gram. By measuring the power levels that cause heating of tissue, and then building in a safety margin of at least ten times, the Federal Communications Commission arrived at a maximum permissible SAR of 1.6 mW/g for the brain, averaged over any one-gram cube of tissue. The limit for parts like the hand and the ear is 4.0 mW/g averaged over any ten-gram cube of tissue.[11] Some other countries, such as Canada, also apply these limits.[12] These limits are the world's most stringent.

Some countries are more forgiving in their SAR limits than the USA. The

International Commission on Non-Ionizing Radiation Protection recommends a limit for brain tissue of 2.0 W/kg averaged over any 10 grams. Not only is the maximum higher, but the larger averaging volume allows for a small point to have a high field if the immediate surroundings have low fields. Many European countries adhere to this more permissive guideline. In all cases, these limits are not based on any specific harm that is being avoided, but in the notion that heating is the only biological effect that can be measured. Whether that heating is harmful is not addressed. But the rules are set and cellphone designers must meet the established SAR limits, which means that they must measure the SAR caused by their designs.

A common method for measuring SAR is with a simulated brain medium, which can be simply water with salt and sugar. Purified water has almost no conductivity of its own, so the salt increases the conductivity to match that of brain tissue at the frequency of the phone being measured. The sugar increases the water's electrical permittivity, which is a measure of how strongly a medium responds to an electric field. Taken together, the conductivity and permittivity define a material electrically. The experimenter adds salt and sugar, taking periodic measurements of the conductivity and permittivity until the target values are reached. If the values are too high, more water is added to dilute the mixture and the process begins again. Sometimes a gelling agent is added to solidify the mixture and keep it from moving inside a plastic head model.

When I was making SAR measurements, preparing the liquid was the most time-consuming activity since the mixture had to be completely mixed. The salt and sugar tended to settle at the bottom, making that area too dense and the top too dilute. So frequent mixing was necessary, and the mixing had to be done slowly, since any air bubbles would also change the results. A few minutes of stirring were usually adequate to then perform about ten minutes of measurements.

An electric field probe moving within the simulated brain liquid takes the actual SAR measurements. The operator pours the liquid into a bowl shaped like half of a human head. For the purposes of the measurement, the head contains all brain tissue underneath the skin. A phone attached to the underside of the bowl against the simulated ear and mouth acts as the source. The measurement probe is a thin rod with small field sensors at the tip. The sensors, only a few millimeters across, measure the field strength at one point, which the system uses to calculate SAR. A typical measurement station has a robotic arm that scans the probe through the liquid, taking point-by-point measurements through a three-dimensional grid. The measurement is mechanical and precise, but the results can change widely with even small variations in the phone placement.

The phone positioning in relation to the artificial head introduces the greatest variation in SAR. The concern is not with the phone radiation, which decreases relatively slowly with distance, but with the stronger, but also more short-range, near fields. The power in the near fields drops with at least the fourth power of distance, so moving the phone a few millimeters can significantly change the results. The thickness of the artificial ear or the distance of the microphone to the mouth could determine whether a phone meets the SAR limit or not.

When I was taking these measurements, the point of maximum SAR was often inside the cheek rather than the ear, due to phone positioning. To take a measurement we would put the phone's earpiece directly against the ear and then move the mouthpiece toward the simulated mouth, leaving the phone making contact with the mid-cheek. For a solid-body handset, not a flip-phone type, the antenna at the top would then be at an angle away from the head, while the phone body would be against the cheek. Unsurprisingly, we usually measured the maximum SAR to occur directly inside the cheek. There is, of course, no brain tissue at that location, but rules are rules, and we had to find ways to decrease this fictional brain SAR. Other phone orientations would produce different SAR patterns inside the head model, and there is no way of knowing in advance how people will hold the phone.

Published sources and websites provide lists of measured cellphone SAR's, but they are of limited use. Those who have carried out the measurements know there is too much variability not only in the results but in how those results correspond to real usage. Comparing the SAR results of phones with different shapes is particularly vague since the positioning next to the head could be completely different. This is not to imply that SAR measurements are pure theater. They catch handsets that are true outliers, putting abnormally high amounts of energy into the head. But when comparing the SAR values of cellphones that meet the limits, sizeable differences do not necessarily indicate which models are safer.

Accepting the great variability in SAR results, the engineering and scientific communities, as well as the public, would still like to know what possible effects cellphone fields could have. Many researchers have been moving forward in looking for biological effects.

Direct testing for the effect on biological tissue of the electric and magnetic fields similar to what surrounds a cellphone is difficult and has produced mixed results. First there is the question of *in situ* versus *in vivo* measurements. *In situ* experiments consist of exposing cells in a dish or a test tube to fields. The setup has to be carefully designed so that the fields are evenly distributed across the cells, without concentrated field points. Cells in isolation also do not have the support systems of cells in a living organism, such as cooling, waste removal, and any other healing effects provided by flowing fluids and surrounding cells. To include these factors, researchers turn to *in vivo* experimentation, which presents other problems that add variability to the results. An animal study must include careful, which means time-consuming and expensive, monitoring of the subjects. Researchers must weigh all food and droppings, note

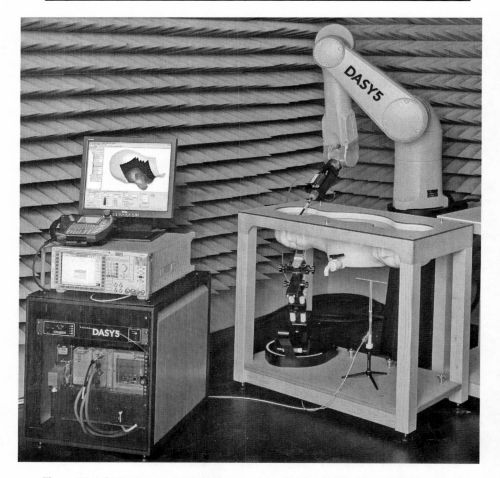

Figure 22: A SAR measurement station consists of a physical head model and a robotic field probe; image used courtesy of Schmid & Partner Engineering AG.

exercise and sleep times, account for complicated factors such as stress, and handle many other details. Even well-executed experiments can leave ambiguity in the conclusions.

One difficulty that laboratory tests encounter is the rarity of cancer and tumors. For the case of cells in a dish, actually creating a cancerous cell from several minutes of exposure to an antenna broadcasting at low power is unlikely. Experimenters instead search for changes that they believe raise the risk of eventually becoming cancer if those cells were in a living organism. But cancer is still largely a mysterious phenomenon, so whether that risk will be realized is not understood. "Only 10 minutes on a mobile phone could trigger cancer, scientists believe," was the title of a newspaper article from 2007 reporting on, and probably exaggerating, the results of one *in situ* study that measured certain chemical changes with field exposure.[13] And looking for full tumors in live test animals is no easier.

Many experiments search for fragmentation of the cell nucleus as a possible precursor to cancer. In response to damaging stimuli, and under certain conditions, the nucleus of a cell can break into pieces called micronuclei. Once a cell's nucleus breaks, that cell's function is compromised and it often dies, although in some cases the damaged DNA could make the cell cancerous. A review paper of 64 studies found odds ratios of 1.4 to 75.3 connecting the presence of micronuclei and cancer in people.[14] This is a wide range of values, with the high-end odds ratio of 75.3 showing a clear link while the low odds ratio of 1.4 would indicate an indeterminate connection. As with much in this subject, the answer is not immediately apparent. Part of the variability arises from the method of measuring the DNA damage.

Researchers measuring this fragmentation have relied on a relatively new method called the comet assay. The basic procedure is to place the cell between electrodes which create an electric field. A complete cell and nucleus is electrically neutral and will not move in the field. Micronuclei, however, have a negative charge and move toward the positive electrode. The higher the degree of fragmentation, the more charged the micronuclei are and the farther they will move. The micronuclei form a trail emerging from the mass of the cell and pointing to the positive electrode, giving the appearance of a comet when viewed under a microscope. Hence the name comet assay, although the technical appellation is "single-cell microgel electrophoresis." The length of the tail indicates the amount of fragmentation, so the result of a comet assay is a length in micrometers.

A study published in 1995 used the comet assay technique to find micronuclei in rat brain cells that had been exposed to cellphone fields.[15] Leading the investigation were two professors from the University of Washington, including the researcher who had first presented the comet assay as a micronuclei measurement technique in 1988. They placed antennas broadcasting at 2.45 GHz next to rats, with the transmissions done in two microsecond pulses with 550 pulses per second. The power level was set to give an estimated whole-body SAR average of either 0.6 W/kg or 1.2 W/kg, which are both considerably less than the FCC limits on brain SAR. After two hours of exposure, they placed the rats in a box of dry ice for sixty seconds, and then decapitated them and removed their brains. They cut the brains into small pieces and repeatedly washed them in a chemical solution to remove blood cells, and then placed the brain cells into a gel between two electrodes. Applying 18 volts to the two electrodes for sixty minutes created the comet shapes for measurement, and they did find micronuclei.

The study found a trend of increased micronuclei comet tail lengths with field exposure. Samples from eleven rats not exposed had comet lengths of approximately 170 micrometers, while cells from eight rats in the 0.6 W/kg SAR group showed longer lengths of 180 micrometers. Finally, cells from eight rats in the 1.2 W/kg group had comet tail lengths of 190 micrometers. So they did find a progression of comet tail length as the antenna power increases. These were for assays performed immediately after exposure.

Assays performed four hours after the exposure showed lengths of 150, 175 and 250 micrometers for the three groups. The trend is even clearer in this case, but may be due to effects encountered during storage, or by separation from the complete organism's maintenance systems. The experimenters also performed variations such as broadcasting a continuous wave from the antenna rather than pulses. In that case, cells from seven rats with no exposure showed comet tail lengths of 100 micrometers, and cells from eight rats that were exposed had comet tail lengths of 120 micrometers. Again, this is a clear trend, but how these numbers translate into cancer is unknown.

Subsequent studies by other researchers have not found these levels of fragmentation. The 1995 study found significant amounts of micronuclei in nearly every brain cell that had been exposed to even modest field levels. Such a large and widespread effect should be easy to identify, but it has not been. Three experimental studies published in 1997 and 1998 that tried to reproduce the results found the same comet tail lengths for cells with and without exposure to the fields.[16] These results were for both cells exposed while in a dish and for cells exposed while in a rat brain and then removed for measurement. Pronouncing one study as more correct than another is difficult, since there are so many variables and effects involved in the experiments.

The inability of researchers to find a clear mechanism for electric and magnetic field induced diseases through experimentation does not, of course, mean that they do not exist. With mysterious illnesses such as cancer, such a discovery may be a long way in the future, if it even exists. More fruitful for the present is to leave the myriad biological suspects in the laboratory and venture into the marketplace. The question still remains: whatever the causes may be, do cellphones increase disease rates?

The Search for Connections

The field of epidemiology examines disease rates in order to draw conclusions about possible causes, without specifying all of the biological details. One example is the aforementioned smoking studies, which demonstrated a high rate of lung disease among smokers and left the discovery of the reasons smoking may be harmful to other scientists. While this removes many of the difficulties in finding disease causes, by entering the real world, rather than the laboratory, epidemiology deals with other complications.

People are exposed to numerous environmental and lifestyle factors, so the effects of cellphones are difficult to isolate. Perhaps a cellphone user is more likely to be in a socioeconomic class, or live in a location, or use other products that lower or raise cancer rates. And once found, the results may need interpretation to be meaningful. One definite risk factor for cancer, for example, is age. So a rise in the cancer rate of a population might be showing that people are living longer.

Epidemiology is devoted to accounting for these confounding factors, usually by dividing subjects into groups based on similar characteristics and doing the comparisons within the groups. The hope is that a well-designed epidemiological study involving a large enough population of subjects can mitigate the confounding factors and provide valid conclusions showing disease causality. Epidemiologists began applying these techniques to electric and magnetic field effects in the 1970's, with interesting results.

A turning-point in popular concern over the health effects of electric and magnetic fields was a 1979 epidemiological study linking power lines and childhood leukemia. The study, conducted in the Denver area in 1976 and 1977, involved visiting the residences of 344 cancer patients under age 19 and the residences of 344 non-cancer patients as the control group.[17] The epidemiologist divided the residences into a low-current configuration and a high-current configuration groups based on visible wiring. Transmission lines carry voltages of several hundred kilovolts which primary transformers reduce to 13 kilovolts for each neighborhood, and then secondary transformers reduce the voltage again to 240 Volts and fan out the lines to individual residences. The highest currents in the system are between the primary and secondary transformers, so residences near those lines got the high-current configuration appellation. The study searched for a link between high-current configurations and leukemia cases.

The observations did show a sizable odds ratio for these two factors. Of the subjects that lived continuously in one residence their entire lives, 48 leukemia cases and 26 controls lived near high-current configurations, which is a ratio of 1.85. In the low-current configurations were 61 leukemia cases and 102 controls, which is a ratio of 0.6. The odds ratio is therefore 1.85/0.6 = 3.1. The authors found the same trend when taking into account urban/suburban groups, economic differences, age of mother, sex of patient, sibling order (leukemia is higher in first-born) and traffic congestion on the street.

The main limitation of the study, which the authors acknowledged, is that it is based on potentially high currents and magnetic fields as suggested by observed wiring, not on field measurements. The authors also pointed out that their conclusions suggest an increase in the expected childhood leukemia rate from one in one thousand to two or three in one thousand (0.1 percent to 0.3 percent). Also, since this study is epidemiological, they offer no hypothesis explaining specifically how magnetic fields may promote cancer. Perhaps the effect is indirect, such as carcinogens in soil, piping, paint or other sources being activated by the currents. Although the study may not have been definitive, the link between electricity and cancer had found new publicity.

The study received wide publicity and quickly entered the popular consciousness as a new source of worry. Writer Paul Brodeur used it as the centerpiece of several *New Yorker* articles and subsequent books, such as *Currents of Death*,[18] about the threat of electric and magnetic fields. The debate about the effects of power lines may never be settled since their expected effect is small and there are many variables involved, such as the fact that people move frequently. But certainty is not required to generate fear.

When dealing with cellphones, epidemiologists generally look for three types of tumors: meningioma, glioma and acoustic neuroma. Meningioma is a class of tumors that grow in the meninges, which are the brain's outer layers. According to the Cancer Brain Tumor Registry of the United States, the occurrence rate is 7.8 cases per 100,000 people in a year, largely concentrated in the elderly. Meningiomas are usually non-lethal, with 75 percent being asymptomatic. The cells in the brain that are responsible for thinking are the neurons, and they are supported by glial cells, which is where gliomas originate. Gliomas, unlike most meningiomas, are tumors that grow quickly and spread to other sites, and usually return after being removed through surgery. The rate of occurrence is 9 per 100,000 and the prognosis is usually poor. Gliomas are ranked in increasing severity by grades I through IV, with approximately 2 percent of patients over age 65 and 30 percent of patients under age 45 surviving two years after a grade IV diagnosis. Acoustic neuroma is a slow-growing tumor on the auditory nerve that can cause hearing loss, tinnitus and dizziness if it grows large enough, and has an annual occurrence rate between 1 and 20 in one million. This tumor is found primarily in people over fifty years old, and the number of incidences has been rising for several decades, which may be an indication of better diagnosis.[19] Of these tumors, the glioma is the most dangerous and is what most people think of as brain cancer.

In addition to these three types of tumors, some studies have also examined cancerous tumors in the salivary glands, called the parotid glands, at the base of the jaw under the ears. These tumors also have an occurrence rate of approximately one in one hundred thousand per year, and the survival rate varies widely with the type of tumor and its stage of development at the start of treatment. The studies examining these types of tumors have been numerous, both independently and as part of larger research projects.

The European-based Interphone project provided guidance for many epidemiological studies dealing with cellphones in the late 1990's through the early 2000's. Not a study itself, Interphone was a set of guidelines and a means to share resources between several researcher groups working independently in Australia, Canada, Denmark, Finland, France, Germany, Israel, Italy, Japan, New Zealand, Norway, Sweden, and the UK. The studies were designed and run separately, but most followed the same overall procedure. Patients with meningioma, glioma or acoustic neuroma were identified and invited to participate, along with a control group. The researchers then gathered information from the subjects about their cellphone usage and other relevant information through a questionnaire or an interview. Having the subjects provide information about past behavior is vulnerable to recall bias, but is convenient for the participants. After creating their data sets, the groups would then compile the statistics into charts and odds ratios for publication. No strong link between cellphones and cancer emerged in the published studies.

As an example, one large and broad study in Denmark surveyed 420,095 cellphone users between 1982 and 1996 based on existing records.[20] Two phone companies offered the researchers access to their subscriber data, which covered 723,421 users. The researchers excluded business phones and subscriptions not linked to someone listed in Denmark's Central Population Register. The study was publicized, giving the population the option of not being included in the study, although only 53 subscribers asked to be removed. The researchers then compared the remaining 420,095 users with the Danish Cancer Registry to identify patterns. Since they had a full range of information, the researchers did not restrict the study to brain tumors, and also looked at other types of cancer, such as those of the colon, stomach, and liver. There was no increase in the incidence of cancers among cellphone users. For brain cancer, the study expected 142.8 cases among the 357,550 male subjects and found 135 cases. The 62,545 female subjects were statistically expected to yield 18.5 cases, and the study found 19 cases. In both cases the odds ratio is near 1.0, meaning that the study found no increased risk of brain cancer from cellphone usage. This is, however, only one study trying to make sense of a large phenomenon. Fortunately, a host of published studies are available.

The case-control studies generally show odds ratios around 1.0, although with some outliers. Table 10-1 lists the reported odds ratios of several studies into the link between cellphone use and acoustic neuromas. Table 10-2 does the same for meningioma and Table 10-3 for glioma. The studies vary significantly in size, as shown by the number of tumor cases included in each, and the results also vary. Some found odds ratios that were significantly less than 1.0, indicating cellphone use may actually prevent tumors. This is unlikely, and those results demonstrate the difficulty in dealing with such rare and complex phenomena.

TABLE 10-1: MEASURED ODDS RATIOS FOR ACOUSTIC
NEUROMA AND CELLULAR PHONE USAGE.[21]

Years of Study	Number of Cases	Odds Ratio	Description
1994–1998	5	1.9	5 years use
1997–1999	11	1.7	3–6 years use
1999–2002	14	1.8	10 years use
	12	3.9	≥ 10 years ipsilateral use
1994–2004	360	0.9	All cases
	23	1.8	ipsilateral use

Years of Study	Number of Cases	Odds Ratio	Description
	12	.9	contralateral use
1997–2003	130	1.7	> 1 year of use
	20	2.9	> 10 years use
	10	3.5	> 10 yrs ipsilateral use
2000–2004	51	0.7	Regular use
	4	0.8	> 8 years use
	20	0.9	ipsilateral use

TABLE 10-2: MEASURED ODDS RATIOS
FOR MENINGIOMA AND CELLPHONE USAGE.[21]

Years of Study	Number of Cases	Odds Ratio	Description
1994–1998	6	0.9	≥ 5 years use
2000–2002	118	0.7	Regular use
	5	1.3	≥ 10 yrs ipsilateral use
	3	0.5	≥ 10 yrs contralateral use
2000–2002	67	0.8	Regular use
	6	1.0	≥ 10 years use
2000–2003	104	0.8	Regular use
	5	1.1	≥ 10 years use
1997–2003	347	1.1	> 1 year use
	38	1.5	> 10 years use
	15	2.0	> 10 yrs ipsilateral use

TABLE 10-3: MEASURED ODDS RATIOS
FOR GLIOMA AND CELLPHONE USAGE.[21]

Years of Study	Number of Cases	Odds Ratio	Description
1994–1998	11	0.6	≥ 5 years use
1996	119	1.5	Analog or digital use
	40	2.1	Analog use
	11	2.4	Analog use, 1–2 years
	11	2.0	Analog use, > 2 years
2000–2002	214	0.8	Regular use
	15	1.6	≥ 10 yrs ipsilateral use
	11	0.7	≥ 10 yrs contralateral use
2000–2002	47	1.1	Regular use, low-grade glioma
	6	1.6	≥ 10 yrs use, low-grade glioma
	59	0.6	Regular use, high-grade glioma
	8	0.5	≥ 10 yrs use, high-grade glioma
2000–2004	508	0.9	Regular use
2000–2003	138	1.0	Regular use
	12	2.2	≥ 10 years use
1997–2003	65	1.4	> 1 yr use, low-grade glioma
	7	1.5	> 10 yrs use, low-grade glioma
	2	1.2	> 10 yrs ipsilateral use, low-grade glioma
	281	1.4	> 1 yr use, high-grade glioma

Years of Study	Number of Cases	Odds Ratio	Description
	71	3.1	>10 yrs use, high-grade glioma
	39	5.4	>10 yrs ipsilateral use, high-grade glioma
2000–2004	867	0.8	Regular use
	77	1.4	≥ 10 yrs ipsilateral use

Some studies have examined the side of the head that tumors appear in relation to cellphone usage. This is an approximate way to establish a dose-dependent effect, since the fields are weaker on the side of the head opposite to the handset. The Tables include some of the study results, with ipsilateral tumors being on the same side of the head as the cellphones, and contralateral tumors being on the opposite side. These studies introduce more recall bias, since patients with tumors may be more likely to remember ipsilateral cellphone usage. Many of the studies find a modest increase in tumor occurrence, but when tumors exist they are more likely to be ipsilateral than contralateral.

As a general conclusion, there is no definite trend of danger from cellphone usage, at least not one large enough to dent their spread. An odds ratio in the single digits represents an increase of several cases in 100,000, which is difficult to separate from statistical noise. A high odds ratio, such as 10 or higher, would be a clearer trend and would probably have been found by now. Whether cellphones are safe is a matter of personal interpretation of the data, but they are not unsafe enough to motivate most people to stop using them.

The Battle in the Courtroom

The January 21, 1993 episode of television interview show *Larry King Live* introduced the public to two new aspects of cellphones, fear and lawsuits. David Reynard of St. Petersburg, Florida, discussed his lawsuit against phone maker NEC and service provider GTE Mobilnet. His wife had died less than a year earlier at the age of 33 from a brain tumor that was located around the area where she held her cellphone. Although a U.S. District Judge dismissed the suit in 1995 for lack of evidence, by then the case had received wide coverage and was part of the cellular phone story. Other lawsuits soon followed, leaving courts trying to determine scientific fact.

For several decades scientific evidence had to meet the Frye standard to be admissible in American courts, originating in a 1923 decision by the Federal Circuit Court of the District of Columbia. James Fry appealed his second-degree murder conviction on the basis that he had not been allowed to use the results of a blood pressure deception test as evidence. That test measured the subject's blood pressure in response to questions as an early form of what would become a polygraph test. After another half-century of research and testing, the polygraph would gain some degree of acceptance, but in the 1920's it was an unknown development. The Court ruled against the appeal, letting the conviction stand on the basis that scientific evidence must be accepted by the relevant community in order to be admissible.

The Frye standard does not demand complete agreement among scientists in the field, but does seek to disqualify fringe theories. The standard also alleviates the judge and jury from scientific decision making. Expert witnesses with new theories may not use the court as a forum to argue for their own research and why others are wrong. Scholarly journals and conferences establish the scientific consensus, and the role of expert witnesses is only to explain that accepted truth to the jury. The Frye standard held until the 1990's in the Federal Court system, until pressure to allow more viewpoints into the courtroom won out.

The Daubert standard supplanted the Frye standard in the federal courts, giving the courts more discretion to use scientific testimony that is not generally accepted in the literature. This standard originated in 1993's *Daubert v. Merrell Dow Pharmaceuticals Inc.*, in which the parents of two children born with birth defects sued, saying the anti-nausea drug Bendectin was responsible. The defense presented over 30 studies involving 130,000 subjects, all of which reached the conclusion that *in utero* exposure to Bendectin does not correspond to a higher rate of birth defects. In response, the plaintiffs brought expert witnesses who, on the basis of their own interpretation of the published data, testified that a link does exist. Since the plaintiff's experts were not explaining peer-reviewed and published conclusions, the court disallowed their evidence due to the Frye standard. But on appeal the Supreme Court ruled that Frye is too restrictive and that a judge could consider other factors and evaluate scientific evidence on its own merit. The case went back to the circuit court which again ruled that the plaintiff's evidence was not admissible, but the Supreme Court's new precedent was established.[22]

The Supreme Court further strengthened the conclusions of *Daubert* with the 1997 ruling in *General Electric Co. v. Joiner*. Joiner was an electrician who experienced regular exposure to PCBs while working with GE electrical transformers, and sued after developing lung cancer. Since he had a history of cancer in the family and was a smoker, Joiner argued that while exposure to PCB's may not have caused his lung cancer, it may have accelerated its onset. Further obscuring Joiner's claim, while studies have shown a link between PCB's and some types of cancers, they had not found a connection with lung cancer. Joiner's expert witnesses, however, presented their own unpublished data and reinterpreted the published data to argue that a link does exit. The court ruled against this testimony and decided the case for GE. The 11th Circuit Court of Appeals in Atlanta then overturned the ruling, concluding that the jury should have been allowed to decide between the differing testimonies. The Supreme Court then overturned the appeal and reinstated the original decision in an eight-to-one ruling that the judge does have the power to evaluate scientific evidence and choose what is admissible.[23]

As Chief Justice William Rehnquist predicted in his dissent on *Daubert*, judges are now called upon to be amateur scientists. This has lead to wide variability between judges as they reach different conclusions. Some judges, for example, disallow epidemiological evidence that does not show at least a factor of two increase in risk. But the factor of two is an arbitrary standard, with journals accepting studies showing lower risk increases.[24] With the variation of standards between courtrooms, cellphone litigants have a hope of finding the right judge that will rule in their favor, although so far that has not happened.

Some well-publicized lawsuits have emerged through the years, without yet harming the cellular phone industry. A Baltimore man with a brain tumor sued Motorola and other companies in the year 2000 for $800 million. The case was significant for two reasons. First, the plaintiff was a neurologist, and therefore an expert on the brain. More importantly, he was represented by attorney John Angelos, who had achieved billion-dollar rulings against tobacco companies. The Federal District Court judge still stopped the case in 2002, citing lack of evidence.[25]

Base Station Concerns

Base stations present a less immediate health risk due to the low power of their surrounding fields. Unlike a handset, which is centimeters from the body, base-station antennas are typically in elevated locations several meters from anyone. The power in the near-fields decreases with distance, d, at the rate of at least $1/d^4$, so they are negligibly small except for immediately next to the antenna and transmission lines. For considering the effects of base stations, the radio waves become important.

Rather than the near electric and magnetic fields, the power is in the radiated electromagnetic waves, so a cellular phone tower is similar to a broadcast radio tower. While a radio tower may broadcast with thousands of watts, a cellular base station puts out tens of watts. But cellular base stations are more numerous than radio stations. The net effect is that the ambient power of broadcasts from radio towers and from cellular base stations are approximately equal in most locations. And they are also usually quite low. The power that wireless receivers encounter, whether radio, television, or cellphones, is typically less than one microwatt.

Concerns about the possible negative health effects of cellular phone towers have been particularly prominent in the UK. In the year 2000, there were approximately 300 campaigns to remove towers, usually near schools. The campaigns have had some successes, but have encountered difficulty due to the strong demand for cellular phone coverage.[26]

Attention in the USA has not been as focused on towers as on the handsets, since the Telecommunications Act of 1996 may have preempted much of the controversy. This was one of the laws enacted by the 104th Congress, which saw the first Republican majority in both houses in almost fifty years, and was one of a group of new, often business-oriented, laws. Section 704, while affirming the right of state and local governments to make decisions about tower placement, limited the process to an approved set of criteria. If a tower meets FCC specifications, no other supposed environmental effects can be taken into account. Like the Frye standard, this law takes the responsibility of scientific decision-making away from the legal realm.

Driving While Talking

Those who have spent any time on the road since the late 1990's are familiar with the phenomenon of talker-drivers. A car is being driven in a way that is a little off: too slow, not responsive to conditions, listing to one side of the lane. Upon passing, the driver is almost invariably on the phone. This selfish act is annoying, but the harm may extend beyond inconvenience. Talking on cellphones while driving certainly seems to be a distraction, and since 90 percent of automobile collisions are caused by driver error,[27] the distraction of cellphones may be a public safety issue.

The problem is that conversing on a cellphone requires more cognitive effort than listening to the radio or speaking to someone in the car.[28] First, the listening itself requires effort since the audio from a cellphone can be weak when compared to the background automotive noise. Conversation can also be more difficult over the phone since the two participants are not experiencing the same environment. Someone riding along can change the volume and pace of the conversation to match driving conditions, but over the phone the two talkers have no idea what is happening on the other end. The distraction arises because the driver has to mentally withdraw from the surroundings to participate in the remote conversation.

An influential study published in 1997 examined the link between cellphone use and automobile collisions as a cross-over study. This type of study was invented to examine possible negative effects of drugs when a control group is not available, so the same subjects act as both the test group and the control group, crossing between the two groups as time passes. A study may try to determine, for example, if a drug increases the risk of seizure within two hours of consumption by compiling seizure records for users. If the subjects take the drug twice daily, then for four hours they are in the test group and for the remaining twenty hours they are in the control group. If the drug does not increase seizure risk, then four out of twenty-four, or one sixth of the recorded seizures would take place in the test group time. This result corresponds to an odds ratio of one, while if more than one sixth of the seizures occur in the test group time, the odds ratio would be larger. Unlike taking a pill, however, cellphone users vary widely in how they make calls while driving.

The publicized conclusion of the study found that driving while speaking on a cellphone increased the risk of collision as much as driving while intoxicated. The researchers interviewed people who came to the North York Collision Reporting Centre in Toronto from mid–1994 to mid–1995, yielding 699 people who were cellphone users and had been in a collision. Of the subjects, 37 had been using their cellphones while driving on the day before their collisions, which was the control period. The authors therefore expect 37/699 = 0.0529 of drivers with cellphones to be driving while calling at that time of day. Yet 170 subjects had used a cellphone in the 10-minute period up to the collision, giving a ratio of 170/699 = 0.243. The increase over the expected value is approximately four, which is the same as driving while intoxicated. Interestingly, while this study is often cited as justification for mandating hands-free phone kits, it found a risk increase of 3.9 for handheld cellphones and an increase of 5.9 for hands-free users.[29]

A more recent Australian study found similar results. That study surveyed people involved in collisions reporting to hospital emergence rooms in the Perth area in the years 2002 to 2004. Also a cross-over study, the authors used the subjects' previous driving experiences as the control group. They found that for collisions involving injuries, the odds ratio for handheld cellphone users is 4.9, while for hands-free users it is a slightly more modest 3.8.[30] Like the epidemiological studies into biological effects, these investigations look for an increased risk without pointing to specific causes. To find what about cellphones may cause collisions, others turn to experiments in controlled environments.

Researchers have attempted to create laboratory tests to simulate cellphone use while driving, but with limited success. The problem may be that the subjects know they are under examination and can concentrate accordingly. Collisions on the road probably occur when the driver becomes accustomed to the environment and confident that nothing unexpected will happen, which is not the case in a laboratory. In one study, for example, subjects sat in a station with two pedals to simulate a brake and accelerator. There was no steering wheel or view other than a light. The subjects kept pressing the accelerator until a red light came on, at which point they moved to the brake. The study measured reaction time in silence, with a radio playing, during conversation, while using a handheld cellphone and while using a hands-free phone kit. The change in reaction time was slight but noticeable. The mean time with no distractions was 392 milliseconds, with the radio it was 408 milliseconds, and the mean times with conversation taking place were in the 450 to 470 millisecond range. Traveling at 100 kilometers per hour (62 mph), a 50 millisecond delay corresponds to approximately 1.4 meters, which could be enough to cause a collision if following another car closely.[31] So this experiment did find a degradation of performance, although it was probably hampered by simplifying a complicated situation.

Laboratory studies have become increasingly elaborate, including three-dimensional scenes of traffic projected onto large curved screens in front of the subjects and feedback forces to the steering wheel and pedals based on simulated traffic. In one such study the researchers told the subjects they were testing new driving software and let them use the driving stations for thirty minutes at a time with varying levels of distraction. The study found that driving incidents, including crashes, increased when going from no conversation to conversation in person, and increased again when conversing on a cellphone. The study also found no increase in incidents during conversation when the subjects were pilots, who have training and experience with handling multiple stimuli and tasks while driving.[32] This is consistent with other studies that found the performance of the subjects in areas such as reaction time and maintaining a constant speed while conversing improves with practice.[33]

Yet another way that cellphone use could make driving more dangerous is with increased aggression, and researchers have tried to examine that aspect as well. A 2001 study that used a written questionnaire to gauge attitudes toward cellphone-using drivers found no increase in aggressive feelings toward them as opposed to other drivers going too slowly, too quickly, not moving after a stoplight had turned green, or other frustrating behaviors. When questioned, people did not admit to particular animosity to drivers focused on their conversations.

In 2006, researchers tested these attitudes with a particularly annoying scientific study. Driving what the authors call a "low-status, sun-faded yellow, 1970 Dodge Omni hatchback," the experimenter either appeared to be concentrating on driving or having an exaggerated cellphone conversation, while a video camera in the rear, hidden by a pile of laundry, noted the facial expressions of the following driver. In the second phase of the study, the driver would fail to move at stoplights that had turned green while in front of a waiting car. Noting that conducting such an experiment in a Los Angeles rush hour could lead to explosive externalities, the researchers performed this experiment in a small North Dakota town. Observing the facial expressions of 135 subjects, the study found that female drivers appeared to be more angered by the cellphone usage than male drivers.[34]

Despite the perceived risks, increased cellphone usage has not yet resulted in higher collision rates. In the decade from 1995 to 2005, the number of cellphone subscribers in the USA increased from 34 million to 208 million, a sixfold increase. According to National Highway Traffic Safety Administration (NHTSA) statistics, 42,065 people were killed and 3,483,000 people were injured in automobile collisions in 1996. For 2006 the corresponding numbers are 42,642 and 2,575,000, which shows a significant rate decrease since the number of registered motor vehicles increased during the same period from 201 million to 252 million.[35] In a 2005 survey, the NHTSA estimated that of the 974,000 vehicles on the road at any moment during daylight hours, 6 percent were being driven by drivers using a cellphone.[36] The saving grace may be that while intoxicated drivers often go faster than usual, drivers using cellphones are apt to drive slowly, leading to property damage but not to serious injuries.

Society and Social Interaction

An irony of cellphones is that they allow people to contact others more readily, but also to withdraw from personal contact. Using cellphones while walking, waiting, and even while interacting with others is commonplace, although most of these conversations are probably unimportant. People seemed to get along fine without the cellphone in the thousands of years of human civilization before 1980. There are unique uses for cellphones, such as emergency calls, or relating important information when not near a wired phone. But if those were the only uses for cellphones, industry revenue would be a tiny fraction of its current level. The business of cellular phones depends on frequent chatter and the public is happy to oblige. The usage of communications products generally increases faster than the number of users.

Metcalfe's Law states that the value of a communications system rises with the number of points of contact. The law is named after Robert Metcalfe, a pioneer in the field of computer-to-computer communication, who displayed the genesis of the law in talks around 1980. For a decade this principle went unnamed and largely unnoticed, until the internet boom of the mid–1990's brought it to prominence. The original statement of the law concerns a communication network with N members. The members could be computers, radio transmitter/receivers, telephones, or some other equipment. According to Metcalf's Law, while the cost of the communication network is proportional to N, its value is proportional to N^2, which is the number of pair combinations between the members. When a new member joins, the cost is the fixed price of the equipment alone, but the member gains communication access to all of the other members. The value of the system is therefore not in the equipment, but in the connections, and the value rises at a faster rate than the cost.

While a communications system may be expensive to start, Metcalf's Law predicts that if enough members join, at some point the system will become profitable. The application to the excesses of the internet boom is clear, and the law was sometimes invoked as a justification for heavy investment into companies with little revenue. The internet boom ended as sufficient revenue did not appear and companies collapsed. The biggest loss was internet equipment manufacturer Cisco Systems Inc., which lost 89 percent of its market capitalization from 2000 to 2002, a $580 billion drop. The problem with the simple form of Metcalfe's Law may be that most members of a communication system are only interested in contacting a few other members, so the number of useful connections is much less than N^2. Writers attempting to rehabilitate the law have suggested that the value of the network rises in proportion to $N \times \log(N)$, which has a slower growth rate than a square-rate increase.[37]

Despite the limited economic truth of Metcalfe's Law, it has entered the realm of sociology as a statement that as the number of communications points increases, the communication taking place also increases.[38] Or put another way, the ability to communicate increases the amount of communication that takes place. As people get cellphones, they make more calls, partly to justify the cost, but also because the means are available.

Increased communications may be an annoyance and a luxury in the advanced nations, but in the developing world it offers important benefits. Large segments of the world's population live in areas that do not have wired telephone systems and will probably not have them into the foreseeable future. For them, a wireless phone is the only way to call for emergency services. And business also greatly benefits. Producers of goods can take orders remotely, and buyers can shop remotely for the best deal. The communication of price information leads to the allocation of goods to avoid local shortages and surpluses. Farmers, for example, can take their produce to the market with the highest prices, and fishermen at sea can come back to land when the price of fish is high. The improvement in efficiency can make a noticeable improvement in the economy.

According to current estimates, increasing the wireless penetration in a country by 10 percent causes a growth in the Gross Domestic Product by approximately 0.5 percent. The source is a survey of cellphone use in China published in 2006. Based on direct observation and interviews, the study estimated that a cellphone improves the economic productivity of a worker by an average of 6 percent. A taxi driver, for example, could more efficiently use his time. For the year 2005, while direct economic activity in the wireless industry added $24 billion to China's GDP, the indirect contribution due to the improved efficiency was $84 billion. The study concludes that investment in the wireless industry gives a return three times higher than the outlay.[39]

Never Alone

The analog cellphones of the 1980's to mid–1990's did not encrypt their calls, so the conversations could be heard by anyone in the area with the right equipment. Since the cellphones were FM transmitters, the equipment required was just a radio scanner that could operate in the cellular frequency band. Hobbyists added cellular phone calls to police, fire, aviation, and other audio signals that were freely available for reception. According to *The Monitoring Times*, a magazine in the field, by 1992 there were three million devotees of the scanning hobby, and their conviction was that wireless communication is not private. A court decision in 1992 cleared an Ohio man of charges that he recorded the conversations of city officials with the argument that cellphone callers had no more expectation of privacy than people speaking in public.[40] Intercepting cellular calls was therefore not eavesdropping, but listening to the broadcasts of small, portable radio stations.

Despite high-profile examples of call interception, the sensitive cellphone conversations continued unabated. Recordings of a call in which Virginia governor L. Douglas Wilder belittled Senator Charles S. Robb, a rival in the Democratic Party, reached the public in 1988, to much embarrassment. A 1991 recording of a Spanish Socialist official disparaging the Finance Minister made news in that country. More famously, a retired bank manager and listening enthusiast in Abingdon, England, used an antenna mounted on a 20-foot tall mast in his backyard to record a 23-minute conversation between a man and a woman. Although Buckingham Palace attempted denial at first, the call was between Princess Diana and James Gilbey, a wealthy car-dealership owner. The conversations featured the Princess's complaints about her life, the royal family and her husband, and were made available to the public by the *Sun* newspaper in 1992 on a 95p-per-minute telephone line. Prince Charles joined the fray in 1993 when the British tabloids published transcripts of an intimate 1989 call to Camilla Parker-Bowles. If allowed to talk, people are going to speak freely. Fortunately for the interest of privacy, the second generation of cellphones brought some respite from external listeners.

Digital technology introduced encryption, removing the easy interception by eavesdroppers. In the case of GSM, a third party could still intercept the bits being sent, but would be unable to decipher them without the encryption key. CDMA–based systems add another layer of difficulty, since without the right codes a receiver cannot pick the transmitted bits out of the noise. To be more specific, an eavesdropper on a 2G CDMA cellular system needed a synchronized PN generator and a handset's electronic serial number to find the data bits. The calls are still open to interception, but only with significantly more computational resources than in the 1980's. And the third generation technology has further strengthened the encryption.

A dramatic example of the potential of cellular phones as a locating tool took place on the evening of October 23, 1989 in Boston. At about 8:30 in the evening, Charles Stuart called emergency services saying that a robber had shot both he and his wife in their car.[41] He then lost consciousness, but left the cellular phone active so the call continued. The dispatcher had police cars on the streets turn on their sirens sequentially, and by listening for the loudest sirens heard through the call was able to find the car. Charles Stuart survived, but his wife and their unborn baby did not, and his description of a bearded black man with a raspy voice led to racial tensions in the city. Upon investigation, the story unraveled and Stuart leapt from Tobin Bridge on the fifth of January, soon after his brother admitted to police that he had helped hide the gun and the supposedly stolen jewelry.[42] Although the circumstances were unfortunate, this was also a high-profile demonstration of the usefulness of cellphones for emergency location finding.

Before GPS applications became popular, the FCC's E911 requirement largely drove the locating ability of cellphones. Released in October of 1996, the new rules would take effect in two phases. In Phase One, cellphones sold after March of 1998 must be able to send their phone numbers and cell locations to the public safety system. For Phase II, starting October of 2001 cellphones must be able to provide their position to within 125 meters at least 67 percent of the time. The rules did not specify what the phone would return the other 33 percent of the time, but most cellular phone developers assumed a gradual degradation in accuracy would be adequate.[43] Considering the size of the American cellular phone market, and since other governments were also amenable to location-finding through cellphones, manufacturers around the world began adding this capability. After establishing the goal, developers had to find a way to achieve it.

Cellphones use the signal delay in communicating with base stations to calculate position. Considering that an electromagnetic wave travels at almost exactly 300 meters per microsecond, the propagation time carries distance information. Several base stations, for example, may all simultaneously send a signal. The mobile unit receives the signal and uses the time delay between them to calculate the distance to each base station, and therefore its own position. The process can happen in the other direction as well, with the mobile unit sending a signal and the system calculating the position from the reception delays at the base stations. The second method is usually preferable, since it places the burden of reception and calculation on the base stations and alleviates some of the complexity and price in the mobile unit.

In all cases, the propagation delay must be determined as accurately as possible, which is problematic with small-bandwidth systems. As described in Chapter One, the bandwidth of a system determines the maximum speed of a signal. A low-bandwidth signal is more spread out in time than a high-bandwidth signal. The analog AMPS standard used 30 kHz channels, but considering the 6 kHz spacing, each transmission only had 24 kHz available. The fastest time-domain resolution was therefore 1/24,000 Hz = 42 microseconds, although designers could achieve a resolution of 10 microseconds with more processing.[44] Two signals arriving within 10 microseconds are therefore indistinguishable. Almost all of the multipath copies of the signal, which arrive a few microseconds apart, will register as one indistinguishable mass, leading to uncertainty in position.

The digital systems can find the mobile unit's position more precisely than analog systems due to the higher bandwidth. GSM uses 200 kHz channels, and therefore is capable of finer time resolution of 1/200,000 Hz = 5 microseconds. Even better are the 1.25 MHz channels used by CDMA–based systems which allow for sub-microsecond resolution. The third generation systems use even more bandwidth, further improving the time-domain resolution.

The Global Positioning System would seem to be ideal for this application, but there are difficulties with its use. To determine a location, a GPS receiver must receive the weak signals of at least three satellites. This may not be possible indoors, in a car, when holding the cellphone in certain positions, or in other situations. Even when the handset is outdoors and has an unobstructed view of the sky, the process can take a minute or more. Many cellphones have GPS receivers installed, with the handset filling in moments of lost GPS signal using base station information and its own position calculations based on the last recorded position and velocity.

11

Inside the Cellphone

Despite Herculean efforts to create the best-performing cellphone with the most features, appearance motivates many sales. How a cellphone looks in a display case next to competitors is one of its most important features. Since phones have shrunk to the minimum volume needed to pack in the components, there is not much leeway in phone body design, but there is still room for artfully designed ridges and curves. Some manufacturers create the phone body themselves, while others turn to industrial design companies.

The interesting workings of the cellphone are beneath the surface and encased in the appealing shell. While the cellphone has entered the lives of nearly everyone, the device itself remains mysterious. Previous chapters have elaborated on high-level and general concepts like digital communications and radio waves, but what is actually within the small, plastic shapes that allow them to work?

Creating Integrated Circuits

The heart of the modern cellphone, the parts that perform the functions that define it as a communications device, is a set of *integrated circuits* (IC's, also called chips). As is the case with modern computers, a cellphone consists of several IC's along with the support components needed to carry out functions such as providing power and interfacing with the user.

The importance of the IC is that it puts many components and their interconnections into a small volume and it does so without mechanical placement. The need for this ability became apparent by the late 1960's, as advancements in electronics moved the difficulty in creating large circuits to the physical assembly of the devices. Manufacturers could produce electronic components, such as transistors, in ever-smaller sizes. But how could they be wired together? The components themselves were small, some resembling grains of sand, but someone had to place them onto a circuit board and add the wiring between the leads. The tasks involved were too complicated and precise to automate.

Performed under a magnifying glass, or even a microscope, the assembly process was laborious and error-prone, and an obstacle to creating advanced circuits. The circuits needed to run digital cellphones, containing millions of components, would have been impossible to assemble. The answer came with the realization that the same processes used to create the transistors on the surface of silicon could also add the metal interconnect lines and other components.

Two teams came upon the idea of the IC nearly simultaneously, although from different perspectives.[1] This demonstrates again that most technological development stems from both necessity and the current state of knowledge. Hundreds of researchers in the field were aware of the challenges, knew about the recent advances, and were actively looking for a solution.

The first team, led by Jack Kilby at Texas Instruments, had the idea to make not just transistors, but also other circuit components on a silicon surface. They used regular wires arcing over the chip surface to connect the components for the first prototype devices. The final test chips were not fully planar, but they showed that the idea could work.

The second group, at Fairchild Semiconductor, with Robert Noyce at the lead, placed the emphasis on printed metal lines on the surface to make the connections. Fairchild's application reached the patent office first, leading to the 1961 grant of the patent for the IC. The Texas Instruments invention had come six months earlier than Fairchild's, but years of legal wrangling could not reverse the decision. Most subsequent awards and recognition, such as the National Medal of Science, referred to Kilby and Noyce as co-inventors of the IC. An exception is the Nobel Prize for Physics, which the Nobel committee awarded to Jack Kilby in 2000 since Robert Noyce had died in 1990. From these origins, the production of IC's has developed into an enormous industry.

IC production follows a multi-step process similar to printing, with patterned layers deposited in sequence to build up the components and the connections. The process starts with a thin, less than one millimeter thick, wafer of silicon. Some components, such as transistors, are directly on the silicon surface, so they are created first. The processor places a layer of photosensitive material onto the surface and exposes it to ultraviolet light through a patterned filter. Areas of the material that receive the UV light react to form a second material. Washing the surface with chemicals removes the first type of material while leaving the second, forming a pattern of exposed surface areas. Next is ion implantation, in which ions bombard the entire surface, although they only enter into the exposed areas. A diode, for example, requires two silicon regions with different ionic implants. To simplify the process, the entire chip surface is normally implanted with one type of ion as a default before starting the patterning. Then only one subsequent step of ion implantation overwrites the appropriate regions.

After preparing the silicon surface, creating the metal lines between the components follows similar steps. An applied pattern allows metal deposition into the necessary patterns. Then the processor washes away the pattern and moves to creating the next layer. An IC generally has five to ten layers of interconnect metals, stacked over the surface of the chip and separated by insulating layers. The metal layers themselves are approximately one micrometer thick, so the entire stack of metals and insulators only reaches a height of a fraction of a millimeter above the silicon surface, and the assembly is close to being truly planar. Holes in the insulating layers filled with metal provide the vertical connections between the metal layers and from the lowest layer down to the silicon surface which contains the transistors, diodes and similar components.

The final step in the manufacture of an IC is to encase the delicate layers in a plastic package. Plastic poured around the chip creates the small, flat, black box seen inside electronic devices. The bottom of the package has the metal connections that link the IC to the outside world, which is the Printed Circuit Board on which it lays.

Manufacturing a new chip is expensive, so designers would like to create a working IC on the first try. Typically, the IC comes back to the designer from the manufacturer and testing shows some problems. The designer makes changes, waits for the revised chips and then retests them. The goal of the process, besides making IC's that meet the performance requirements, is to minimize the number of manufacturing iterations. To accomplish this, the designers are dependent on the chip manufacturer's component models.

An IC's design process follows different tracks for the type of circuit, with all methods completely dependent on computer simulation. The starting point is a library of component models. On a computer screen, the designer connects the components together, applies simulated voltages and watches the results. The success of those simulations depends on the exact representation of the components by the models, so those models must be detailed. A transistor in a typical circuit simulation in the 1980's may have been defined by approximately one dozen parameters. Twenty years later a commonly used transistor model contains nearly one hundred parameters. Other circuit components have become equally detailed, although the required level of detail varies with the application.

The design of digital IC's is similar to computer programming. These digital IC's are circuits that process digital information and can therefore contain large numbers of transistors. Laying out millions of components and their interconnects is beyond what a person can efficiently and reliably accomplish, so much of that task is left to automation. The designer specifies the operation of the chip in a format similar to a computer program. For regular computer programming, the program would go to a compiler, which reduces the human-level statements into simple commands and then sends that version of the program to an assembler, which translates those commands into binary machine language. For digital IC design, the final step is to translate the commands into a physical layout of components and interconnects. A good translator produces efficient layouts that use a minimum of area while still meeting the various electrical requirements. Many of the physical aspects of digital chip design are therefore automated, allowing the designer to focus on the algorithms represented by the transistors and other components. Other IC's are not as amenable to automation.

Analog IC design deals with fewer components, but requires fully detailed models and simulations. While digital circuits may contain millions of transistors, circuits such as amplifiers, filters, mixers, and oscillators have a few transistors each. And their design requires exact knowledge of how the circuit responds to the input waveforms. This is where the large component models become necessary. An oscillator, for example, might produce a pure sine wave of one frequency in simulation, with energy in other frequencies a million times smaller. Measuring the physical chip may find that the extraneous frequencies are only one thousand times smaller than the intended wave, which is probably unacceptable. Insufficient component models may be the source of the problem, but there are other parts of the IC that are not as straightforward to describe in simulation.

An area of constant contention is the overall interaction between the components. A model of a transistor, for example, may completely characterize what happens between its terminals, and this model would be complete if the transistor existed in isolation. But there are other transistors nearby, and metal lines carrying signals passing all over the IC surface. Signals can transfer between components through electric or magnetic fields. And, as a semiconductor, the silicon body itself has some conductivity and can carry current. Not including those effects results in an incomplete simulation which may not match the measurements. But accounting for the coupling effects is not yet an exact science, and so the iterative development continues.

The result is an IC that performs all of the required functions under many conditions. Before leaving the simulation stage, the designers test the circuit under different temperature conditions, such as -20 C to 50 C. There are also manufacturing variations to consider since all of the deposited structures could deviate in width, length, thickness or density. With the complexity involved, getting a chip to work perfectly on the first try almost never happens. Measurements of the fabricated chip usually show that it works well for most of its functions, but requires some adjustments. The designers make the changes and send the IC plans back to the fabrication plant to make more chips for testing, hoping that this iteration will be the last. But even a completed IC does not perform its functions in isolation, it needs the support of many other parts.

Printed circuit boards (PCB's) form the backbone of the cellphone's internal parts, since they hold the IC's and other electronic components. The board material is typically a substance similar to fiberglass, with a characteristic greenish tinge. A PCB's surface has metal patterns needed to attach the components, and printed metal lines acting as connections. Most of the connections are on lines in the internal layers, so the surface may appear to contain only the components. Like an IC, the PCB manufacturing process is layer-by-layer, with the fiberglass spacing material alternating with patterned metal layers. Small vertical metal cylinders connect lines on different layers where needed. A PCB could have over a dozen layers, although each layer adds expense, so most cellphone PCB's have four to eight layers. Early cellphones contained several parallel PCB's to accommodate all of the components. As the cellphones have shrunk they may contain only a single PCB, densely populated on both sides with components.

The components around the IC's provide various support functions and usually have some reason not to be integrated. These include the display, speaker, and parts needed to regulate the power given to the IC's. Other components are precise filters that are more exact that what can be achieved on an IC.

One component that has resisted integration is the crystal oscillator, which produces a sine wave at a set frequency to be used as a reference wave for the digital clocks and various high-frequency oscillators. These are made of crystals, usually quartz, that vibrate at a frequency determined by its physical shape. The sine wave from a crystal oscillator is more precise than what an integrated oscillator can produce. The output of a crystal producing a wave with a frequency of 125 MHz, for example, would contain almost no energy at 124.9 MHz or 125.1 MHz. An on-chip oscillator, however, operating at 5 GHz will put a significant amount of energy into waves with frequencies that are over 100 MHz away from the main wave.

The high-frequency on-chip oscillators must work with the lower-frequency crystal oscillators to produce a precise output wave. The example IC oscillator running at 5 GHz produces 40 wave periods for every one wave period created by the 125 MHz crystal oscillator. The start of every fortieth high-frequency wave should therefore closely match the start of the crystal oscillator output. A sub-circuit within the IC compares the two waves and adjusts the 5 GHz oscillator to resynchronize it with the 125 MHz wave. This prevents the output wave from drifting away from an ideal 5 GHz sine wave. The high precision needed for this operation has kept the crystal oscillator from integration into the IC's, and other components also remain individual for the same reason.

The switches in the signal path, called *duplexers*, remain as discrete components due to the requirements they must meet. The sole function of a duplexer is to switch connections between the terminals. A three-terminal duplexer, for example, with incoming line A and output lines B and C switches the connection of A between B and C as specified by a control voltage. The signal passing through may be high-power waves traveling to the antenna, or incoming low-power received waves. In either case, the loss through the duplexer must be low. Furthermore, when the duplexer connects A to B, the leakage into C must be as low as possible. This isolation goal renders the duplexer particularly difficult to integrate into the IC's.

The duplexers perform two tasks in a cellphone. The first is to switch between transmit and receive paths at the antenna. This ensures that the transmitted signal goes to the antenna rather than back into the receive path. Conversely, the duplexer sends the received waves from the antenna into the receive signal path, rather than wasting power by sending it into the transmit path. The other separation is between frequency bands, such as cellular and PCS. The bands have different filters, power amplifiers and other components, requiring duplexers to switch the signals between the paths.

A dual-band cellphone uses both sets of duplexers to perform both functions in turn. One duplexer switches between the transmit and the receive paths for the cellular frequency band, and another does the same for the PCS frequency band. Rather than linking directly to the antenna, the terminals of the two duplexers lead to a band-switching duplexer. The terminal of that duplexer then goes to the antenna. A cellphone therefore contains several duplexers as individual components.

With the integration of radio functions onto IC's, most of a cellphone's workings occur in a small group of chips. Taken together, the IC's form a

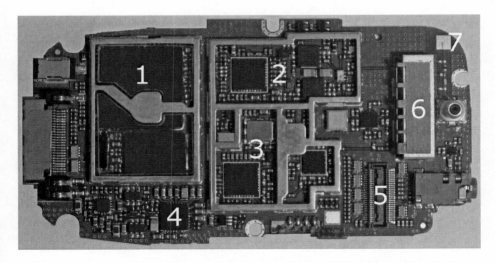

Figure 23: Populated PCB from a cellphone circa 2005: 1. Digital (in enclosure), 2. Transmit and 3. Receive (in separate enclosures), 4. Power control, 5. Connector to the display, 6. Filter, and 7. Antenna contact.

chipset, around which a manufacturer builds the cellphone. The manufacturer purchases the chipset, places them on a PCB with the required supporting components, adds peripheral devices such as a display, keyboard, microphone and speaker, places the assembly into a plastic body and has produced the phone. The industrial flow of creating a cellphone is like the computer industry, with several key similarities. A fundamental parallel is that there is little overlap between the companies that design and produce the IC's, and the companies that manufacture the cellphones.

One of the first tasks for a cellphone designer is to pick a chipset. Several companies offer complete ranges of chipsets, from basic, budget models to expensive, state-of-the-art versions. As is the usual case with technology, the inexpensive chipsets are similar to the expensive chipsets of only a few years previously. The manufacturers often use chipsets from two or more companies in a single assembly to create what they feel is the best overall product.

The IC companies, of course, would like the manufacturers to buy their complete chipset, with the strongest enticement being increased integration. One IC that does the work of two or more IC's saves money and space, even if the single IC is larger and more expensive than one of the IC's it is replacing. The pace of integration is ongoing, but the functions that the cellphone must perform are also expanding.

A cellphone of circa 2000 contained a chipset of approximately five or six main IC's. The largest was the digital chip that performed the processing and

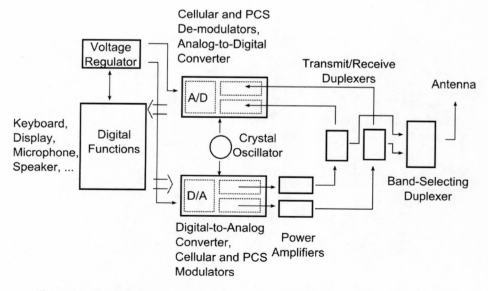

Figure 24: Simplified arrangement of a dual-band cellphone showing the functions of the chipset.

interfaces with the user. A common companion IC is a memory chip for the large files needed to do the processing and run the applications. On the analog side, which was often on the other side of the PCB from the digital, one IC performs modulation and another performs demodulation. A third IC regulates the voltage supplies needed by the other IC's and by the handset components such as the display and speaker. Another IC may perform the initial amplification upon reception before sending the signal to the demodulating chip. This does not include the power amplifiers, which are usually placed individually on separate chips. Also present would be chips that perform filtering and switching.

A few years later a cellphone with a full range of functions may contain the same number of chips, even with the high level of integration. The transmit and the receive circuits are probably combined into one IC, which may also include the separate reception amplifier IC. But then there may be one or more new IC's for Bluetooth, GPS, video downloading and other features. And so the integration may continue indefinitely.

Liquid Crystal Displays

Liquid crystals form the basis of cellphone displays and are therefore worthy of some examination. The name itself seems to be a contradiction: can a material be a liquid and a crystal at the same time? The answer is a qualified affirmative, since liquid crystals flow like liquid, but optically they share some properties with crystals.

Liquid crystals were discovered in the nineteenth century as materials that have two melting points. The first observation of this phenomenon was in 1888, when an Austrian botanist tested a material now known as cholesteryl benzoate. He found that the substance melts at 145 C into an opaque liquid, then changes again into a clear liquid at 179 C. Further testing by others showed that the intermediate state has the optical characteristics of a crystal.[2]

What defines a crystal is the regular arrangement of the constituent atoms. In salt (NaCl), for example, the sodium (Na) and chorine (Cl) atoms are arranged as the corners of a cube, which repeats in all directions throughout the structure. Due to this geometric regularity, an electromagnetic wave passing through the atomic lattice would experience a different structure with different directions of travel. Even when considering one travel direction, the material has a different effect depending on the direction of the electric field within the wave, also known as the wave's polarization direction.

This is in contrast to non-crystal structures, where the atoms do not have a regular arrangement. An electromagnetic wave may experience more density for a few atoms as it travels, and then it may find fewer atoms for a while after that. For a random placement of atoms, the material effects average over the propagation distance to a value that is constant for any direction of travel and polarization. Materials without a regular atomic structure therefore generally appear to have properties that are independent of direction. So in optical terms, the important feature of a crystal is that the atoms are in a fixed and repeating arrangement.

Materials in a liquid crystal state exhibit the optical properties of crystals while remaining liquids. The atoms in a liquid crystal group into molecules, which are usually electrically neutral but in this case there is enough electrical force between the molecules to keep them in a regular arrangement. The intermolecular force is not as strong as in a solid crystal, so an externally applied force can still deform the mass like a liquid. This is an interesting quality but seemed to have no application for several decades.

Liquid crystals remained a scientific oddity until the 1960's, when RCA began research into their use in displays, creating the first LCDs. Researchers found that an applied electric field could re-order the molecules in the liquid crystal and change the optical properties. By switching from an arrangement that allows light to pass to one that reflects light, a liquid crystal could act as a shutter. Without mechanical parts, a liquid crystal based shutter could be useful, although the high temperature needed to enter the liquid crystal state was prohibitive. As is often the case, with a pressing need, progress soon followed. More research found compounds that could achieve a liquid crystal state at room temperature.

The developments led to a press conference at RCA headquarters in May of 1968 to announce that their new LCD technology would be lighter, smaller, and consume less energy than other types of displays. Despite the potential, RCA subsequently dropped the development of LCDs, choosing instead to continue with cathode-ray tube displays, in which the company had large investments. While this decision may appear to lack foresight, it would take three more decades for LCDs to reach their potential and begin to earnestly replace the cathode-ray tube displays. So RCA's decision has justification, but it did allow for others to take over the LCD field and to dominate the market that did eventually emerge.

After RCA, the development of LCDs moved to Japan, where the Sharp Corporation was interested in adding them to their calculators.[3] Sharp had produced the first transistor-based desktop electronic calculator in 1964, weighing a hefty 25 kg. By 1969 the calculator was about 25 times smaller, but Sharp sought to create a truly pocket-sized calculator. That meant finding a new type of display, since the florescent tubes used to form the numbers accounted for much of the size, power-consumption and cost.

Sharp approached RCA about buying LCDs, but RCA had stopped development almost completely, so Sharp set out to create LCDs on its own. This led to two years of research, during which Sharp had to rediscover some of what RCA had found but kept secret, such as the formula for a room-temperature liquid crystal. The result was an essential part of the Elsi Mate EL-805, the first pocket calculator, which weighed only 200 grams and could run for over one hundred hours on a single AA battery. The low-power LCD would remain a staple of consumer electronics after that, until the late 1990's when large, color displays became common.

The common LCD since the 1970's has been based on a twisted nematic liquid crystal structure. Nematic means that the liquid crystal molecules arrange into planes, with the molecules of each plane lined up with each other, but with less influence from one plane to the next. In a twisted nematic display, grooves in the top and bottom glass plates hold the first and last layers at a ninety-degree orientation to each other. The molecules of the intermediate layers arrange to form a gradual transition in direction from the top to bottom.

The effect of the twisted nematic structure is to rotate the polarization of the electric field of an electromagnetic wave that passes through by ninety degrees. The layers accomplish the rotation by absorbing and re-emitting the wave with a slightly different polarization. Assume, for example, that the electric field of an incoming wave is aligned at a few degrees off of the molecular orientation. By definition, the electric field causes charges to move, although they are restricted to travel along the molecules. Since the alignment of the electric field and molecules is not the same, some of the wave's energy will pass through unchanged, but most can transfer into the motion of charges in the molecules. Those moving charges then act as antennas, creating a new electromagnetic field with an electric field pointing in the same direction as the molecules. By repeating this process with many layers, the twisted nematic layers turn the polarization of at least some of the wave passing through by a full ninety degrees.

The rotation of the wave's electric field is interesting, but it becomes useful when combined with crossed polarizers. These polarizers are filters that only allow waves with an electric field pointing in one specified direction to pass, while reflecting other waves or dissipating their energy as heat. One polarizer placed before the first layer has the same orientation of zero degrees. This polarizer acts as a gate that only lets waves pass that are candidates for rotation. The second polarizer is after the last layer and also shares its orientation of ninety degrees. Of the waves that made it past the first polarizer, only those that the nematic layers fully rotated can pass the second polarizer. This establishes a specific process that an electromagnetic wave must follow to transmit through the structure.

An applied electric field can remove the twist from the nematic structure, and therefore stop the transmission of waves through both polarizers. The plates holding the liquid crystal also contain a coating of indium tin oxide, which is a transparent conductor. Placing a voltage on those conductors creates an electric field that overrides the intermolecular electric field that orients the nematic layers. Without the twisted layers, waves that pass one polarizer are not rotated and therefore do not pass the second polarizer. Once the externally applied electric field switches off, the inter-molecular electric fields reorder the liquid crystal layers into the twisted structure and light can once again pass through both polarizers. This process happens quickly and can uses a low-magnitude electric field, so the power drain is minimal. To improve the speed and power savings, LCDs typically use a super-twisted nematic structure, where the layers rotate a wave's electric field by 270 degrees. With the larger rotation, the transmission process is more vulnerable to disruption with a smaller applied electric field. A large factor in the power-saving capability of the LCD is that it does not create its own light.

The common LCD uses light from the surroundings and a backing mirror. When the liquid crystal is in its natural state, light can pass through both polarizers, reflect from the backing mirror, and then pass through the polarizers again to exit the display. Applying the electric field, however, causes incoming light to be trapped between the polarizers, creating a black spot in the display. Looking closely at an LCD, the black letters appear to be floating above the back surface, which they are, since that is where the polarizers stop the light. These displays do not generate their own light, so the power drain is

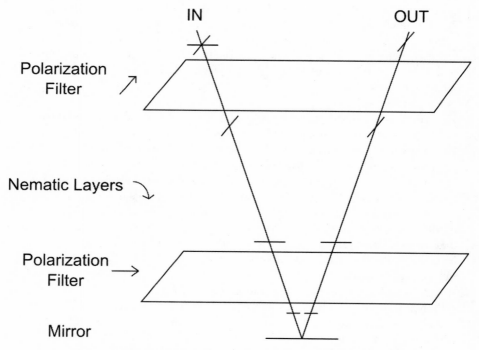

Figure 25: In a Liquid Crystal Display the nematic layers turn the light's polarization so that it can pass both filters (a); an applied electric field disrupts the nematic layers and stops the rotation, so that the filters stop the light (b).

small. The introduction of bright color displays, however, added a light source with the accompanying rise in power consumption.

The displays of cellphones in the 1990's were low resolution by later standards, but also used much less power. Displays had a diagonal measurement of 1.5 to 2 inches, and resolutions of 96 by 65 pixels up to 120 by 160 pixels. These were super-twisted nematic displays that would consume approximately one milliwatt of power. Since the handset used up to several hundred milliwatts to transmit, the display represented only a small portion of the cellphone's power consumption.[4] While these modest displays may have done the job at the time, the increasing capabilities of cellphones demanded better displays, including the ability to show colors.

The primary obstacle to producing color LCDs was countering the distortion caused by the liquid crystal. This problem reduces to recovering white light, since filters could extract any color from the white light. White light passing through a liquid crystal experiences distortion, which is the source of the greenish-grey color that forms the background of standard LCDs. Researchers arrived at a practical solution in the 1980's of placing a film over the LCD that would compensate for the distortion. The first film-compensated super-twisted nematic color LCDs reached the market in the late 1980's.[5] But these were for computer monitors and similar large and expensive applications. The cellphone would have to wait another ten years for color.

Color screens began appearing on cellphones in Asia around the year 2000, and the reticence of the top manufacturers to embrace this feature was an opportunity for companies at the back of the industry to build market share. The perennial king of the cellphone manufacturers, Motorola, had lost its top spot by then to Nokia. The issue had been Motorola's delay in switching from analog to digital phones. In the interim, Nokia saw a 73 percent increase in sales of its GSM–based digital phones between 1997 and 1998. Yet both Motorola and Nokia passed on the color LCD, since it would increase the handset price by about 20 percent. The Asian manufacturers, particularly Samsung, introduced cellphones with color LCDs to the American and European markets in 2002 and they sold well, despite the added cost. Motorola and Nokia reversed their evaluation of color LCDs, but by then it was too late to get products into the stores for the end of 2002. Their color LCD–equipped handsets reached the market in 2003. By then color was no longer a special, premium feature, and prices were dropping.[6]

The Cellphone Battery

Without batteries, portable electronic communications devices, among other inventions, could not exist. Of equal importance, and leading to the same gadget-less world, is the notion that the electrical experimentation and advancements of the eighteenth and nineteenth centuries would have been greatly delayed. At the time there were no city power grids, so any scientist trying to make progress in the field would have had to supply his own electricity and use it immediately. Fortunately, ways to store electrical energy did emerge. The history of the battery begins in the mid–1700's, and follows a circular path so that modern batteries share a defining characteristic with the earliest models.

The first batteries stored electrical charges in two metal pieces separated by glass. First, in 1747, came the Leyden jar, named for the University of Leyden in the Netherlands. This was a glass jar filled with water and coated on the outer surface with metal. A metal wire or thin rod entering the water from the top of the jar was the other metal piece.[7] The two complementary metal elements are *electrodes*, each holding an excess of one type of charge. One metal piece holds the positive charge and the other holds the negative charge.

The electrodes should be close together, so that the attractive electric force holds the charges in place. Since there is a strong force between the two electrodes, there is a high-amplitude electric field there. An electric field contains energy, and it is in the electric field that a battery stores its energy. But if the electrodes touch, they exchange their excess charges, leaving them both electrically neutral.

The early experimenters were not aware of field theory, but they did soon realize that only the electrodes and the glass dividers were necessary, not the entire jar. Batteries then used glass plates, alternating with metals to store the charge. Benjamin Franklin's version had eleven glass plates stacked vertically between electrodes. Since it held electrical charges that would otherwise be fast-moving, he called it a battery, in analogy with ammunition storage.[8]

The next stage of battery development was to use a continuous chemical reaction to generate the excess electrical charges. The chemical battery originated with Allesandro Volta, who built a vertical stack of alternating copper and zinc disks. Separating the metals was cloth soaked in an acidic solution to facilitate the chemical reaction. This eliminated the generator needed to put the charge on the electrodes, but brought the jar back.

A typical early chemical battery would use carbon for both electrodes, with one electrode also coated in zinc, and both immersed in an acid solution. The zinc reacts with the acid and releases electrons, which are the negative charges. Meanwhile, a chemical reaction at the other electrode takes away electrons from the metal and puts them into new molecules in the acid. A wire connecting the two electrodes therefore experiences a current as the excess negative charges in the zinc-coated electrode travel to the other electrode, which has a deficiency of negative charge. The chemical reaction takes place continuously, but loses its power as the acid solution depletes. Once researchers understood the governing principles of the battery, the development became a matter of better packaging and finding the best materials.

The dry-cell battery was ready by 1890 and remained the standard basic design for decades. Gone was the glass jar, and in its place was a zinc cup acting as both the container and an electrode. A paste made by mixing plaster with ammonium chloride replaced the liquid acid. The entire arrangement was sealed into a tight metal container that was both safe and held its charge better than the previous jar-based models. This design continues to the present day, although the materials have changed.

The zinc-carbon batteries had been the most popular, but were displaced by alkaline manganese batteries in the 1960's, which were subsequently joined by nickel cadmium and lithium batteries in the 1970's. The new batteries offered more energy per volume so they could be lighter and smaller. They also featured reversible chemical reactions, which allows for recharging. Another important quality is that these newer batteries maintain a relatively constant voltage as they discharge.

The most recent battery advance is the lithium ion battery, which does not use a chemical reaction at all. Instead, the anode and cathode are both lithium-based materials that exist, at the atomic level, in layers. Between the atomic layers are places to hold electrons, and the electrons can move in and out of those places with no other changes to the atomic structure. Rather than immersion in an acidic chemical, the two electrodes are separated by a plastic film less than 50 micrometers thick. During charging, the applied voltage causes the electrons in one electrode to cross the barrier and enter the other electrode. This creates the excess of positive and negative charge in the two electrodes and the battery is ready for use. Like the Leyden jar, the lithium ion battery stores charge surpluses created by an external electrical source, rather than creating the voltage with a chemical reaction.

By the mid–1990's cellphone battery varieties were of three types. First was the economical and most common variety, nickel cadmium. This battery offered a steady discharge at about 1.5 volts and could be recharged up to 700 times before degrading to 80 percent of capacity. The next type of battery was nickel metal hydride with both positives and negatives in comparison to nickel cadmium. As a benefit, nickel metal hydride batteries had an energy-per-volume ratio about 1.6 times higher than that of nickel cadmium. They would degrade to 80 percent capacity, however, after only 500 recharges.

The last type of battery, and the eventual winner, was the lithium ion battery. First introduced to the market by Sony in 1990, this battery had an energy-per-volume ratio 1.5 times higher than nickel metal hydride and 2.5 times higher than nickel cadmium. It could also withstand 1200 charge cycles before degrading to 80 percent capacity.[9] With these considerable benefits, this type of battery was destined to rise to the top of the market.

The lithium ion battery is the most popular battery for the cellphone industry and will probably continue to be so into the foreseeable future. A typical small cellphone battery weighs 40 grams and contains seven watt-hours of energy, meaning it could provide one watt for seven hours, seven watts for one hour, or any other combination. The maximum average transmission power of a typical 3G cellphone is 0.2 watts, so the battery could supply power for 35 hours of talk time. Obviously, this is not the case, since other parts such as the display and the speaker also consume considerable energy.

The Cellphone Antenna

Of all the components that make up a cellphone, the antenna has the closest association with wireless communication. It is one of the most important parts and one of the least well understood. Adding to the mystery, many of the cellphones of the second generation, and most of the third generation and beyond, have no visible antenna. Although they may be invisible, every radio transmitter and receiver requires an antenna.

Within the plastic bodies of the handsets may be more than one antenna. And to be more precise, the metal of the entire cellphone acts as part of its antennas. The first aspect to explore is therefore what defines an antenna.

Fields exist around any conductor with a current passing through it, and under the right conditions those fields propagate outward as radiation. While a Direct Current, which stays constant in direction and magnitude with time, has a magnetic field around it, surrounding an Alternating Current is both an electric and a magnetic field. These are *near-fields* which drop in amplitude quickly with distance. The majority of the field strength in the near-fields decreases with distance, d, as $1/d^2$. Since the power in an electric or magnetic field is proportional to the square of the field magnitude, the power decreases as $1/d^4$. At this point, the electric and magnetic fields are independent of each other, so the common term EMF stands for Electric and Magnetic Fields. But there is another component to the fields around a cellphone.

Some portion of the fields decouple from the source and travel outward as an independent entity. These are the *far-fields*, which decrease at a rate of $1/d$, and their power decreases as $1/d^2$. In this case EMF is an electro-magnetic field, since the propagating fields consist of an electric field and a magnetic field that support each other as they travel.*

All conductors are antennas to some extent, transforming some of the power that enters as electrical current into radiating electromagnetic waves. An efficient antenna transforms most of the input power into radiating waves, or conversely transforms most of the incoming waves into output power. The goal of antenna design is not only to create an antenna, but to create an efficient antenna.

The geometry of a conductor is what determines if it will be an efficient antenna. As a general rule, the size of an antenna should be half of the wavelength of the transmitted wave. At this length, the antenna is in *resonance*,

---

Yet another common usage of EMF in the technical literature is electro-motive force, which is equivalent to voltage.

meaning that the currents reflecting back and forth between the ends of the antenna add constructively. At off-resonance frequencies, the currents in the antenna add destructively and nearly vanish. From the perspective of the transmission line feeding the antenna, the antenna reflects off-resonance frequency waves back out the feed line, while waves at the resonant frequency enter the antenna and do not come back, since they leave as radiation.

Most radio waves used for cellphones have frequencies of approximately one or two gigahertz, which correspond to wavelengths of thirty and fifteen centimeters, respectively. The length may not be obvious from the antenna's appearance. The large curved structure of a dish antenna, for example, is actually a reflector, with the resonating element a small antenna at the center. The short, stubby antennas used on many cellphones, as another example, contain a length of wire wound into a helix to save space. The size of the antenna determines if it is a good transmitter, and the same applies to its use as a receiver.

An antenna receives as well as it transmits, due to reciprocity between the currents on the antenna and the radiating fields. Each set of electrical currents on a surface corresponds to a set of far-field electromagnetic waves, with either one creating the other. When transmitting, a distribution of currents on the antenna leads to a far-field distribution of outward-traveling waves. Conversely, if a set of incoming waves form the same far-field distribution, then the currents on the antenna will match the first case. But there is a slight caveat to comparing the transmitting and the receiving properties of an antenna.

The reciprocity applies to currents and fields at a single frequency. In the case of cellphones, as with many two-way communication systems, transmission and reception are at different frequencies, so the antenna performance is not identical for both cases. A PCS handset, for example, receives waves with frequencies in the range of 1850 to 1910 MHz and transmits waves with frequencies of 1930 to 1990 MHz. A common design strategy is to set the antenna size so that it resonates at the center frequency, 1920 MHz, and then to design the antenna and some circuit elements so that the performance is still acceptable at the band edges of 1850 and 1990 MHz. This meets the efficiency requirements, but there is another important antenna property to consider.

Antennas increase the signal-to-noise ratio for both transmission and reception as if they were providing amplification, which is a property called *antenna gain*. Like processing gain and encoding gain, described in Chapter Six, the antenna gain is not real gain, which comes from adding power with an amplifier. Antenna gain is instead a relative measure of antenna effects that improve a wireless link as if an amplifier had been added to a reference device.

The antenna gain is in comparison to an isotropic radiator, and originates in *directivity*. An isotropic radiator is a fictional antenna that broadcasts power evenly in all directions. An isotropic antenna spreads its power over the surface of an imaginary sphere, and that sphere then expands as the waves radiate outward. Since the area of a sphere is $4\pi r^2$, with r being the radius, if an isotropic antenna radiates P watts, then the power density at distance d is $P/4\pi d^2$ in units of watts/m^2. The power density continues to decrease with distance from the antenna as $1/d^2$. This is the no-gain case which serves as a baseline for evaluating other antennas.

A non-isotropic antenna increases the radiated power density, but only in some directions. An antenna that only radiates into one hemisphere, for example, would produce radiated waves that spread the power over a surface of area $P/(0.5 \times 4\pi r^2)$. The power density at a distance of d is then $P/2\pi r^2$, or twice that of an isotropic antenna. A receiving antenna located in that hemisphere would receive twice the power, as if the transmitting antenna were isotropic and using an amplifier. But if the receiving antenna were located in the other hemisphere it would find almost no power. Dish antennas used for satellite communications, for example, can have gains of over one thousand but they must be aimed carefully or the transmitted power will miss the satellite.

Directivity also provides gain during reception by screening out noise coming from other directions. An isotropic antenna converts incoming waves from all directions into currents of equal magnitude. A non-isotropic antenna, by contrast, converts incoming fields from some directions more efficiently into currents than fields coming from other directions. Returning to the example of a high-gain dish antenna, only waves originating from the exact direction of the satellite convert into currents. Waves at the same frequency but coming from other directions are effectively filtered out, lowering the received noise and raising the signal-to-noise ratio.

While antenna gain derives from directivity, the two concepts are not equivalent due to the power losses in the antenna. Returning to the previous example, assume the transmitting antenna with a directivity of two also loses one quarter of the input power to heating and reflection. Then one watt of input power becomes $3/4$ watts transmitted. With the directivity concentrating the broadcast into one direction, a receiving antenna would encounter the same power density as transmitted from a loss-less isotropic antenna with an input of $2 \times 3/4$ watts = 1.5 watts. So while the directivity is still two, the antenna gain is 1.5.

One of the most common and useful types of antenna is the dipole antenna. Appearing as a simple metal rod, the dipole antenna is made up of two arms, each with a length of one quarter of the wavelength of the waves it transmits and receives, so the total length is one half of a wavelength. The connection to the circuit is at the center of the antenna, between the two arms. For transmission, two currents of equal magnitude but opposite direction enter the antenna, leading to one current direction flowing through the dipole. Incoming radio waves cause a current to flow in the antenna, which also leads to two oppositely-directed currents leaving through the feed lines.

The dipole antenna broadcasts fields to the horizon around it, with little power going out the direction of the ends. The directivity of a dipole is 1.6, meaning that an antenna placed in the direction of maximum field strength would receive 1.6 times more power than from an isotropic transmitting antenna with the same input power. Conversely, if the distant antenna was transmitting and the dipole was receiving, the signal emerging from the dipole would be 1.6 time stronger than for an isotropic receiving antenna. Considering the losses associated with a real device, the antenna gain of most cellphone dipole antennas is approximately one. This means that the boost in received power created by directivity brings the signal level up to that originating in an ideal, and therefore loss-less, isotropic antenna.

The origin of the directivity may be evident by considering the apparent magnitude of the currents from the perspective of the receiver. For a vertical dipole antenna, a receiver on the horizon sees the currents traveling up and down the full height. A receiver directly over the antenna, however, would only see a constant dot of current. The first receiver would therefore expect the full power of the transmitted waves, while the second receiver would expect none. Receivers at angles between the two would detect intermediate power levels.

Among receivers restricted to the horizon, a dipole antenna appears the same, and is therefore *omnidirectional*. Unlike an isotropic antenna, the vertical dipole antenna sends no power upwards or downwards. For broadcasting, this pattern of radiation is ideal. A central tower can broadcast to the surrounding receivers without specific information about their locations other than that they are located on the horizon. And the system does not waste power by broadcasting upward into the sky.

In a cellphone, the antenna that comes out the top is one arm of a dipole, with the phone body forming the other arm. This is true both for a long, whip-

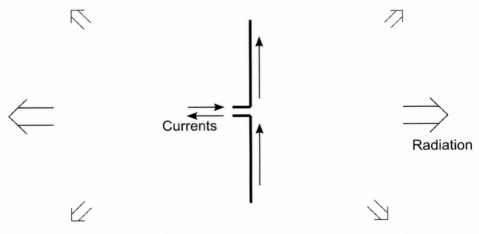

Figure 26: The radiation from a dipole is directed to the horizon and decreases in amplitude with the angle of deviation.

type antenna and for a short stubby antenna. In the case of the stubby antenna, the helix is still a dipole, but is wound to save space and covered with a plastic cap. The phone body, or more specifically, the PCB within the phone, is the other half of the dipole and therefore carries a significant amount of current. While effective, this type of antenna that protrudes from the cellphone body became less common with the advance of cellular phone systems.

As cellular phone systems expand and as the number of cells and base stations increase, users are typically not far from a base station. The antenna performance is then not critical, allowing for smaller antennas placed within the phone body. These internal antennas are typically modules that plug into the phone board, and there may be more than one. Many phones use two antennas placed at different locations in the phone so that if one antenna is experiencing a fade, the other one might be receiving a strong signal. Others use separate antennas to service different frequencies, such as GPS or video downloads.

The lack of an external antenna is good for marketing, but degrades the ability of the cellphone to make calls to some extent. Internal antennas are particularly sensitive to hand placement, since the user's hand can not only block the antenna completely, but also change its electrical characteristics leading to lower efficiency and wasted power. For an environment with a strong signal level, the poorer antenna performance is usually not a problem for voice calls and some data downloads.

The inner workings of the cellphone are evolving to include more features, even as the level of integration increases. Cost is the main factor in handset design, with size important because of its effect on cost. The expectations of the consumer are also relevant, since tolerance for large, brick-style handsets has disappeared. Whatever manufacturers may add to the cellphone, it will remain easily portable. And the features and capabilities are rapidly expanding and multiplying.

12

Cellphones Beyond Phones

The rapid growth in the popularity of cellular phone systems eventually overtook the capabilities of the second generation technology. By the year 2000, urban areas in the developed world were sometimes reaching their capacity limits. The government regulator of communications in the Philippines ordered Global Telecom, a GSM operator, not to add any more subscribers until they upgraded their system. And users in the Tokyo area were experiencing outages in i-mode service.[1]

As usually happens with technology, by the time engineers achieve a goal, a new and more challenging objective is already demanding attention. The 9.6 kbps rate that was adequate for voice transmission is too slow for download-ing music, pictures or video. While transmitting conversations with adequate capacity had been largely accomplished, the systems still needed significant upgrades for the new applications. And the new applications kept advancing.

An economic principle states that supply creates its own demand. When Jean Baptiste Say published this law in 1829 he was writing about aggregate markets, but it also applies in some cases to specific products. Before the cell-phone, most people did not realize they needed to be able to place calls at any time and at any place. Once the cellphones were common and affordable, they became a necessity. The same is true for features like the built-in camera, musi-cal ringtones and email access. Once capabilities are available, people often use and grow accustomed to them.

The trend of development has the phone portion of the cellphone dimin-ishing in relative size and importance as other features gained prominence. Transmitting and receiving voice was the goal of 1980's cellular systems, and increased capacity was the challenge in the 1990's. The industry met those requirements, so by the early 2000's consumers expected good voice quality and broad coverage as a matter of course. The new advancements moved to mul-timedia features such as pictures, music and downloadable television and movies. In many cases, the cellphone has merged with the personal digital assistant, to become a pocket-sized link to the electronic world.

Faced with increasing demand for new features, the International Telecommunications Union set up a committee in June of 1997 to define the goals of the third generation (3G).[2] The first requirement was that there be no degradation in voice quality, meaning that the phone should still operate as such. Then came the data rate requirements of 384 kbps for a slow-moving user and 144 kbps for a user traveling at automotive speeds. There might be more bandwidth in country-by-country frequency allocations for cellular phone use, but for the most part any new cellular phone systems would have to operate within the existing frequency limits. This means that third generation technology must use bandwidth more efficiently than second generation technology did.

Efficient Spectrum Use Through Flexibility

While the transition from first generation to second generation involved a complete revision of the technology while the applications remained mostly the same, the move from the second generation to the third generation reversed those trends. The second generation phones performed the same functions as first generation phones, sending and receiving conversations, but with improved voice quality, higher capacity, fewer dropped calls and common standards across borders. To accomplish this, the basis of the systems fundamentally changed from analog to digital. By contrast, applications for the third generation are more demanding than those of the second generation, while the basis of the technology is similar. The difference is in how the newer standards build and improve upon the previous technology.

One of the technical limitations of the second generation standards was their fixed parameters. Frequency and time slots, power levels, data rates and other parameters were unchanging. The system could update some parameters, but the environment and demands of data transfer change at the millisecond scale, and at that scale everything was predetermined and unmovable. This usually leads to situations where some users do not have enough bandwidth while others have too much. Given the technology available in the 1990's, there was little that could be done. Designers would create a cellular phone system to perform well in the most demanding cases, and for lighter cases the system would overperform.

With advances in the technology, those constraints are disappearing and designers can approach the cellular system from a broader level. The general wireless communication problem is that several users, all with different data rate demands and with varying link quality, would like to use the same block of frequencies. At approximately each millisecond, the system controller decides how to allocate the available resources to optimize communication. The controller could assign to each user a power level, bandwidth, data rate, and even a modulation scheme as the need arose, and then revise the assignments a few milliseconds later as the situation changes. By optimizing the assignments on a fast time scale, the system efficiency stays high, without idle and therefore wasted bandwidth.

The published data rates of post–second generation standards are impressive, but the numbers require some interpretation due to the flexibility involved. The high data rates often assume optimal conditions, such as a few users who can use all the available bandwidth and have an excellent connection to the base station. In practice, these systems must deal with the unknowns of demand and environment. There are limitations on the equipment and on the system's algorithms for optimizing the used bandwidth, so the typical data rates in practice can be significantly lower than the advertised rates.

The United Nations, through the International Telecommunications Union (ITU), began to guide the development of the next generation of cellphones, and wireless personal communications in general, in the mid–1990's. While the United Nations may have limited power over vague issues like creating peace and ending poverty, it can provide a valuable service to international communications standards. The ITU does not write the standards, but acts as a forum where government regulatory agencies can vote on which standards to admit into usage. Originally burdened with the name Future Public Land Mobile Telephone System, in 1995 the developing guidelines took the easier appellation of International Mobile Telecommunication 2000 (IMT-2000). Not a single standard, IMT-2000 is a group of standards covering cellular phones and fixed cordless phones.

When the ITU met in June of 1998 to set the direction of third generation development work, ten potential standards emerged, one of which was for cordless phones. Of the nine cellular phone standards, one called UWC-136 was a TDMA–based standard that would build on the GSM and D-AMPS standards. All of the other eight standards used CDMA in some capacity to manage the link between the mobile unit and the base station.[3] As had happened with the second generation standards, two groups emerged as the leading contenders for the world's markets.

A European third generation standard emerged after some struggles between competing factions made up of different companies and even divisions within companies. The cellphone developers at Nokia supported a CDMA–based system due to its many advantages, but the network developers supported GSM because of their extensive experience. The compromise reached was that the wireless part of the system, between the base station and the mobile unit, would use CDMA, while the infrastructure at the base station and further into the system would be similar to GSM. Ericsson had similar ideas and partnered with Nokia to support this strategy. NTT was for taking GSM completely out of the new standard, but joined the coalition in order to present a united front. One month after Nokia, Ericsson and NTT announced their joint effort, Siemens, Alcatel and Nortel presented their own 3G proposal. To decide the matter, the European Telecommunications Standards Institute held a vote in January of 1998, with the Nokia/Ericsson proposal receiving 61 percent of the vote. The rules required a 71 percent vote, so there was no clear winner. Negotiations produced a single standard with elements from both of the proposals.[4]

The third generation standard that serves as the successor to GSM is the Universal Mobile Telephone Standard (UMTS*). Another name that occasionally appears in technical contexts is WCDMA, referring to Wideband–CDMA. WCDMA gets its name by using channels of five megahertz each, which is significantly more than 2G CDMA's 1.25 MHz channel size. While 2G CDMA used a chip rate of 1.2288 Mcps, UMTS has a constant chip rate of 3.83 Mcps. The flexibility is in the number of chips that replace a data bit. In 2G CDMA, one bit became 64 chips, while UMTS allows the system controller to vary the ratio as need and conditions dictate.

On the American side, 2G CDMA grew into the Third Generation standard called CDMA2000. Since the 2G version was already using CDMA, the 3G version is similar but improved. For operation in low-demand situations, CDMA2000 reverts to 2G CDMA operation with 1.25 MHz frequency channels. But the new standard also offers the user a peak data rate of 3.1 Mbps on the forward link (base to mobile) and 1.8 Mbps for the reverse link (mobile to base), although average data rates are approximately one third of the peak. This is where the added flexibility of the third generation becomes useful, as the system can allocate more resources, such as bandwidth and power, to mobiles operating near the peak rate.

In CDMA2000, the system controller can adjust the data transmission rate in 20 millisecond increments as conditions allow. These adjustments include added abilities to use the available bandwidth more efficiently. At the highest end of data transfer, a mobile unit can use three 1.25 MHz channels to create a 3.75 MHz channel, and the chip rate rises from 1.2288 Mcps to 3.6864 Mcps.[5] The system can change the user's data rate and change the number of chips that represent one data bit.

By 2001, cellular phone networks were approaching or at their capacity limits and represented enormous investments by the service providers. GSM and 2G CDMA had 350 million and 110 million subscribers, D-AMPS and PDC had a combined total of 90 million subscribers, and first generation analog systems still had 110 million users.[6] Service providers were not in a position to discard their systems and launch a third generation network in one step.

While second generation systems had their limitations, their most important feature was that they worked. The burgeoning popularity of cellphones

---

*UMTS is not to be confused with IMTS (Improved Mobile Telephone Service), the successor to MTS introduced in the 1960's for pre-cellular car phones.

made voice traffic into veritable money fountains. Non-voice data transfer was slow, but the demand represented a small part of the business. Some urban areas had reached capacity, but there were other remedies besides completely replacing the technology, such as adding more cells. The industry therefore provided a more gradual, and palatable, way to introduce third generation technology to existing systems.

A series of add-ons to second generation systems that allowed them to continue operating as before while adding new features formed the bridge to the third generation. A system could devote a small part of its spectrum to these additions, for high-speed data transfer, and the rest of the spectrum would still carry the voice calls on the second generation system. This mixed system is the 2.5G since it is a transitional stage. The path that 2.5G offers is different for the various second generation starting points.

The first GSM extension was *high-speed circuit-switched data*, which added no cost to the base stations, since the advances were in the software, but did require the user to buy a new handset. This system used improved channel encoding techniques to increase GSM's data rate from 9.6 kbps to 14.4 kbps. Also, while GSM restricted each user to one time slot of the eight slots in a frame, this standard allowed a user to take up to four consecutive time slots, yielding a data rate of 57.6 kbps, although only a maximum of two users could operate in a frequency channel in this mode.[7] This extension to GSM was simple to implement, and the improvement was minimal.

The next step in the transition was *general packet radio service* (GPRS), which began to significantly change the basis of GSM. The circuit-switched methods assign each mobile unit a designated communication channel, which can be a frequency band or time slot, to use as it sees fit. The packet-switched methods, by contrast, follow an internet-style of digital communications in which the users send groups of bits, the packets, through a common channel. The GPRS system uses whatever spectrum was left over from the GSM voice channels as the common channel to transmit packets, with the base station dynamically allocating the GPRS spectrum as the GSM usage changes. The maximum download rate, under ideal circumstances, is 171.2 kbps.[8] While originally meant for GSM, GPRS is also compatible with D-AMPS and PDC.

After GPRS came Enhanced Data Rates for GSM Evolution (EDGE), which was an advanced form of GSM, rather than an external add-on. Perhaps inevitably, different versions of EDGE competed for acceptance. The first EDGE, later called EDGE Classic, began as a proposal to the European Telecommunications Standards Institute in 1997, and was ready for use in 1999. Then a group called the Universal Wireless Communications Consortium published a version in March of 2000 called EDGE Compact. As the name implies, EDGE Compact would use 600 MHz wide channels rather than the 2.4 MHz channels of EDGE Classic. In return, EDGE Compact required adding complexity to control the power and timing more closely. EDGE Classic won when the European Telecommunications Standards Institute picked it over the more complicated alternative in January of 2001.[9]

The EDGE standard is still a TDMA–based system that is in most respects identical to GSM, but achieves a higher data rate through advancing some details. Like GSM, EDGE uses eight time slots of 0.577 milliseconds to send 148 symbols, of which 116 are data. Rather than GSM's four-level modulation scheme that communicates two bits for each symbol, EDGE uses eight-level phase shift-keying for modulation, so each symbol represents three bits. In addition, EDGE allows a user to take up to all eight time slots, although then there could be only one user in the frequency channel. GSM offers a raw bitrate of 270 kbps, which EDGE increases to a maximum ideal download speed of 547.2 kbps, although in practice the maximum is about 384 kbps. As with power, the system keeps each mobile unit's bandwidth at the lowest possible level. A download starts at the highest possible coding rate, and then the system lowers the parameters incrementally until the bit error rate reaches an unacceptable level, and then goes back one level.

While GSM needed a complete revision to create UMTS, 2G CDMA already had most of the technology needed for third generation operation in place. As mentioned earlier, the differences come down to added flexibility at the millisecond scale, so that the system could better use the available spectrum in a continuously changing environment.

A modification of the existing standard served as the transitional stage for 2G CDMA. The common designation is IS-95B, since 2G CDMA had the serial number IS-95. Recall that in 2G CDMA, the base station transmits to many users over the same frequency band, but using a different Walsh code for each user. The mobile unit then applies its assigned Walsh code to extract its message. With IS-95B, the system can assign up to eight different Walsh codes to a user. These eight Walsh codes act as eight parallel communication channels, so the maximum bitrate becomes 8 channels × 14.4 kbps/channel = 115.2 kbps. Due to limitations in installed systems the actual maximum bitrate was 64 kbps.[10]

The first incarnation of a third generation standard in this flow was CDMA2000 1×, offering twice the voice capacity of 2G CDMA and a higher data rate. The listed maximum rate was 307 kbps, but typical systems achieved rates up to approximately 144 kbps. Each user in this system was still taking only one 1.25 MHz channel, but the allocation was more efficient due to the added ability of the system to optimize the settings quickly. As an added benefit of this efficiency, the time between battery charges significantly increased, reaching a factor of two in standby mode.

An extension appeared under the name CDMA2000 1×EV-DO with added capabilities for data transfer. The "EV" represents "Evolution," and the "DO" could either mean "Data Only" or "Data Optimized." As the name implies, an EV-DO system is an add-on to an existing CDMA–based system, and is primarily intended for data transfer. In ideal conditions, data rates of up to 2.4 Mbps are possible, although in typical usage the maximum is several hundred kilobits-per-second.

An associated standard that includes regular calls is CDMA2000 1×EV-DV, with "DV" meaning data and voice. A system using this standard offers twice the capacity for voice calls as IS-95B, and data transfer up to 144 kbps. Unanswered is whether a 1×EV-DV system is better than an IS-95B system with some spectrum set aside for a tandem 1×EV-DO system. That is something each service provider evaluates individually.

The ultimate landing place that a CDMA–based evolution to third generation technology progresses toward is CDMA2000 3×. The significant development here is the addition of wide-band CDMA. Under this standard, a single user can simultaneously communicate through three of the 1.25 MHz channels. The channels could be scattered throughout the band, or they can be adjacent and form one 3.75 MHz channel. With this mode, CDMA200 3× is comparable in its capabilities to UMTS.

The 3G Spectrum Auctions

With the increasing awareness of the importance of cellphones, or as they were becoming, personal wireless devices, governments that had spent decades insisting no spectrum was available began to allocate more frequency bands. With some local variation, most countries found approximately 100 MHz, split into 50 MHz for the forward link and 50 MHz for the reverse link, at around 2 GHz. Governments by then were universally accepting the auction method of distribution, although with varying results.

Lack of competition was the main obstacle that the auction organizers had to overcome. The size of the new spectrum allocations generally equaled that of the existing cellular phone spectrum in each country. And with the number of new licenses matching the existing licenses, the established service providers had a clear advantage. The current licensees could each take one new license, leaving nothing for new entrants. In many cases, this is exactly what happened.

The first European 3G auction occurred in early 2000 in the United Kingdom and was a clear success. At the time, the UK had four established licenses, and put five new licenses up for auction. That four of the licenses would go to the existing providers was a given, but the presence of an extra license was the opportunity that attracted nine more bidders. The auction also benefited from its timing during the high of communication funding. The result was a total sale price of 39 billion Euros, or 650 Euros for each occupant of the UK. This was the first auction and would also serve as the high-water mark.

The next auction, in the Netherlands, was not as competitive and therefore not as successful. There were five new licenses but also five existing operators. One new company, Versatel, participated but left after receiving a legal notice from one of the other bidders, Telfort. According to Telfort, Versatel had no real chance of winning and was only in the auction to bid up the price. Therefore, Telfort would hold Versatel liable for what it considered damages if it continued to bid. The Dutch government allowed this reasoning, perhaps fearful that without Telfort the auction would collapse. In the end, the auction raised 5.9 billion guilders, much less than the expected 21 billion guilders, and equivalent to only 170 Euros per population. This auction was the start of a downward trend.

The Italian auction started with high hopes from the government that the process would raise 25 billion Euros, but soon fell apart. Three days after the auction began in late 2001, with six bidders trying for five licenses, one of the bidders, Blu, dropped out. The final revenue from the auction was 12.2 billion Euros. The Italian government tried to go after British Telecom, which owned 21 percent of Blu, in court for spoiling the auction, but the suit did not last.

As the listing of results in Table 11-1 shows, the revenue generated decreased significantly with time. The first auctions had the benefit of taking place near the height of the technology bubble, when money poured into communications projects. With the bust of 2001, the money dried up. The predictions for the Swiss auction for example, began at 1,000 Euros per capita soon after the UK's successful auction. By the start of the auction, this expectation had been cut in half, and the final result was a modest 20 Euros per capita.[11] As with the Internet, while ambitious plans were still in place, the overheated expectations had given way to more realistic revenue projections. Service providers found that they could continue to meet most of the current demand with second generation systems, further reducing the motivation to expend large resources for a conversion to third generation technology.

TABLE 11-1: RESULTS OF EUROPEAN UMTS (3G)
AUCTIONS OF 2000–2001, IN CHRONOLOGICAL ORDER.[11]

Country	Revenue in Euros per Capita
United Kingdom	650
Netherlands	170
Germany	615
Italy	240
Austria	100
Switzerland	20
Belgium	45
Denmark	95
Greece	45

More Radios in the Handset

As development of the cellphone continued, handsets that were more multifaceted wireless communication platforms rather than telephones became common. Cellphones already had multiple transmitters and receivers by the late 1990's to operate in the different frequency bands. An American cellphone, for example, could operate in the original cellular band at 824 to 894 MHz or in the PCS band of 1850 to 1990 MHz. While the circuits for operation in the different frequency bands may exist on the same chip, they are independent radios.

As has happened before, while engineers master the art of integrating these radios into the same handset, more features become essential. A user may want to simultaneously make a cellular call, use a Bluetooth-based headset, be downloading data such as music or video, and be transmitting music to a nearby FM stereo system. The number of wireless links could be large. Two of the popular wireless features requiring separate radios are GPS and Bluetooth.

Development of Navstar GPS began in the 1970's as a replacement for earlier, more primitive systems. The Transit and the Cicada systems, belonging to the USA and the USSR, respectively, followed the same principles of operation. A user would first have to wait for one of the few orbiting satellites to appear over the horizon, which could take as long as two hours. For the few minutes that a satellite was overhead, the unit would receive the satellite's transmitted position and velocity information and could calculate its own position. The obvious drawback was the limited availability of the satellites, as well as the limited precision when using a single beacon to determine position. The receiver had to already have information, such as its own velocity, to reach a conclusion. As such, the system was useful mainly as a broad check against other navigational methods for ocean-going vessels.[12]

The two countries set about replacing these systems with the more advanced GPS and GLONASS systems. The first GPS satellite launch was in 1978, and the first of the GLONASS satellites entered orbit in 1982. Both systems reached operational status in the mid–1990's, although GLONASS fell into disrepair with the dissolution of the Soviet Union. No one had the resources to replace decaying satellites and the system became unusable around the turn of the century. Other systems are under development, but for the first decade of the twenty-first century, GPS has had no competition in satellite positioning and it has performed well, with an operating method that significantly improved on its predecessors.

GPS overcomes vague positioning information by using multiple satellite signals for each position calculation. The satellites orbit the earth in one of six paths, with four satellites spaced along each path, giving a total of 24 satellites. Their purpose is to continuously broadcast their on-board time and position. The satellite orbits are approximately 20,000 km away from the earth, and recalling that radio waves travel at about 0.3 kilometers per microsecond, there will be a resolvable time delay between transmit and receive, and between the received signals from different satellites. If the received signal from a satellite shows a 70 millisecond delay, for example, then the receiver can calculate that the satellite is 70,000 microseconds × 0.3 km/microsecond = 21,000 km away.

Obtaining this information from multiple satellites enables the receiver to calculate a position.

The number of satellites from which the receiver can detect a wave is vital
to the location-finding calculations. With three satellites, the receiver can tri-
angulate its position in three dimensions. With the information from four satellites the receiver does not even need the exact current time, but can use the
relative delays from the satellites to construct the current position. Alternatively,
if the receiver has an exact elevation map, thereby removing one of the three
dimensions, then three satellites are enough to calculate position without the
exact time. As circuit manufacturing technology improved and designers could
place more functionality into a small space, the GPS receiver came to be found
with the cellphone.

From the perspective of the cellphone, GPS is another low-power signal
to pick out of the noise. While a received signal from a cellular base station
may be as low as 10 femtowatts (10×10^{-15} watts) the GPS signal is generally 0.1
fW. The received GPS power is well below the baseline noise floor that radio
engineers assume for a receiver operating at room temperature.*

To extract a usable signal from the noise, the GPS system uses the processing gain deriving from spread-spectrum communications. GPS is CDMA–
based, with all the satellites using the same frequency band but with different
assigned codes. Cellular phone systems use 1.2288 Mcps to transmit 16 kbps,
meaning that 64 chips represent one bit. That redundancy is the processing
gain, equivalent to placing an amplifier in the communication link with an
amplification of sixty-four. GPS tops these numbers by using a chip rate of 1.023
Mcps to transmit only 50 bps, yielding a processing gain of over 20,000. Even
with this processing gain, however, the signal is not by any means strong.

The first challenge in placing a GPS receiver within a handset is the
antenna, which only efficiently receives power at its resonant frequency band.
An antenna may work efficiently in the PCS band, for example, of 1850 to 1990
MHz. At other frequencies the antenna acts as a filter that prevents waves from
entering the receiver. So the GPS signal, which is at 1575 MHz, would attenuate by a factor of one hundred to one thousand in passing through the antenna.
Some antenna designs reduce that attenuation at the price of sacrificing a little performance in the cellular phone band. Other phone designs add another
metalized area within the phone body to act as a separate GPS antenna. But
once the signal makes it past the antenna it is still weak and vulnerable to interference.

The second problem to overcome is demodulating the signal in the close
presence of other signals. The economics of cellphone design dictate that the

*In logarithmic scale, the minimum received power for a cellular phone is approximately
-140 dBW = 10^{-14} watts and a typical GPS received power is -160 dBW. The noise floor at room
temperature for a bandwidth of 1 MHz is -144 dBW.

GPS demodulation take place on the same crowded chip used to both modulate signals for transmission and demodulate incoming signals. The GPS signal path through the chip may be only a millimeter away from other signals following their own path, leading to interference. One solution is to turn off the other signals, take a GPS reading, and then turn the signals back on. But this has drawbacks to both the GPS information and the cellphone's data transmission, so chip designers are left trying to integrate the GPS circuit while keeping interference at a minimum.

The Bluetooth standard emerged in the late 1990's, gaining immediate industry acceptance.[13] Teams within a company working on a project frequently assign it a colorful name for internal reference, while marketing comes up with the product name shown to the world. Bluetooth, named after a tenth century Danish King, was a project at Ericsson to create a new wireless standard for interconnecting devices, and the nickname endeared enough to become official. Recognizing the potential of the new technology, Nokia, Toshiba, IBM and Intel joined with Ericsson in 1998 to create the Bluetooth Special Industry Group, which oversees Bluetooth development. Besides offering a useable technology that met a need, the Group offered the further enticement of free licensing. Membership in the group quickly swelled to thousands of companies, and the number of Bluetooth devices produced has easily surpassed one billion. The hundreds of millions of cellphones including Bluetooth have made up a significant piece of that number.

The first chore in establishing a new radio service is to find spectrum, and Bluetooth got around this issue by using the only free spectrum available. The American FCC set aside several small frequency bands for common usage and the International Telecommunications Union has encouraged other countries to follow this example. Called the Industrial, Scientific, Medical and Domestic Bands (or ISM bands), these are free for unlicensed, short-range usage. But not all of the bands are ideal for portable wireless. Operation at frequencies below one gigahertz requires large antennas, while radio waves at frequencies above several gigahertz experience significant loss in propagation. This leaves the 2.45 GHz ISM band as the common wireless communication band, and the band has quickly become crowded with applications.

A downside in using the free ISM band is that Bluetooth must separate its signal from the competition. Microwave ovens, for example, operate at 2.45 GHz not because this is a special frequency for heating, but to be within the ISM band. Many non–Bluetooth wireless devices, such as wireless microphones, also work in this band. Other large users are the wireless computer networks that are becoming ubiquitous. And other Bluetooth networks may also be operating in the area, providing more interference. Some of these applications are short range, extending only a few meters, but others, especially the computer networks are longer range. Usage of the 5.8 GHz ISM band is increasing, but the multitude of users remains in the 2.45 GHz band. Bluetooth systems use a type of spread-spectrum communication to separate its signal both from other applications and from other nearby Bluetooth systems.

Bluetooth uses frequency-hopping and encryption keys to establish a network. While CDMA–based systems spread the bandwidth by converting each data bit into several chips, Bluetooth increases the bandwidth by rapidly changing the link frequency. The data rate is one Mbps, requiring a 1 MHz-wide channel. Bluetooth has between 23 and 79 channels available, varying with the size of the ISM band in different countries. The network switches operation among these channels 1,600 times per second, using a pseudorandom pattern. As a basis for the frequency-hopping pattern, the network uses the unique 48 bit number, assigned during manufacturing, of the hub device. Several Bluetooth networks could therefore coexist with almost no overlap between their transmissions. For added security, the network encrypts its data using shared binary keys.

The common application of Bluetooth in cellphones is for external speakers and microphones. Given the short separation distance, typically within one meter, reception is usually not challenging. The transmit power of these devices is a low one milliwatt, and the antennas used for transmit and receive do not have to be particularly efficient. If only a fraction of one microwatt appears at the reception circuit, this is still relatively strong when compared with incoming cellular signals in the femtowatt range.

The Personal Electronic Device

Besides the added radios, the digital functionality of the cellphone is also expanding. This may be an inevitable product of the advancing state of digital IC processing. A measure of the compactness of IC's is the minimum possible transistor gate length, with the gate being the terminal of the transistor that controls the current flowing between the other two terminals. In the early 1990's, the finest gate length used by typical digital IC's was 0.5 micrometers. By the mid–2000s, the minimum gate length was usually 0.065 micrometers, a decrease by almost a factor of ten. And this is only in one dimension. Two-dimensional arrays of transistors could contain almost one hundred times more of the smaller transistors. In the digital world, more transistors translate to more memory and processing power, and therefore more functionality.

As the technology advanced, formerly separate industries in consumer electronics found themselves in direct competition with each other. The more advanced cellphones could offer the features of a Personal Digital Assistant. And the companies that made Personal Digital Assistants could add a wireless chipset to copy the cellphones. Another overlap became possible with the digital IC's available by the mid–2000's, that of the personal computer.

Most of the digital IC in a cellphone a few years into the 2000's is devoted to non-cellular phone features. Graphics processors for the display, audio processors for music, and a more powerful general processor for running applications like games became standard. In the memory category, several gigabytes easily fit within a few square centimeters. The cellphone and Personal Digital Assistant companies had no reason not to enter the personal computer market by adding some of the capabilities available in a notebook computer. And the personal computer companies, conversely, could purchase a wireless chipset and enter the cellphone market, which is what happened.

Handsets that combined cellular phones with the capabilities and usage of a personal computer appeared on the market, such as Apple Computer's iPhone in 2007. With the latest processors and four to eight gigabytes of memory, the iPhone had more computing power than a desktop computer of ten years earlier. And it overcame one of the fundamental problems in cellphones, the small display, by eliminating the keypad. While not large in comparison to a television or a notebook computer, the larger display was usable for watching video and running computer applications. Other manufacturers brought out their own cellphones with high memory and processing power, and they soon became common.

With the added capabilities the cellphone has been evolving beyond itself. Whether referred to as a cellphone, Personal Digital Assistant, or portable computer, it is an electronic device that people can easily carry and provides a connection to information and the world at large.

As noted throughout this history, anytime an opportunity is available to generate revenue, someone will find a way to use it. An electronic device that hundreds of millions of people carry, that can download new applications or content at anytime and from anyplace, and has copious spare memory and processing power, is too great a target to pass up. An industry devoted to computer applications meant for cellphones promptly appeared.

Governments no longer see the cellular phone as an unnecessary luxury. A cellular phone industry not only adds money to the economy through its own revenue, but also by increasing efficiency with more communication. The cellular phone has earned priority in the electromagnetic spectrum. Of importance to the governments, however, is not just money, but the will of their populations. And the people want cellphones.

The largest changes brought by the cellphone, and the process is still ongoing, is to society. People may not need cellphones in an absolute sense. But they like cellphones and the improvements the devices make to their lives enough to approximate need. The cellphone is not only here to stay, but will grow and evolve together as part of the social changes that technology inspires.

Chapter Notes

Introduction

1. Sharon LaFraniere, "Cellphones catapult rural Africa to 21st century," *New York Times,* 25 Aug. 2005, p. A1.

2. Joel Stashenko, "Judge's removal recommended for prolonged tirade over courtroom cell phone," *New York Law Journal,* online, 28 Nov. 2007.

Chapter 1

1. Carl B. Boyer, *A History of Mathematics, 2nd ed.* (New York: John Wiley and Sons, 1991): p. 162.

2. Ibid., p. 252.

3. J. L. Walsh, "A closed set of normal orthogonal functions," *American Journal of Mathematics,* (Jan. 1923): pp. 5–24.

4. Boyer, op. cit., p. 510.

5. John F. Rider, *An Introduction to Frequency Modulation* (New York: John F. Rider, 1940): p. 6.

6. John R. Carson, "Notes on the theory of modulation," *Proceedings of the IRE,* No. 10 (1922): pp. 57–64.

7. Theodore S. Rappaport, *Wireless Communications: Principles and Practice* (New York: Prentice Hall, 2002): p. 256.

8. Rider, op. cit., p. 93.

9. Ibid., p. 94.

10. Magdalena Salazar-Palma, Tapan K. Sarkar, and Dipak L. Sengupta, "A chronology of developments of wireless communication and supporting electronics," *History of Wireless* (Hoboken: John Wiley, 2006): p. 127.

11. Don V. Erickson, *Armstrong's Fight for FM Broadcasting: One Man vs. Big Business and Bureaucracy* (University of Alabama Press, 1973): p. 90.

12. Rider, op. cit., p. 94.

13. Erickson, op. cit., p. 45.

14. Ibid., p. 70.

15. Don V. Erickson, *Armstrong's Fight for FM Broadcasting: One Man vs. Big Business and Bureaucracy* (University of Alabama Press, 1973).

16. Albert Abramson, *The History of Television: 1880 to 1941* (Jefferson, NC: McFarland, 1987): pp. 257–261.

17. Erickson, op. cit., p. 95.

18. Ibid., p. 90.

19. Christopher H. Sterling and John Michael Kittross, *Stay Tuned: A History of American Broadcasting, 3rd Ed.* (Mahweh, NJ: Lawrence Erlbaum Associates, 2002): p. 278.

20. Ibid., p. 501.

21. IEEE Vehicular Technology Society Committee on Radio Propagation. "Coverage prediction for mobile radio systems operating in the 800/900 MHz frequency range," *IEEE Transactions on Vehicular Technology,* (Feb. 1988): pp. 3–72.

Chapter 2

1. Ismo V. Lindell, "Wireless before Marconi" *History of Wireless* (Hoboken: John Wiley, 2006): p. 7.

2. Phillip Dray, *Stealing God's Thunder: Benjamin Franklin's Lightning Rod and the Invention of America* (New York: Random House, 2005): p. 84.

3. Lindell, op. cit., p. 10.

4. Jeffrey Sconce, *Haunted Media: Electronic Presence from Telegraphy to Television* (Durham, NC: Duke University Press, 2000): p. 32.

5. Salazar-Palma, et al., op. cit., p. 55.

6. Ibid., p. 12.

7. James Clerk Maxwell, *A Treatise on Electricity and Magnetism, 3rd Ed.* (New York: Dover, 1954): p. 436.

8. Sterling and Kittross, op. cit., p. 24.

9. Ibid.: p. 27.

10. Ibid., p. 28.

11. "Like Bill Gates, Marconi made waves," *Toronto Star*, 10 Dec. 2001, p. E1.

12. Ibid.

13. Nikola Tesla, "Apparatus for trans-mission of electrical energy," U.S. Pat. No. 649,621. Issued 15 May 1900.

14. Ben Klemens, *Math You Can't Use: Patents, Copyright, and Software* (Washington, D.C.: Brookings, 2006): p. 62.

15. Kirk Teska, "Patently obvious," *IEEE Spectrum* (Dec. 2006): pp. 56–58.

16. Margaret Cheney and Robert Uth, *Tesla: Master of Lightning* (New York: Barnes and Noble, 1999): p. 68.

17. Sterling and Kittross, op. cit., p. 28.

18. Rider, op. cit., p. 88.

19. Sconce, op. cit., p. 74.

20. Sterling and Kittross, op. cit., p. 66.

21. Ibid., p. 74.

22. George R. Town, "Frequency allocations for broadcasting," *Proceedings of the IRE* (1962): pp. 825–829.

23. Sterling and Kittross, op. cit., p. 102.

24. Salazar-Palma, et al., op. cit., p. 71.

25. Sterling and Kittross, op. cit., p. 12.

26. Adam Burgess, *Cellular Phones, Public Fears, and a Culture of Precaution* (New York: Cambridge University Press, 2004): p. 58.

27. W. R. Young, "Advanced Mobile Phone Service: introduction, background, objectives," *Bell System Technical Journal* (Jan. 1979): pp. 1–14.

28. Daniel E. Noble, "The history of land-mobile radio communications," *Proceedings of the IRE* (May 1962): pp. 1405–1414.

29. Ibid.

30. Ibid.

31. Anton A. Huurdeman, *The Worldwide History of Telecommunications* (Hoboken: John Wiley, 2006): p. 286.

Chapter 3

1. W.R. Young, op. cit.

2. Huurdeman, op. cit., p. 519.

3. W.R. Young, op. cit.

4. Huurdeman, op. cit., p. 519.

5. W. R. Young, op. cit.

6. Penelope Stetz, *The Cell Phone Handbook: Everything You Wanted to Know About Wireless Telephony (But Didn't Know Who or What to Ask), 2nd edition* (Newport: Aegis Publishing, 2002): p. 9.

7. W.R. Young, op. cit.

8. Ibid.

9. Jon Agar, *Constant Touch: A Global History of the Mobile Phone* (Cambridge: Icon Books, 2003): p. 49.

10. Fred Guterl, "Ericsson bets on a cellular world," *IEEE Spectrum* (Feb. 1991): pp. 48–51.

11. Dan Steinbock, *The Nokia Revolution: The Story of an Extraordinary Company That Transformed an Industry* (New York: AMACOM, 2001): p. 295.

12. Ibid., p. 92.

13. Ibid., p. 10.

14. Ibid., p. 39.

15. Ibid., p. 46.

16. Agar, op. cit., p. 25.

17. Ibid., 72.

18. John Beck and Mitchell Wade, *DOCOMO: Japan's Wireless Tsunami* (New York: AMACOM, 2003): p. 88.

19. William C. Y. Lee, *Lee's Essentials of Wireless Communications* (New York: McGraw-Hill, 2001): p. 3.

20. W. R. Young, op. cit.

21. William C. Y. Lee, op. cit., p. 5.

22. W. R. Young, op. cit.

23. William C. Y. Lee, op. cit., p. 5.

24. Huurdeman, op. cit., p. 520.

25. William C. Y. Lee, op. cit., p. 10.

26. Franklin H. Blecher, "Advanced Mobile Phone Service," *IEEE Transactions on Vehicular Technology* (May 1980): pp. 238–244.

27. William C. Y. Lee, op. cit., p. 36.

28. W. R. Young, op. cit.

29. Blecher, op. cit.

30. William C. Y. Lee, op. cit., p. 121.

31. W. R. Young, op. cit.

32. William C. Y. Lee, op. cit., p. 105.

33. Ibid., p. 121.

Chapter 4

1. Stetz, op. cit., p. 9.

2. Most of the details of AMPS given here are from W. R. Young, op. cit., Blecher, op. cit., and V. H. MacDonald, "Advanced Mobile Phone Service: the cellular concept," *Bell System Technical Journal* (Jan. 1979): pp. 15–41.

3. William C. Y. Lee, op. cit., p. 37.

4. Rappaport, op. cit., p. 66.

5. Tele Danmark Mobile AS, Telecom Finland Ltd, Telenor Mobile AS, and Telia Mobitel AB, NMT Doc 450–3: Technical Specifications for the Mobile Station (1995).

6. Huurdeman, op. cit., p. 523.

7. William C. Y. Lee, op. cit., p. 47.

Chapter 5

1. Huurdeman, op. cit., p. 519.
2. William C. Y. Lee, op. cit.
3. Beck and Wade, op. cit., p. 88.
4. Steinbock, op. cit., p. 97.
5. Guterl, op. cit.
6. Huurdeman, op. cit., p. 523.
7. Agar, op. cit., p. 52.
8. Huurdeman, op. cit., p. 523.
9. Agar, op. cit., p. 78.
10. Ibid., p. 83.
11. Huurdeman, op. cit., p. 524.
12. Ibid., p. 523.
13. Agar, op. cit., p. 53.
14. Huurdeman, op. cit., p. 524.
15. James B. Murray, *Wireless Nation: the Frenzied Launch of the Cellular Revolution in America* (Cambridge: Perseus Publishing, 2001): p. 11.
16. Ibid., pp. 46–47.
17. Ibid., p. 71.
18. Ibid., p. 26.
19. Bob Davis, "Dialing for dollars: Lottery for franchises for cellular phones mars debut of system — FCC's drawings are a boon to a few, loss to many, bring the U. S. no money — the widow is out $10,000," *Wall Street Journal*, 21 July 1986, p.1.
20. Alexei Barrionuevo, "How MCI got lost amid the competition," *New York Times*, 15 Feb. 2005, p. A1.
21. Davis, op. cit.
22. Murray, op. cit., p. 114.
23. "Cellular mobile phone debut," *New York Times*, 14 Oct. 1983, p. D1.
24. Associated Press, "Motorola phones," *New York Times*, 14 March 1984, p. D4.
25. Eileen White, "Selecting the right mobile phone service requires comparison of costs, equipment," *Wall Street Journal*, 10 Dec. 1984, p. 1.
26. Ibid.
27. Ibid.
28. "Cellular mobile phone debut," op. cit.
29. Janet Guyon, "Cellular phone companies call business a tough one, with profits years away," *Wall Street Journal*, 25 June 1985, p. 1.
30. Murray, op. cit., p. 88.
31. Brenton R. Schlender, "Cellular-phone franchising deals attract investors— and criticism," *Wall Street Journal*, 24 July 1985, p. 1.
32. Ibid.
33. Ibid.
34. Davis, op. cit.
35. Murray, op. cit., p. 132.
36. Davis, op. cit.
37. Ibid.
38. Murray, op. cit., p. 37.
39. Ibid., p. 240.

40. Dan Richman, "The fall of AT&T Wireless," *Seattle Post-Intelligencer* 21 Sept. 2004.
41. William C. Y. Lee, op. cit., p. 131.

Chapter 6

1. Salazar-Palma, et al., op. cit., p. 71.
2. William Stallings, *Wireless Communications and Networks* (Upper Saddle River, NJ: Pearson Prentice Hall, 2005): p. 214.
3. Rappaport, op. cit., p. 411.
4. Andreas S. Spanias, "Speech coding: a tutorial review," *Proceedings of the IEEE* (Oct. 1994): pp. 1541–1582.
5. Bishnu S. Atal, "The history of linear prediction," *IEEE Signal Processing Magazine* (Mar. 2006): pp. 154–157.
6. Ibid.
7. Claude E. Shannon, "Communication in the presence of noise," *Proceedings of IRE* (1949): pp. 10–21.
8. Blecher, op. cit.
9. Robert A. Scholtz, "The origins of spread-spectrum communications," *IEEE Transactions on Communications* (May 1982): pp. 822–854.
10. Ibid.
11. Ibid.
12. Nicholas Farrell, "Hedy Lamarr: movie queen, sex siren. and rocket scientist," *Mail on Sunday* (6 Feb. 2000): pp. 58–59.

Chapter 7

1. Many of the specific details of GSM contained in this chapter are from Moe Rahnema, "Overview of the GSM system and protocol architecture," *IEEE Communications Magazine* (April 1993): pp. 92–100.
2. These system capacity estimates are from David D. Falconer, Fumiyuki Adachi, and Bjorn Gudmundson, "Time division multiple access methods for wireless personal communications," *IEEE Communications Magazine* (Jan. 1995): pp. 50–57.

Chapter 8

1. William C. Y. Lee, op. cit., p. 137.
2. Agar, op. cit., p. 64.
3. Ibid., p. 57.
4. William C. Y. Lee, op. cit., p. 150.
5. Agar, op. cit., p. 63.
6. William C. Y. Lee, op. cit., p. 66.
7. Ibid.
8. Franklin P. Antonio, Klein S. Gilhousen, Irwin M. Jacobs, and Lindsay A. Weaver Jr., "OmniTRACS: a commercial Ku-band mobile

satellite terminal and its applicability to military mobile terminals," *Military Communications Conference* (Oct. 1988): pp. 761–764.

9. Bill Frezza, "Succumbing to technoseduction," *Network Computing*, online (April 1995).

10. Many of the details of Qualcomm's early history are from Dave Mock, *The Qualcomm Equation: How a Fledgling Telecom Company Forged a New Path to Big Profits and Market Dominance* (New York: AMACOM, 2005).

11. William C. Y. Lee, op. cit., p. 174.

12. Bill Frezza, "CDMA: Blazing a trail of broken dreams," *Network Computing*, online (April 1996).

13. Mock, op. cit.

14. William C. Y. Lee, op. cit., p. 189.

15. Richman, op. cit.

16. Steven V. Brull, Neil Gross, and Catherine Yang, "Cell phones: Europe made the right call," *Business Week* (Sept. 1998), p. 107.

17. Stetz, op. cit., p. 21.

18. Murray, op. cit., p. 271.

19. Andrew Backover, "NextWave stubbornly clings to life: scrappy company's comeback story rides on founder's tenacity," *USA Today* (2 July 2001), p. 1B.

20. Albert R. Karr, "Hint: For 10 million, write a 10, then six zeros, then a little dot," *Wall Street Journal* (29 Jan. 1996), p. B1.

21. Murray, op. cit.

22. Huurdeman, op. cit., p. 410.

23. Ibid.

24. G. Christian Hill and David P. Hamilton, "After lofty hopes, Iridium is falling to Earth," *Wall Street Journal* (15 July 1999), p. B1.

25. Jagdish N. Sheth and Rajendra Sisodia, "Manager's journal: Why cell phones succeeded where Iridium failed," *Wall Street Journal* (23 Aug. 1999), p. 14.

26. Ibid.

27. Klemens, op. cit., p. 18.

28. Sheth and Sisodia, op. cit.

29. William C. Y. Lee, op. cit., p. 75.

30. Mock, op. cit.

Chapter 9

1. Steinbock, op. cit., p. 124.

2. "Oy Nokia of Finland posts 89 percent decline in its pretax profit," *Wall Street Journal* (21 June 1991), p. A5.

3. Charles McCoy, "Tandy to make and sell cellular phones under agreements with three concerns," *Wall Street Journal* (11 May 1984), p. 1.

4. Steinbock, op. cit., p. 262.

5. David Pringle, Jesse Drucker, and Evan Ramstad, "Cellphone makers pay a heavy toll for missing fads," *Wall Street Journal* (30 Oct. 2001), p. 1.

6. Steinbock, op. cit., p. 213.

7. Beck and Wade, op. cit., p. 79.

8. Agar, op. cit., p. 95.

9. Beck and Wade, op. cit., p. 84.

10. Ibid., p. 88.

11. Ibid., p. 86.

12. Ibid., p. 123.

13. Kei-ichi Enoki, "i-mode: the mobile internet service of the 21st century," *2001 IEEE International Solid-State Circuits Conference* (2001).

14. LaFraniere, op. cit.

15. Don Clark, "Kyocera of Japan agrees to acquire Qualcomm's wireless-phone business," *Wall Street Journal* (23 Dec. 1999), p. 1.

16. Ibid.

17. Mock, op. cit.

18. Suzanne McGee and Randall Smith, "Qualcomm soars on analyst's grand prediction," *Wall Street Journal* (30 Dec. 1999), p. C1.

19. David J. Goodman and Robert A. Myers, "3G cellular standards and patents," *IEEE WirelessComm 2005* (2005).

20. Hakon Urkin Steen, "The fragmentation of standards in mobile digital broadcast carriers," *Sixth International Conference on the Management of Mobile Business* (2007).

21. Agar, op. cit., p. 85.

22. Murray, op. cit., p. 277.

23. Richman, op. cit.

24. Catherine Greenman, "Too many phones, too little service," *New York Times* (19 Aug. 1999), p. B1.

25. Richman, op. cit.

26. Ibid.

27. Details of the history of patents come largely from Adam B. Jaffe and Josh Lerner, *Innovation and Its Discontents: How Our Broken Patent System is Endangering Innovation and Progress and What to do About It* (Princeton, NJ: Princeton University Press, 2004).

28. Jaffe and Lerner, op. cit., p. 100.

29. Klemens, op. cit., p. 69.

30. Ibid.

31. Teska, op. cit.

32. Klemens, op. cit., p. 19.

33. Melody Petersen, "Drug maker is set to ship generic Prozac," *New York Times* (2 Aug. 2001).

34. Steinbock, op. cit., p. 189.

35. Mark A. Lemley and Carl Shapiro, "Patent holdup and royalty stacking," *Texas Law Review* 85 (2007), pp. 1991–2049.

36. Jaffe and Lerner, op. cit., p. 61.

37. Ibid., p. 72.

38. "Qualcomm Business Model: A Formula for Innovation and Choice," report from Qualcomm website (Aug. 2006).

39. Lemley and Shapiro, op. cit.

40. Goodman and Myers, op. cit.

41. William Cook, "Frand or foe," *Managing Intellectual Property* (1 June 2006), p. 31.

Chapter 10

1. Joel Greenberg, "Slaying blended technology and guile," *New York Times* (10 Jan. 1996), p. A3.

2. Traffic Safety Facts: 2006 Data (National Highway Traffic Safety Administration, 2006).

3. 2004 Surgeon General's Report — The Health Consequences of Smoking (Department of Health and Human Services, 2004).

4. Harvey A. Risch, Geoffrey R. Howe, Meera Jain, J. David Burch, Eric J. Holowaty, and Anthony B. Miller, "Are female smokers at higher risk for lung cancer than male smokers?," *American Journal of Epidemiology* 138(5) (Sept. 1993), pp. 281–293.

5. Prachi Patel D. Predd, "Swedish study links cellphones to brain tumors," *IEEE Spectrum* (Dec. 2004), pp. 56–58.

6. Adam Burgess, "Mobile phones and service stations: rumour, risk and precaution," *Diogenes* 54(1) (2007), pp. 125–139.

7. Caroline Williams, "No evidence for cellphone mast illness," *Newscientist.com* news service, 25 July 2007.

8. 2004 Surgeon General's Report — The Health Consequences of Smoking, op. cit., p. 45.

9. J. E. Moulder, L. S. Erdreich, R. S. Malyapa, J. Merritt, W. F. Pickard, and Vijayalaxmi, "Cell phones and cancer: what is the evidence of a connection?," *Radiation Research* 151 (1999), pp. 513–531.

10. Ibid.

11. FCC OET Bulletin 65, Supplement C (Federal Communications Commission, 2001).

12. Safety Code 6: Limits of Human Exposure to Radiofrequency Electromagnetic Fields in the Frequency Range from 3 kHz to 300 GHz (Industry Canada, 1999).

13. David Derbyshire, "Only 10 minutes on a mobile phone could trigger cancer, scientists believe," *Daily Mail* (UK) 30 Aug. 2007.

14. Maranne Berwick and Paolo Vineis, "Markers of DNA repair and susceptibility to cancer in humans: an epidemiologic review," *Journal of the National Cancer Institute* 92(11) (2000), pp. 874–897.

15. Henry Lai and Narendra P. Singh, "Acute low-intensity microwave exposure increases DNA single-strand breaks in rat brain cells," *Bioelectromagnetics* 16(2) (1995), pp. 207–210.

16. Moulder, et al., op. cit.

17. Nancy Wertheimer and Ed Leeper, "Electrical wiring configurations and childhood cancer," *American Journal of Epidemiology* 109(3) (1979), pp. 273–284.

18. Paul Brodeur, *Currents of Death* (New York: Simon and Schuster, 2000).

19. Halle Collatz Christansen, Joachim Schuz, Michael Kosteljanetz, Hans Skovgaard Poulsen, Jens Thomsen, and Christoffer Johansen, "Cellular telephone use and risk of acoustic neuroma," *American Journal of Epidemiology* 159(3) (2004), pp. 277–283.

20. Christoffer Johansen, John D. Boice Jr., Joseph K. McLaughlin, and Jorgen H. Olsen, "Cellular telephones and cancer — a nationwide cohort study in Denmark," *Journal of the National Cancer Institute* 39(3) (2001), pp. 203–207.

21. Lennart Hardell, Michael Carlberg, Fredirk Soderqvist, Kjell Hansson Mild, and L. Lloyd Morgan, "Long-term use of cellular phones and brain tumours: increased risk associated with use for >= 10 years," *Occupational and Environmental Medicine* 64 (2007), pp. 626–632.

22. Edward P. Richards and Charles Walter, "Science in the supreme court: round two," *IEEE Engineering in Medicine and Biology Magazine* 17(2) (1999), pp. 124–125.

23. Ibid.

24. Sharon Begley, "Ban on 'junk science' also keeps jurors from sound evidence," *Wall Street Journal* (27 June 2003), p. B1.

25. "Suit linking cancer, cellphone use fails," *Wall Street Journal* (1 Oct. 2002), p. D2.

26. Burgess, op. cit., p. 83.

27. Donald A. Redelmeier and Robert J. Tibshirani, "Association between cellular-telephone calls and motor vehicle collisions," *New England Journal of Medicine* 13(7) (1997), pp. 453–458.

28. James Hunton and Jacob M. Rose, "Cellular telephones and driving performance: the effects of attentional demands on motor vehicle crash risk," *Risk Analysis* 25(4) (2005), pp. 855–866.

29. Redelmeier and Tibshirani, op. cit.

30. Suzanne P. McEvoy, et al., "Role of mobile phones in motor vehicle crashes resulting in hospital attendance: a case-crossover study," BMJ (doi:10. 1136/bmj. 38537. 397512. 55), 2005.

31. William Consiglio, Peter Driscoll, Matthew Witte, and William P. Berg, "Effect of cellular telephone conversations and other potential interference on reaction time in a braking response," *Accident Analysis and Prevention* 35 (2003), pp. 495–500.

32. Hunton and Rose, op. cit.

33. David Shinar, Noam Tractinsky, and Richard Compton, "Effect of practice, age, and task demands, on interference from a phone task while driving," *Accident Analysis and Prevention* 37 (2005), pp. 315–326.

34. Andrew R. McGarva, Matthew Ramsey, and Suzannah H. Shear, "Effects of driver cell-phone use on driver aggression," *Journal of Social Psychology* (2006), pp. 133–146.

35. Traffic Safety Facts: 2006 Data, op. cit.

36. Donna Glassbrenner, Driver Cell Phone Use in 2005 — Overall Results, (National Highway Traffic Safety Administration, 2005).

37. Bob Briscoe, Andrew Odlyzko, and Benjamin Tilly, "Metcalfe's law is wrong — communications networks increase in value as they add members — but by how much?," *IEEE Spectrum* 43(7) (2006), pp. 34–39.

38. Burgess, op. cit., p. 68.

39. Kushe Bahl, et al., "Wireless unbound: the surprising economic value and untapped potential of the mobil phone," McKinsey and Company white paper (2006).

40. Anthony Ramirez, "Eavesdroppers troll for salable chat, but it's a big pond," *New York Times* (27 Sept. 1992), p. A6.

41. Peter S. Canellos and Irene Sege, "Couple shot after leaving hospital; baby delivered," *Boston Globe* (24 Oct. 1989), p. 1.

42. Kevin Cullen, Sean Murphy, and Mike Barnicle, "Stuart dies in jump off Tobin bridge after police are told he killed his wife," *Boston Globe* (5 Jan. 1990), p. 1.

43. Jeffrey H. Reed, Kevin J. Krizman, Brian D. Woerner, and Theodore S. Rappaport, "An overview of the challenges and progress in meeting the E-911 requirement for location service," *IEEE Communications Magazine* (April 1989), pp. 30–37.

44. Ibid.

Chapter 11

1. A detailed account of the integrated chip's history is presented in T. R. Reid, *The Chip: How Two Americans Invented the Microchip and Launched a Revolution*, (New York: Random House, 2001).

2. Hirohisa Kawamoto, "The history of liquid-crystal displays," *Proceedings of the IEEE* (April 2002), pp. 460–500.

3. Ibid.

4. Jyrki Kimmel, Jukka Hautanen, and Tapani Levola, "Display technologies for portable communication devices," *Proceedings of the IEEE* (April 2002), pp. 581–590.

5. Kawamoto, op. cit.

6. Pringle, Drucker, and Ramstad, op. cit.

7. Dray, op. cit., p. 44.

8. Dray, op. cit., p. 55.

9. Neil Scholey, "Rechargeable batteries for mobile communications," *Electronics and Communication Engineering Journal* (June 1995), pp. 93–96.

Chapter 12

1. "G-Whizz: Ten Reasons Why 3G is Delayed," (Credit Suisse First Boston [Europe] Limited, 2001).

2. William C. Y. Lee, op. cit., p. 104.

3. Malcolm W. Oliphant, "The mobile phone meets the internet," *IEEE Spectrum* (Aug. 1999), pp. 20–28.

4. Steinbock, op. cit., p. 219.

5. Oliphant, op. cit.

6. Rappaport, op. cit.

7. Ibid.

8. Ibid.

9. Rao Yallapragada, Vera Kripalani, and Anil Kripalani, "EDGE: a technology assessment," *2002 IEEE International Conference on Personal Wireless Communications* (Dec. 2002), pp. 35–40.

10. Rappaport, op. cit.

11. Paul Klemperer, "How (not) to run auctions: The European 3G telecom auctions," *European Economic Review* (2002), pp. 829–845.

12. P. Daley, "Navstar GPR and GLONASS: global satellite navigation systems," *Electronics and Communication Engineering Journal* (Dec. 1993), pp. 349–357.

13. Chatschik Bisdikian, "An overview of the Bluetooth wireless technology," *IEEE Communications Magazine* (Dec. 2001), pp. 86–94.

Glossary of Terms

Antenna gain: The increase in broadcast field strength or received power relative to using an isotropic antenna.

Advanced Mobile Phone Service (AMPS): The analog cellular phone standard used in the USA.

Bandwidth: The range of frequencies of the sinusoidal waves needed to adequately represent a signal; or the range of frequencies of the waves that a communication channel can transmit.

Base station: The transmitter, receiver and associated equipment that the cellular system uses to communicate with the mobile units within a cell.

Bit: A binary digit; the two states of a bit are usually represented as "1" and "0."

Cell: The area over which clear and reliable radio communication between the base station and the mobile units is possible.

Cellular phone (cellphone): a device that sends and receives calls, like a telephone, but does so wirelessly, and that uses a cell-based system in order to increase system capacity and to decrease broadcast power. The original term, cellular phone, has been shortened in general use to cellphone since the rapid popularization of the technology in the 1990s.

Channel encoding: Representing digital data with other digital numbers in order to add error detection and error correction capabilities.

Chip (digital data transfer): The transmitted bits in a digital communication system; several chips could correspond to one data bit.

Code-Division Multiple Access (CDMA): Digital communication technique in which messages use the same frequency band and are separated by orthogonal codes.

Decibel (dB): Unit for logarithmic representation of a number, divide by ten to find the factor of ten represented; 0 dB$=10^0=1$, 10 dB$=10^1=10$, 20 dB$=10^2=100$, 30 dB$=10^3=1000$, etc.

Decomposition (signals): Finding the constitutive parts of a signal; the parts can be Walsh codes for a digital signal, or sine and cosine waves for an analog signal.

Duplexer: A device that switches the connection of an input line between more than one output line.

Electric field: A representation of the force that a test charge would experience when placed in the vicinity of electric charges.

Electrodes: Battery terminals with complementary excess electrical charge; in a chemical battery the electrodes react with an acidic solution to produce excess charge.

Electromagnetic wave: Radio waves; waves consisting of electric and magnetic fields that support each other and travel independently of their original source.

Encoding gain: The improvement in the reception of a digital message when using error-correction codes, relative to not using error-correction.

Fades: Dips in a received radio waves power due to movement and shadowing (slow fades) and cancellation between arriving waves (fast fades).

Far-fields: Radiated electromagnetic waves far (at least several wavelengths) away from the source antenna; the amplitude of the far-fields decreases at a rate of $1/d$, so the energy in the fields decreases as $1/d^2$.

Fourier series: The set of sine and cosine waves of different frequencies, and their individual weightings, that sum to form an analog signal.

Frequency: The number of times a periodic signal repeats in one second, reported in cycles-per-second or in hertz (Hz).

Frequency-Division Multiple Access: Communication technique that separates users by assigning each a unique frequency channel.

Generations (cellular): General grouping of cellular phone technology, consisting of the first generation (analog), the second generation (digital), and the third generation (revised digital).

Global System for Mobile Communication (GSM): The second generation cellular phone standard that uses TDMA to increase capacity.

Handoff: Changing the assigned base station for a mobile unit as it moves from one cell to another.

Induction: The creation of an electric current with a magnetic field.

Integrated circuit (IC): Microscopic electric circuit placed onto the surface of a semiconductor such as silicon.

Interleaving: Shuffling the order of transmitted digital numbers in order to spread the effects of noise bursts and increase the effectiveness of error correction.

Inter-symbol interference: Ambiguity caused by digital streams arriving through paths with different time delays leading to symbols overlapping out-of-sequence.

Linear/Nonlinear devices: A linear device has a straight-line input/output of power and does not change the bandwidth of a signal; a nonlinear device has a curved input/output plot and creates waves with new frequencies when used to transmit a signal.

Linear prediction: The representation of a sequence of numbers by the first few numbers and coefficients to calculate the remaining numbers; used in audio compression.

Liquid-crystal display (LCD): A display that uses a liquid-crystal medium to rotate the polarization of light in order to pass through filters.

Magnetic field: A representation of the force that a test current would experience when placed in the vicinity of electrical currents.

Mixing (waves): Multiplying waves together; mixing a high-frequency carrier wave with a low-frequency signal produces amplitude modulation.

Modulation: Varying the amplitude, frequency or phase of a wave to carry information.

Near-fields: Electric and magnet fields in the immediate vicinity of electrical currents; the near-fields drop in amplitude at least as fast as $1/d^2$ for distance d, so the energy in the fields decreases at the rate of $1/d^4$.

Omnidirectional antenna: Antenna that transmits or receives waves from all angles on the horizon with equal efficiency.

Orthogonal: The absence of common components between signals; two signals are orthogonal if their correlation is zero.

Power amplifier: Device that amplifies the small signals in the circuits to the higher power levels needed for transmission.

Printed circuit board (PCB): The board that holds the integrated chips and other components of a cellular phone.

Processing gain: The improvement in the reception of a digital signal when using spread-spectrum techniques, relative to retaining the signal's original bandwidth throughout transmission.

Pseudo-random noise (PN): A signal with low autocorrelation created by a predictable process.

QPSK: Digital modulation technique that uses a sinusoidal wave with four possible phase shifts to represent symbol states.

Quadrature: Two sinusoidal waves are in quadrature if they have a ninety degree phase difference; waves in quadrature are orthogonal.

Rake receiver: Radio receiver used in CDMA with multiple parallel correlators, each processing separate parts of the incoming waves.

Resonance (antennas): A state in which the waves of electrical current reflecting between the ends of an antenna add constructively; an antenna in resonance can radiate or receive energy more efficiently than in an off-resonance state.

Shift-keying: Applying discrete changes to a wave's amplitude, frequency or phase to indicate digital signals.

Sinusoidal wave: Periodic wave that can be either a sine wave or a cosine wave; described by an amplitude and a frequency.

Specific absorption rate (SAR): The power absorbed by biological tissue from electric and magnetic fields; measured in Watts-per-kilogram or milliwatts-per-milligram.

Standard (cellular communications): The collection of parameters and requirements that define a cellular phone system; e.g., AMPS, GSM, UMTS, etc.

Supervisory audio tone: Single tone broadcast through calls in analog cellular system to indicate that the call is connected; not sent to the speaker, so the user is unaware of this tone.

Symbol: A digital number that takes one of several discrete states; usually translated into bits for comparisons (e.g., a symbol that takes eight states represents three bits).

System controller: The equipment and personnel that operate a cellular system; the system controller communicates with the mobile units through the base station and acts as the gateway to the wired telephone system.

Time-Division Multiple Access (TDMA): A digital communication technique in which messages use the same frequency band and are separated by timeslots.

Walsh codes: A set of orthogonal digital numbers with that can represent any digital number.

Selected Bibliography

Abramson, Albert. *The History of Television: 1880 to 1941*. Jefferson, NC: McFarland, 1987.

Agar, Jon. *Constant Touch: A Global History of the Mobile Phone*. Cambridge: Icon Books, 2003.

Atal, Bishnu S. "The history of linear prediction." *IEEE Signal Processing Magazine*. Mar. 2006: pp. 154–157.

Beck, John, and Mitchell Wade. *DOCOMO: Japan's Wireless Tsunami*. New York: AMACOM, 2003.

Blecher, Franklin H. "Advanced Mobile Phone Service." *IEEE Transactions on Vehicular Technology*. May 1980: pp. 238–244.

Boyer, Carl B. *A History of Mathematics*, 2nd ed. New York: John Wiley and Sons, 1991.

Brodeur, Paul. *Currents of Death*. New York: Simon and Schuster, 2000.

Burgess, Adam. *Cellular Phones, Public Fears, and a Culture of Precaution*. New York: Cambridge University Press, 2004.

Cheney, Margaret, and Robert Uth. *Tesla: Master of Lightning*. New York: Barnes & Noble, 1999.

Dray, Philip. *Stealing God's Thunder: Benjamin Franklin's Lightning Rod and the Invention of America*. New York: Random House, 2005.

Erickson, Don V. *Armstrong's Fight for FM Broadcasting: One Man vs. Big Business and Bureaucracy*. Tuscaloosa: University of Alabama Press, 1973.

Hardell, Lennart, Michael Carlberg, Fredirk Soderqvist, Kjell Hansson Mild, and L. Lloyd Morgan, "Long-term use of cellular phones and brain tumours: increased risk associated with use for >= 10 years," *Occupational and Environmental Medicine*. 64 (2007): pp. 626–632.

Huurdeman, Anton A. *The Worldwide History of Telecommunications*. Hoboken, NJ: John Wiley, 2006.

Jaffe, Adam B., and Josh Lerner. *Innovation and Its Discontents: How Our Broken Patent System Is Endangering Innovation and Progress and What to do About It*. Princeton, NJ: Princeton University Press, 2004.

Kawamoto, Hirohisa. "The history of liquid-crystal displays." *Proceedings of the IEEE*. April 2002: pp. 460–500.

Klemens, Ben. *Math You Can't Use: Patents, Copyright, and Software*. Washington, D.C.: Brookings, 2006.

Lee, William C.Y. *Lee's Essentials of Wireless Communications*. New York: McGraw-Hill, 2001.

MacDonald, V.H. "Advanced Mobile Phone Service: the cellular concept." *Bell System Technical Journal*. Jan. 1979: pp. 15–41.

Maxwell, James Clerk. *A Treatise on Electricity and Magnetism, 3rd Ed.* New York: Dover, 1954.

Mock, Dave. *The Qualcomm Equation: How a Fledgling Telecom Company Forged a New Path to Big Profits and Market Dominance*. New York: AMACOM, 2005.

Murray, James B. *Wireless Nation: the Frenzied Launch of the Cellular Revolution in America*. Cambridge: Perseus Publishing, 2001.

Noble, Daniel E. "The history of land-mobile radio communications." *Proceedings of the IRE*. May 1962: pp. 1405–1414.

Rahnema, Moe. "Overview of the GSM system and protocol architecture." *IEEE Communications Magazine*. April 1993: pp. 92–100.

Rappaport, Theodore S. *Wireless Communications: Principles and Practice*. New York: Prentice-Hall, 2002.

Reid, T. R. *The Chip: How Two Americans Invented the Microchip and Launched a Revolution*. New York: Random House, 2001.

Rider, John F. *An Introduction to Frequency Modulation*. New York: John F. Rider, 1940.

Sarkar, Tapan K., et al. *History of Wireless*. Hoboken, NJ: John Wiley, 2006.

Scholtz, Robert A. "The origins of spread-spectrum communications." *IEEE Transactions on Communications*. May 1982: pp. 822–854.

Sconce, Jeffrey. *Haunted Media: Electronic Presence from Telegraphy to Television*. Durham, NC: Duke University Press, 2000.

Spanias, Andreas S. "Speech coding: a tutorial review." *Proceedings of the IEEE*. Oct. 1994: pp. 1541–1582.

Stallings, William. *Wireless Communications and Networks*. Upper Saddle River, NJ: Pearson Prentice-Hall, 2005.

Steinbock, Dan. *The Nokia Revolution: The Story of an Extraordinary Company That Transformed an Industry*. New York: AMACOM, 2001.

Sterling, Christopher H., and John Michael Kittross. *Stay Tuned: A History of American Broadcasting*, 3rd ed. Mahweh, NJ: Lawrence Erlbaum Associates, 2002.

Stetz, Penelope. *The Cell Phone Handbook: Everything You Wanted to Know About Wireless Telephony (But Didn't Know Who or What to Ask)*, 2nd ed. Newport: Aegis Publishing, 2002.

Young, W. R. "Advanced Mobile Phone Service: introduction, background, objectives." *Bell System Technical Journal*. Jan. 1979: pp. 1–14.

Index